U0645807

深圳大学"鹏城法学前沿系列"编辑委员会

主　任　黄亚英

委　员　（以姓氏拼音为序）

蒋慧玲　魏秀玲　杨献军　姚秀兰　叶兴平　应飞虎

易松国　钟明霞　曾月英　邹平学　左德起

作者简介

　　韩平，1980 年生于湖北省武汉市。2002 年毕业于大连海事大学法学院。2003 年在英国布里斯托大学获法学硕士学位。2007 年在英国格拉斯哥大学获法学博士学位。曾任华南国际仲裁院和深圳仲裁委员会仲裁员。现任深圳大学法学院副教授。主要著作包括《国际私法》（合著），《中国国际私法学》（合著）。在多份法律刊物发表文章，如《法学》、《法学评论》、*Frontiers of Law in China* 等。

鹏城法学前沿系列

中英仲裁法比较研究

A Comparative Study of the Chinese Arbitration Law and
the Arbitration Laws of the UK

韩 平 著

厦门大学出版社 国家一级出版社
XIAMEN UNIVERSITY PRESS 全国百佳图书出版单位

图书在版编目(CIP)数据

中英仲裁法比较研究/韩平著.—厦门:厦门大学出版社,2019.8
(鹏城法学前沿系列)
ISBN 978-7-5615-7565-9

Ⅰ.①中… Ⅱ.①韩… Ⅲ.①仲裁法－对比研究－中国、英国 Ⅳ.①D925.704
②D956.157

中国版本图书馆 CIP 数据核字(2019)第 179166 号

出 版 人	郑文礼
责任编辑	李 宁

出版发行 厦门大学出版社

社　　址	厦门市软件园二期望海路 39 号
邮政编码	361008
总　　机	0592-2181111　0592-2181406(传真)
营销中心	0592-2184458　0592-2181365
网　　址	http://www.xmupress.com
邮　　箱	xmup@xmupress.com
印　　刷	南平市武夷美彩印中心

开本	720 mm×1 000 mm　1/16
印张	19.75
插页	2
字数	448 千字
版次	2019 年 8 月第 1 版
印次	2019 年 8 月第 1 次印刷
定价	88.00 元

本书如有印装质量问题请直接寄承印厂调换

厦门大学出版社
微信二维码

厦门大学出版社
微博二维码

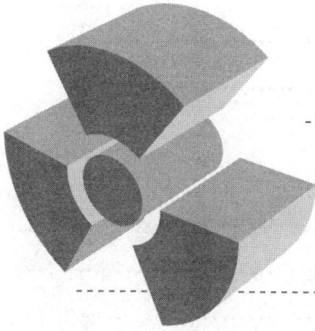

Table of Contents

中英仲裁法比较研究
A Comparative Study of the Chinese Arbitration
Law and the Arbitration Laws of the UK

中英仲裁法比较研究
A Comparative Study of the Chinese Arbitration
Law and the Arbitration Laws of the UK

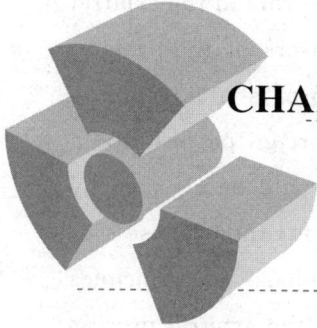

CHAPTER 1

INTRODUCTION

Arbitration is a device whereby parties to a legal dispute agree to refer it to the binding resolution of one or more persons. In China, although the process of asking a third party to decide a dispute has a long history, arbitration in proper sense has not existed until recently. Arbitration legislation first appeared early in the 1990s, the first legislative version concerning arbitration, the first edition of the Civil Procedure Law of the People's Republic of China being produced in 1991(hereinafter referred to as "the PRC Civil Procedure Law 1991"), the latest edition of the Civil Procedure Law has been produced in 2017 (hereinafter referred to as "the PRC Civil Procedure Law 2017")and the first edition of the Arbitration Law of the People's Republic of China only being promulgated in 1994, coming into force in 1995 (hereinafter referred to as "the PRC Arbitration Law 1994"), and the latest edition in 2017 (hereinafter referred to as "the PRC Arbitration Law 2017"). Although the laws of the People's Republic of China have made great advances, but still even now, in some areas of the law the provisions are far from perfect. It will be seen that many provisions are obscure or contradictory, that there are overlapping legislative regimes and supervisory jurisdic-

中英仲裁法比较研究
A Comparative Study of the Chinese Arbitration
Law and the Arbitration Laws of the UK

tions, and that agencies of the state play a very intrusive role in the arbitral process. Reform would be useful to benefit domestic users of the system. Moreover, given China's developing trade relations, reform is vital if foreign users are to have confidence in the Chinese system. Foreign parties would struggle to understand how the system operates and would be alarmed by much of what they did understand. There may be room for the Chinese system to be extensively modernized, placing proper emphasis on principles such as the autonomy of the parties and the freedom of the arbitral process from improper state interference. Fortunately, arbitral systems across the world have been so modernized over the last two decades as a result of the influence of the Model Law on International Commercial Arbitration (hereinafter referred to as the "Model Law") which was adopted by the United Nations Commission on International Trade Law (hereinafter referred to as UNCITRAL) in 1985, and amended in 2006. This thesis will consider whether the Model Law, which has been adopted in Scotland, or more recent and comprehensive measures such as the English Arbitration Act 1996 (hereinafter referred to as the "1996 Act") have lessons for China.

Every system must concede a role to its judicial authorities, not only in terms of assistance and support, but also supervision of that process. On the other hand, if the level of judicial control is too high, the confidence of users of the system will be damaged. Foreign parties may indeed choose to avoid arbitrating in such a system. Consequently, it is crucial to reconcile the autonomy of the arbitration process with the interest of national courts in ensuring the integrity of process and the protection of public interest. It will be argued that China often fails to offer proper support and supervision in some areas, while unduly restricting the autonomy in others.

The areas to be explored are:

(1)The arbitration agreement and its form. Will the law permit separate arbitration agreements as well as arbitration clauses, and if so, will there be any consequences which flow from the different forms. Will all arbitration agreements have to have a certain fundamental content? Will the law say anything about the incorporation of arbitration agreements from other contracts?

(2) The staying of legal proceedings. How should the law direct a court to react, when a party to litigation pleads the existence of an arbitration agreement? Must it stay the proceedings or will it have discretion? When should it have discretion?

(3) The creation of the arbitral tribunal. Should the law have rules as to the number of arbitrators, and who should be allowed to be an arbitrator? Surely it should have default rules to deal with situations where the parties have not agreed upon key specifics of the arbitral tribunal or where the procedures agreed by the parties break down.

(4) The revocation of arbitral authority and its consequences. I will discuss in the part about disqualifications and challenges, removal of arbitrator by the court, time for challenge, responses to challenge.

(5) The arbitral immunity. Should arbitrators have complete immunity, and if not for what manner of behaviour and to what extent should they be liable?

(6) The jurisdictional matters and the doctrine of separability. Should the arbitral tribunal have the competence to rule on its own competence? Should an arbitration clause in the principal contract remain valid where that contract turns out to be invalid?

(7) The conduct of the proceeding, including the powers of the tribunal and the courts. The issues dealt with here are discretion of the parties/arbitral tribunal, the opportunity of being treated equally and presenting his case, evidence, location of arbitral proceedings, power to order interim measures of protection, language, statements of claim and defence, supplementary claims and defences, form and scope of hearings, advance notice of hearings and meetings, copies of evidential material.

(8) The arbitral award. The contents include the types of award, sub-

中英仲裁法比较研究
A Comparative Study of the Chinese Arbitration
Law and the Arbitration Laws of the UK

stance of award, e. g. power to award damages and interests, power to a-
ward expense, power to make other orders, delivery of an award, correction
of an award, effect of an award.

(9)challenging awards. Unlike other literatures on this subject, my research will not just discuss the grounds and procedures for challenging an a-
ward, but also elaborate the substantial principles to resolve the challenges,
including comprehensive references to the sources of each individual principle, and the theoretical underpinnings of the remitting awards for reconsideration, a remedy for challengeable arbitration awards.

CHAPTER 2

BACKGROUND OF CHINESE ARBITRATION LAW

The reason why Chinese arbitration law takes its current form is mainly because of Chinese traditional legal culture and the historical development of Chinese legislation. Chinese traditional legal culture is closely related to Chinese traditional culture, being affected by its economic base and polity.

I. Tradition and Culture

Before the ending of the Qing Dynasty (the Qing Dynasty was the last dynasty of Chinese feudal history, and ended in 1911), Chinese feudal society had existed for more than two thousand years, based on a centralized feudal monarchy. A centralized feudal monarchy needs a steady and powerful ideology as a theoretical support. Furthermore, in Chinese feudal society, the autarkic "smallholder economy" (also called the natural economy) is the main form of economy. Its characteristics were decentralization, conserva-

中英仲裁法比较研究
A Comparative Study of the Chinese Arbitration
Law and the Arbitration Laws of the UK

tism and stability. As a result of decentralization, relationships between producers were very weak. The strongest organization in society was the governing group. The strongest relations were those within the governing group and between that group and the governed. The emperor carried out high-level systematization within the governing group across a huge territory.[1] Moreover, due to their conservatism and desire for stability, people were accustomed to deferring to authority.

Commodity exchange was extremely underdeveloped, so that there was no basis for a society ruled by law to come into being. In the process of production, the basic unit was the family, the aim of production was to satisfy its needs. Individuals did not exchange merchandise. As a result, it was impossible for the basic principle of exchange, which is the principle of equality, to come into being. Neither were individual rights recognized. The order of production was based on the status of the family, the status of individual person was of no importance. The basic obligation of individuals was obedience. Civil and commercial law, dealing with production and exchange between equals, could not come into being where there was no equality.[2] Thus no civil or commercial law existed in China before the end of the feudal period.

Chinese traditional culture has a profound content. Some of that content is splendid, but some is not beneficial for the development of Chinese law. In the Spring and Autumn and Warring States Periods (770—221BC), a school of thought called Confucianism emerged in China. The philosophy of Confucianism had the most profound historic significance for Chinese culture, and

---

① Li Peizhi,Zhao Fujiang, Wang Xiuying, The Defects of Chinese Traditional Legal Culture and the Constitution of a Modern Society Ruled by Law, 23(5) Hebei Law Science,2005,157-158.

② Tian Wei, Gao Hong, Chinese Traditional Legal Culture in the Process of Making the Society Ruled by Law, 5(2) Journal of Hebei Vocational College of Public Security Police,2005,32.

inevitably for Chinese legal culture. Even today the philosophy of Confucian-ism plays an important role in Chinese life, and to some degree hampers the process of the legal modernization of China. Firstly, Confucianists advocated vigorously the three cardinal guides and the five constant virtues as specified in the feudal ethical code. The three cardinal guides are: the ruler guides the subject, the father guides his son, and the husband guides his wife. The five constant virtues are benevolence, righteousness, propriety, wisdom and fi-delity. The effect of the guides and virtues is that individuals forfeit person-ality. The will of the individuals is subordinate to the will of the family. This philosophy still influences contemporary Chinese law, including arbitration law, in that it says little about rights, but much about obligations. Chinese arbitration law infringes the principle of party autonomy more often than the Model Law or the 1996 Act. Secondly, Confucianists also emphasized that morality should be regarded as important and economic benefit unimportant. Morality and individual economic benefit were regarded as mutually opposed to each other. The notion of individual rights was suffocated. The notion of obligation prevailed. As a result, even today, parties' rights and autonomy are not protected well by Chinese law. Thirdly, in traditional culture, the harmony of people and providence (the will of the sky), of people and socie-ty, and of people and nature were regarded as very important. The notion that providence and people were integrated and should work together is in the mainstream of Chinese traditional culture. The sky, land, everything on earth, and the people are an integrated entity; with the sky dominating that entity. It was for the emperor to actualize the entity. The emperor was domi-nating the people and everything on earth on behalf of the sky. Therefore, people must obey the will of the emperor, and the emperor was supposed to obey providence.[1] The ancient Chinese people believed that referring dis-

---

①   Li Peizhi, Zhao Fujiang, Wang Xiuying, The Defects of Chinese Traditional Legal Culture and the Constitution of a Modern Society Ruled by Law, 23(5) Hebei Law Sci-ence, 2005, 158.

中英仲裁法比较研究
A Comparative Study of the Chinese Arbitration
Law and the Arbitration Laws of the UK

putes to litigation would disturb the harmony of both society and the universe. Moreover, to protect popular harmony within the people and avoid hurting each other's feelings, people preferred to resolve problems by conciliation, rather than referring disputes to litigation. Fourthly, Confucianists deemed ethics as the most effective means of regulating popular behavior, as they resonated in peoples' minds. By contrast, they deemed law, which is enforced through the exercise of power, as inauthentic, unilateral, and of limited effect. In their opinion, although law can force a person to do or refrain from doing something, it cannot make a person act on his own initiative. Thus, in their eyes, law was much less effective than ethics.[1] This is why Chinese civil and commercial law (including arbitration law) is underdeveloped even though Chinese cultural history is very long. Fifthly, Confucianists considered that language and writing are simply tools to express feelings, and thus less important than inner experience. Sometimes, certain things can only be understood by the heart, and cannot be expressed verbally. Although this view might be beneficial for the development of Chinese literature and art, it is harmful for that of Chinese law. Some Chinese laws are thus much terser and oversimplified in comparison with the laws of other countries.

Moreover, in Chinese traditional ancient legal culture, there was no concept that rational and just procedure is necessary for resolution of disputes. Consequently, legislators have not given much attention to questions of arbitral procedure, so that procedural rules in the Chinese arbitration law have some defects.

The emperor dominated ancient China. His will was law, and could not be questioned.[2] The highest power in the country was thus unrestricted. Of-

---

① Zhu Chanlin, Reform in China's Traditional Legal Culture, 2 Journal of Qinghai Junior Teachers' College, 2005, 95.

② Ke Wei, A Creative Evolution: From Traditional Legal System to Modern Legal System, 25(1) Inner Mongolia Social Science, 2004, 73.

ficials should carry out his will. The different ranks of officials themselves had different privileges. The higher the rank of the official was, the more privileges he would have. Those privileges also apply to his family members.[1] By contrast, the common people were simply the objects of the law. Thus, not every one was equal before the law. The law was simply a tool to control the people. The idea that common people should be ruled and controlled by government still influences today's Chinese arbitration law. For example, many issues which would be more sensible for the arbitral tribunal to determine are actually controlled by a public institution known as arbitration agency.

Ⅱ. Historical Development

During the Qing Dynasty its government appointed a very learned scholar, Shen Jiaben, as judicatory. He perused European, American and Japanese codes, as well as the current legal doctrines of these countries, borrowing those provisions which suited the monarchy of China for the laws of the Qing Dynasty. He created a new framework of constitutional and criminal law. Yet this led to a conflict inside the government, which was called "conflict between ethics and law". In this conflict, Shen Jiaben and his supporters claimed that the new framework of constitutional and criminal law was beneficial for China. However, many other officials disagreed with them, claiming that rights based on framework infringed Chinese tradition. This conflict in the end was only resolved by all parties accepting that the new framework would be ignored in practice. This experience suggests that Western law based on commodity exchange cannot easily be transplanted to

---

[1] Li Guangyu, A Comparison on the Characteristics of Chinese Law with Those of Western Law, 24 Journal of South-Central University for Nationalities (Humanities and Social Science Edition),2004,155.

中英仲裁法比较研究
A Comparative Study of the Chinese Arbitration
Law and the Arbitration Laws of the UK

Chinese "smallholder economy". Although an important legal reform had seemingly been effected, nothing really changed. The smallholder economy remained, while commodity exchange was still very underdeveloped. The way of life and mode of thought of the people did not change. People still resolved disputes by virtue of village rules, nongovernmental agreements and ethics and morality as of old. No one used the new law. Thus there was no condition for the new framework of constitutional and criminal law to be put into practice. Yet although these political reforms failed, the new laws promoted the transformation of Chinese legal system.

After the end of Qing Dynasty, the Northern Warlords (1912—1927) employed the new laws, except for those provisions which conflicted with democracy. Thus in 1925, the government made the first civil law in Chinese history, based on those laws. After the Kuomintang Government replaced Northern Warlords, it continued to use the civil law rules and resultant case law. From 1929 to 1931, the Kuomintang compiled a set of Six Codes, governing such matters as the constitution, civil law, criminal law, civil procedure, criminal procedure, and court organization. This was based on the civil law of the Northern Warlords and the legal systems of continental Europe.

Essentially, the Six Codes was the fruit of the combined wisdom of the law experts of the Qing Dynasty, the Northern Warlords, and the Kuomintang, based on researching into the law and folk-customs of the country. The Six Codes continued to be used during the War of Resistance Against Japan (1931—1945) and the War of Liberation (1945—1949). In 1949, since the Communist Party considered that its ideological difference from the Kuomintang should be emphasized, the Six Codes was abolished. This abolition led to discontinuity in Chinese civil law.

In October of 1949, the People's Republic of China (hereinafter referred to as the PRC) was founded. Chinese law did not advance even a little from 1949—1978. This is one main reason why Chinese law is so underdeveloped, comparing with the law of the West.

The Chinese legislative process did not resume until the end of the "Great Cultural Revolution". Deng Xiaoping became the leader and introduced the guiding principles that democracy should be developed and legislation should be strengthened. From 1979, legislation, legal education, and the operation of the legal system regained importance.

Deng Xiaoping opened a door for the Chinese people to learn from the West. Economic reform began in the 1980s, with the planned economy being formally abandoned in 1992, and the aim of the reform of the economy being defined as a system establishing "socialist market economy".

The former legal system based on a planned economy was clearly unsuitable for the development of the market economy. Lessons could clearly be learned from the legal systems of Western countries with developed market economies. The market requires to be regulated by law. People who compete in the market must know that the rules of the game should be obeyed. Given the pace at which economic change must be achieved, it has proved much more convenient to adopt effective rules from the laws of Western countries than to develop original Chinese rules.

When any sort of market economy is introduced, disputes will invariably arise between individual economic actors, and an effective means of resolving those disputes must be available. Parties may prefer not to resort to the courts, particularly if they are foreign parties. Arbitration is a mechanism which allows disputes to be conclusively adjudicated without resorting to the courts, and thus is particularly valuable in an emergent market economy with developing foreign trade relations. A well-developed arbitration law is thus vital to the development of the Chinese economy. There were and there still are many defects of the Chinese arbitration law and the Chinese arbitration system. For example, although from the 1980s, foreign arbitration in China followed the principle that arbitration is a nongovernmental activity which should be chosen by the parties, and an arbitration award is fi-

中英仲裁法比较研究
A Comparative Study of the Chinese Arbitration
Law and the Arbitration Laws of the UK

nal, ① before the promulgation of the arbitration law, domestic arbitration in China was very much controlled by administrative bodies.

Supervision of arbitrations involving Chinese and foreign parties was inaugurated in the 1950s. In 1954, the Government Administration Council passed a "decision" which established an arbitration commission for external trade within the international trade promotion commission, formulating temporary regulations to govern its operation. In December 1958, the State Council passed another "decision" establishing the maritime arbitration commission within the international trade promotion commission, along with corresponding arbitration rules. From the beginning, foreign arbitration in China followed the principle that arbitration is a nongovernmental activity which should be chosen by the parties, and that an arbitration award is final. ② However, the historical development of domestic arbitration is more complex. Between 1955 and 1966, the parties to economic contracts could only apply to the economic arbitration commission to resolve disputes by arbitration. The court was not allowed to deal with such disputes. A party who disagreed with the arbitral award could only appeal to the higher administrative department. The practice of resolving contractual disputes by administrative measures is typical of a highly planned economy. From 1978 to 1982, before the promulgation of the economic contract law, although China resumed arbitration, the system was confused and there was no uniform procedure. According to the "Combined Notice as to Several Problems of Managing Economic Contracts" and the "Trial Regulation of Contract Arbitral Procedure of Industrial and Commercial Administrative Management De-

---

① Cheng Zhongqian, Origination from, Development of and Prospects for Arbitration, 9 Journal of Arbitration Research of the Guangzhou Arbitration Commission, 2005, 47.

② Cheng Zhongqian, Origination from, Development of and Prospects for Arbitration, 9 Journal of Arbitration Research of the Guangzhou Arbitration Commission, 2005, 47.

partments" both issued by the Industrial and Commercial Administrative General Department on 8 September 1979 and 2 May 1980, that body would arbitrate any dispute. It can be seen that state agencies were playing a role as arbitrators at this stage. Confusingly, it would hold two sets of proceedings, and a party might only appeal to the court if he disagreed with the second arbitral award which was the final award. However, once the economic contract law was passed, a dispute could no longer be arbitrated twice. There was only one arbitral award, which was final, subject to an appeal to the court. Indeed after the passing of the new economic contract law in 1993, an appeal to the court was no longer open.

Before the promulgation of the arbitration law, arbitration could only be conducted through arbitration agencies which in turn were attached to administrative organs. Thus arbitration agencies dealing with economic contracts were attached to Industrial and Commercial Administrative Management Departments; those dealing with real estate were attached to Real Estate Management Departments; those dealing with technology contracts were attached to Technology Commissions; and those dealing with disputes arising from labour relations were attached to Labour Administration Departments. In fact, the parties were not entitled to appoint arbitrators. The arbitrators were the officers of those departments. Thus, essentially, the government exercised significant control over arbitration. Moreover, before the passing of the arbitration law, there were 14 statutes, 82 administrative regulations, and 190 local regulations dealing with arbitration, although most of the regulations dealt with administrative rather than economic arbitration. Additionally, an arbitration agreement is not a necessary precondition for commencing a commercial arbitration. Where there was no arbitration agreement before or even after a dispute arose, a party was still allowed to refer the dispute to arbitration. The fact that arbitration was an administratively directed activity conflicted with the principle of party autonomy, removing a key advantage of arbitration, as seen from the common interna-

中英仲裁法比较研究
A Comparative Study of the Chinese Arbitration
Law and the Arbitration Laws of the UK

tional standpoint.① Fortunately, after the promulgation of the arbitration law, state agencies stopped appointing arbitrators and playing a role in the arbitration process. Article 14 of the PRC Arbitration Law 2017 provides that an arbitration shall be conducted independently according to law, free from interference by administrative organs, social groups or individuals. Article 14 provides that an arbitration commission shall be independent of and not be subordinate to any administrative organ.② Furthermore, the parties are entitled to appoint arbitrators and party autonomy has been protected in this regard. However, As a result of historical development of arbitration in China, even nowadays, some of the legislators still retain the idea that arbitration is an administrative activity which requires to be controlled. Accordingly some provisions of arbitration law do not protect party autonomy sufficiently, while arbitration agencies continue to have too much power. Even the PRC Arbitration Law 2017 shares these defects and others.

III. Policy Debate

In 1991, the Legality Working Commission of the Standing Committee of the National People's Congress embarked on a project to create a new arbitration law. During the process of research and consultation, six issues were examined in detail —the question of arbitrability, the role of arbitration agencies, the position of arbitration agreements, how jurisdictional issues should be resolved, the relationship between arbitration and litigation, and the degree of state supervision of arbitration. After full discussion, the

---

① Cheng Zhongqian, Origination from, Development of and Prospects for Arbitration, 9 Journal of Arbitration Research of the Guangzhou Arbitration Commission, 2005, 48.

② Article 14 of the PRC Arbitration Law 2017.

first edition of the arbitration law was passed in August, 1994.① Certainly, the policy debates during the process of law making might determine more directly the content of the arbitration law. Unfortunately, the details of the policy debates as to the Chinese arbitration law are confidential, so that no definitive answer can be given as to why the law adopted its particular form.

It can be seen that, by reason of the culture and tradition of China, commercial law, including arbitration law, was not well developed and in particular no arbitration law existed before the Constitution of the PRC. After the Constitution of the PRC and before the promulgation of the Arbitration Law 1994 and the accompanying the CIETAC Rules, although there were some arbitral regulations or rules, some rules of they were odd and unreasonable. While the PRC Arbitration Law 2017 and the CIETAC Rules are much better than the previous regulations or rules, they are still far from perfect.

The United Kingdom is a developed western country and its arbitration laws are extremely developed. It is submitted that it is particularly useful to look to the United Kingdom for a paradigm which may be followed, as it offers two models for consideration —the Arbitration Act 1996 in England (the 1996 Act), and the UNCITRAL Model Law on International Commercial Arbitration (the Model Law) which has been adopted in Scotland. At first sight it may seem odd to suggest that China seek to borrow legislative models from a very different social and legal order. However, the Model Law is, of course, not Scottish, but a legislative framework which has been specifically devised to be adaptable to the widest possible variety of legal cultures. Equally, the 1996 Act, which in large measure is directly inspired by the Model Law, marks a significant departure for the English legal system, going against the grain of much of the previous law. To a significant extent it

---

① The Civil Law Office of the Legality Working Commission of the Standing Committee of the National People's Congress and the Secretary Office of CIETAC (eds.), All Sets of the PRC Arbitration Law, Beijing: Publishing House of Law, 1995, 13.

中英仲裁法比较研究
A Comparative Study of the Chinese Arbitration
Law and the Arbitration Laws of the UK

is directed towards attracting international arbitrations to England. While the Model Law requires to be general and adaptable as possible, and deliberately avoids framing provisions on areas which may be thought to be controversial, the 1996 Act can deal with a number of issues not addressed by the Model Law or deal with issues more specifically than the Model Law. Furthermore, it can do so from the standpoint of a system which has long experience as an attractive forum for international arbitration. For such reasons the 1996 Act and the Model Law are excellent and obvious models for a country seeking —as dozens of other states have done over the last 20 years — to adopt a modern arbitration regime which will immediately be comprehensible to potential foreign users.

CHAPTER 3

A THEORETICAL UNDERPINNING

I. Introduction

In order sensibly to compare the role of the courts in arbitration under Chinese and UK law, some sort of theoretical underpinnings are needed. This chapter thus focuses on two overarching issues. The first one is the role of the state in supervising arbitration, viewed as a process that occurs out-with the formal dispute resolution mechanisms established by the state. The second issue, which flows from the first, would be the respective roles of the court and arbitral tribunal in arbitration. The discussion of the first issue encompasses party autonomy in making and enforcing arbitration agreements, the balance between mandatory and default rules in arbitration, procedural controls, substantive controls. The discussion of the second issue encompasses the competence-competence principle, and the comprehensive su-

中英仲裁法比较研究
A Comparative Study of the Chinese Arbitration
Law and the Arbitration Laws of the UK

pervision theory versus the procedural supervision theory.

II. The Role of the State in Arbitration

A. Nature of Arbitration

In order to analyse whether, and if so why, the court shall play a role in arbitration, the nature of arbitration shall be discussed. The extent to which the state should supervise the arbitral process, if at all, must depend on the essential nature of arbitration. Bernard[1] propounded three theories on that issue in 1937. Under the first theory, the arbitration agreement and the arbitral award are separate, and the latter should be regarded as akin to a court judgment. Under the second theory the award derives from the agreement, so that they are inseparable. Thus the arbitral award is essentially a contract rather than a court judgment. The third theory is a compromise between the first two, and claims that an arbitral award can be regarded as akin to a court judgment only when a court order is needed for its enforcement.[2] These three theories are now respectively known as the "Jurisdictional Theory", the "Contractual Theory" and the "Mixed or Hyrid Theory".[3] In the 1960s, a fourth theory developed, known as the "Autonomous Theory". All are discussed below.

---

① Lew, Julian D. M., Applicable Law in International Commercial Arbitration, New York: Oceana Publications, Inc.,1978,51-52.

② Lew, Julian D. M., Applicable Law in International Commercial Arbitration, New York: Oceana Publications, Inc.,1978,51-52.

③ Yu Honglin, Total Separation of International Commercial Arbitration and National Court Regime, 5(2) J. Int'l Arb. 1988,148; Georgios I. Zekos, Problems of Applicable Law in Commercial and Maritime Arbitration, 16(4) J. Int'l Arb. 1999,177; Gunther J. Horvath, The Duty of the Tribunal to Render an Enforceable Award, 18(2) J. Int'l Arb. 2001,147-148.

Jurisdictional Theory: it claims that arbitration operates within a framework of law, and a state has the power to control and regulate all the arbitrations happening in its jurisdiction. While the theory concedes that arbitration is based on the agreement of the parties, it insists that matters such as the validity of the arbitration agreement and award, the powers of arbitrators, and the enforceability of awards, all depend on the law of the place of arbitration and the law of the place of enforcement of the arbitral award. An arbitration agreement will be valid and an arbitral award will be enforceable only if both laws, the law of the place of arbitration and the law of the place of enforcement, recognize that the parties have the right to refer the dispute to arbitration, that the arbitrators have jurisdiction over the case concerned, and that the arbitral award is enforceable. In other words, arbitral jurisdiction and the validity of the arbitration process ultimately depend on the law of the place of enforcement.[1]Moreover, certain supporters of this theory insist that adjudication is a sovereign function of courts, and only courts have the power to administer justice. The reason why the law permits the parties to have recourse to arbitration is that the law wants the arbitration to perform a court-like function. The only difference between arbitrators and judges is that arbitrators are appointed by the parties and judges by the state. Since the powers and functions of arbitrators and judges are extremely similar, the arbitral award should be regarded as a sort of judgment, and should have the same effect.[2] The theory limits the autonomy of arbitrators and emphasizes the power of the state law, requiring the arbitral award to be consistent with the law of the place of enforcement.

Contractual Theory: this theory emphasizes the contractual character of arbitration. Its supporters give three main reasons why the essence of arbi-

①   Han Jian, Theory and Practice on Modern International Commercial Law, Beijing: Law Press, 2000.

②   Klein, F. E., consideration sur 1' arbitrage en droit international priv Bale: Heilbing & Lichtenhahn, 1955, 105-112.

中英仲裁法比较研究
A Comparative Study of the Chinese Arbitration
Law and the Arbitration Laws of the UK

tration is contractual. First of all, arbitration is based on the agreement of the parties. Where there is no arbitration agreement, no party can force the other to arbitrate, except in the rare instances of compulsory arbitration.[①] Secondly, all issues regarding the constitution of the arbitral tribunal can be decided by the agreement of the parties, including the appointment of arbitrators, the time and place of arbitration, etc. The parties may also agree on the arbitral procedure, while domestic arbitration law only provides default rules to deal with situations where the parties don't agree on such issues.[②] Thirdly, the reason why an arbitral award is recognized and enforced is because of the binding force of the arbitration agreement.[③] The arbitral award is made by the arbitrators as the agents of the parties, and thus is itself an agreement made by the agents on behalf of the parties.[④] Each party has an obligation to enforce the award, otherwise the other party can apply to the court for enforcement. Such enforcement is different from the enforcement of a court judgment, and is essentially the enforcement of a contract. Therefore, it is concluded that an arbitration agreement is simply a contract based on the consensus of the parties[⑤], and not an exercise of delegated sovereign power. This theory sees domestic law as creating a framework for the arbitration. Thus the court will not enforce an arbitration agreement, except, under the law of the forum, the court has exclusive jurisdiction over the sub-

---

① Stone, Morris, A Paradox in the Theory of Commercial Arbitration, 21 Arb. J. 1966,156; Wallace, E. V., Drafting a New York Arbitration Agreement (No.3, N. Y. Continuing Legal Education),1967.

② Eisemann, Frederic, L'arbitre-partie, in International Arbitration: Liber Amicorum for Martin Domke, Hague: Martinus Nijhoff,1967,79.

③ Niboyet, J. P., Trait de Droit International Privé Française, tomes V, VI. Paris: Sirey, 1950, 1284.

④ Lew, Julian D. M., Applicable Law in International Commercial Arbitration, New York: Oceana Publications, Inc.,1978,55.

⑤ Domke, Martin, Commercial Arbitration, Englewood Cliffs: N. J. Prentice-Hall, 1965,2.

ject matter of the dispute. Nor will it enforce an arbitral award which is in conflict with public policy. When arbitrators are dealing with the problem of choice of law, they should conduct the arbitration according to the parties' explicit expression of will. Where there is no such expression, they are guided by their deduction of the parties' implied choice.

Mixed or Hyrid Theory: this theory asserts that arbitration has both a jurisdictional and a contractual character. In 1952, Sauser-Hall explained this theory in detail[1], pointing out that arbitration cannot transcend the legal system, and there must always be laws which determine the validity of arbitration agreements and the enforceability of arbitral awards. He also considered that arbitration derived from private contracts, and that the appointment of arbitrators and the rules governing the arbitral process should mainly stem from the agreement of the parties. As a result, he believed the jurisdictional and contractual character of arbitration correlative and indivisible.[2] Supporters of this theory insist that although the jurisdictional and contractual theories are diametrically opposed, they can work in a concerted way to explain the essence of arbitration. Thus the arbitration agreement is a contract, and its validity should be determined in accordance with contractual principles. If according to the law of the forum, the court has exclusive jurisdiction over the subject matter of the dispute, or if the arbitrators conduct the proceedings in defiance of basic principles of equity, or if the award conflicts with the public policy of the forum, the court in which the enforcement is sought will refuse to recognize or enforce the arbitral award. Arbitrators must balance the will of the parties and the law of the place of arbitration. As far as the substantive law which would be used to resolve the dispute is concerned, arbitrators should respect the will of the parties and apply the

---

① Sauser-Hall, Georges, L'arbitrage en Droit International Privé, 44 Annuaire de L'institut de Droit International, 1952, 469.

② Sauser-Hall, Georges, L'arbitrage en Droit International Privé, 44 Annuaire de L'institut de Droit International, 1952, 469.

中英仲裁法比较研究
A Comparative Study of the Chinese Arbitration
Law and the Arbitration Laws of the UK

law chosen by them. Where the parties have made no explicit choice, arbitrators may directly determine the applicable law by virtue of the rules of international conflict of laws. [1]

Autonomous Theory: this theory is advanced by Devichi. [2] It maintains that arbitration is not jurisdictional or contractual, or even mixed, but a completely independent system. [3] In order to determine the essence of arbitration, she considers it is necessary to examine the function and aim of arbitration. This theory views arbitration from a completely different angle from the other three theories. They concentrate on the aspects of arbitration which accord with domestic law and international law, and how the right of the parties to refer the disputes to arbitration and to determine the arbitral process is limited by the law. By contrast, the autonomous theory concentrates on the issues of the arbitration itself, such as the aim of arbitration, the arbitral proceedings, the function of arbitration and the reason why it can have such functions. Devichi suggests that neither the jurisdictional theory nor the contractual theory can correctly reflect the essence of arbitration, while the fact that they are in fundamental conflict precludes them being combined. She also argues that the three traditional theories all impose limits upon arbitration which would restrict certain advantages, which might otherwise lead businessmen to prefer arbitration to litigation, and which would prevent arbitration from developing. The supporters of this theory argue that arbitration was first created and then developed by businessmen, regardless of the law. The law simply affirms arbitration. The autonomy of the parties to determine both substantive and procedural law is based on neither the

① Han Jian, Theory and Practice on Modern International Commercial Law, Beijing: Law Press, 2000, 36.

② Rubellin-Devichi, Jacqueline, L'arbitrage, Nature Jurisdigue Droit Interne et Droit International Privé, Paris: Librairie Gensäle de Droit et Jurisprudence, 1965, 14.

③ Rubellin-Devichi, Jacqueline, L'arbitrage. Nature Jurisdigue Droit Interne et Droit International Privé, Paris: Librairie Gensäle de Droit et Jurisprudence, 1965, 14.

contractual nor the jurisdictional character of arbitration, but on the necessity of commercial custom. Similarly, the reason why arbitration agreements and awards are enforceable is not because they are contracts, or the state in which enforcement occurs gives concessions, but because businessmen across the world would not be able to conduct international commercial relations successfully if arbitral awards were not enforceable. Support for this theory is found in the fact that certain nongovernmental arbitral institutions had been constituted before the existence of the international commercial arbitration conventions.[1] The theory sees arbitration as non-domestic, with the parties having unlimited autonomy. Commercial society is an international environment which can develop its own law, and can act as an international court. Parties can determine both substantive and procedural law. Devichi[2] contends that the unconditional autonomy of the parties makes arbitration supranational and international commercial law can be applied directly. Thus, the parties can choose not only domestic law to govern the substance of their disputes, but also international commercial law or trade customs. They can even choose general principles of justice and equity. Where the parties have made no choice, arbitrators may apply the conflict rules which they consider suitable, or directly apply relevant international law or international rules,[3] instead of applying the conflict rules of the place of arbitration.

The autonomous theory emphasizes the origins of arbitration, but totally ignores current arbitral practice. While that theory suggests that arbitration be non-domestic and the parties have unlimited autonomy, in reality

---

[1] E. g. the ICC was established in 1923 prior to both the Geneva Convention on the Execution of Foreign Arbitral Awards 1927 and the New York Convention of 1958.

[2] Rubellin-Devichi, Jacqueline, L'arbitrage, Nature Jurisdigue Droit Interne et Droit International Privé, Paris: Librairie Gensäle de Droit et Jurisprudence, 1965, 175. See Lew, Julian D. M., Applicable Law in International Commercial Arbitration, New York: Oceana Publications, Inc.,1978,61.

[3] Han Jian, Theory and Practice on Modern International Commercial Law, Beijing: Law Press,2000,41.

中英仲裁法比较研究
A Comparative Study of the Chinese Arbitration
Law and the Arbitration Laws of the UK

neither of these things is true, and the theory cannot explain why this is so. Jurisdictional theory ignores the contractual essence of arbitration and thus is inappropriate. The key issue is then whether arbitration is contractual or hybrid in nature.

In my opinion, it is inappropriate to say that arbitration is judicial. It is a private method of settling disputes, based on the agreement between the parties. Its main characteristic is that it involves submitting the dispute to individuals chosen, directly or indirectly, by the parties. The rules of contract provide the theoretical basis to why arbitration is binding. The principle of respecting matters agreed by the parties —the doctrine of "party autonomy" permeates the whole arbitral proceedings, including performing the arbitration agreement, constituting the tribunal, conducting the process of arbitration and so on. If matters agreed by parties are violated in arbitration proceedings, the award rendered by the tribunal would be set aside or its enforcement refused. Yet it must be conceded that where the agreement allowed one party to be treated unfairly, that might lead to the award being set aside in most states; while if the tribunal ignored that agreement and conducted the proceedings fairly, the award would probably be safe from being set aside.

The fact that the basis of arbitration is contractual is not in dispute. The arbitrators' power to resolve a dispute is founded upon the common intention of the parties. Thus arbitration should be defined by reference to two constituent elements which commentators[1] and the courts almost unanimously recognize. First, the arbitrators' task is to resolve disputes. Second, the source of this judicial role is a contract which means the arbitrators' power to

① Savage, John, Goldman, Emmanuel, Fouchard Gaillard Goldman on International Commercial Arbitration, New York: ASPEN Publishers, Inc.,1999,29; Mustill, Michael J. & Boyd, Stewart C., Commercial Arbitration, 2nd ed., London: Butterworths Law, 1989, 41; Han, Depei (ed.), Current Issues of Private International Law, Wuhan: Publishing House of Wuhan University,2004,332-334.

decide disputes originates in the common intention of the parties rather than being conferred by the state as in the case of courts. Judicial dispute resolution draws its authority from the sovereign which created the court. In arbitration, decision makers are chosen by the litigants, rather than by the community, and the "submission agreement" creates and defines the arbitral power. The arbitral power is often created indirectly, by reference to rules of the International Chamber of Commerce, or of the International Center for the Settlement of Investment Disputes, and the like. While parties create their own dispute resolution mechanisms as an alternation to court settlement, they sometimes ask a court to provide post-arbitration enforcement[1], just as a contract is enforced. Thus, the essential nature of arbitration is contractual, although it could be said that arbitration has a judicial function.

The essentially contractual nature of arbitration allows it to be distinguished from litigation, although the decisions of arbitrators who derive their powers from a private agreement between individuals, not from the state, are binding in the same way as court orders. At the same time, the adjudicative character of arbitration makes it different from other dispute resolution mechanisms, such as conciliation, mediation, settlement and expert proceedings. Judicial intervention in arbitration should refrain from interfering with the exercise of the powers entrusted to arbitrators by the parties and rather be confined to assisting the arbitral process when the need arises. Judicial involvement in arbitration is justified on the basis that the powers of arbitrators derive from the agreement between the parties, rather than being conferred by the state, so that the courts may often have to employ their inherent powers to fill the inevitable gaps.

There are several arguments against the arbitral process being completely independent of national court systems. Firstly, the judiciary is essen-

---

①　Hirsch, Alain, The Place of Arbitration and the Lex Arbitri, 34 Arb. J.1979,43.

中英仲裁法比较研究
A Comparative Study of the Chinese Arbitration
Law and the Arbitration Laws of the UK

tial in guaranteeing the integrity of the arbitration process.[1] Secondly, the authority of arbitrators is conferred by agreement and extends no further, so that there must be safeguards against arbitrators exceeding the authority. Thirdly, parties may want insurance against erratic and unpredictable results.[2] Fourthly, states may want to review arbitral decisions to protect weak parties, third parties, or their national interests. In relation to disputes which the parties have agreed to refer to arbitration, the court serves two functions. On the one hand, the court provides assistance and support and, on the other, it supervises and controls. The control exercised by the court over the arbitral process is the price which has to be paid for the court's support.

B. Areas Where Judicial Intervention Is Needed

Discussed above, although arbitration has a contractual nature, to ensure the integrity of the arbitral process and protect the public interest, the court must support and supervise that process. It is known that the jurisdiction of the court is given by the state. Accordingly, the power of the court to play a role in arbitration is also given by the state. Thus, the role of the court in supervising arbitration is actually state supervision of arbitration, viewed as a process that occurs outwith the formal dispute resolution mechanisms established by the state. There are a number of areas in international arbitration where there are likely to be problems with judicial intervention. These areas are: party autonomy in making and enforcing arbitration agreements; striking a balance between mandatory and default rules in arbitration; control over the arbitral proceedings; control over the substantive issues; and the role of state agencies as arbitrators and in the arbitration

---

[1] Lutz, Robert E., International Arbitration and Judicial Intervention, 10 Loy. L. A. Int'l & Comp. L. J.1988,621.

[2] Although many systems provide no protection against erratic results in the sense that awards that are substantively erroneous must stand.

process. These categories are addressed in the following discussion.

1. Party autonomy in making and enforcing arbitration agreements

An arbitration agreement means an agreement to submit to arbitrate present or future disputes. Parties have autonomy in making and enforcing such arbitration agreements. To protect that autonomy law requires that the will of parties to enter into that agreement should be genuine, so that if a party is coerced into the agreement, it is deemed to be invalid. Law should also protect party autonomy by allowing parties to abandon the arbitration agreement mutually. Moreover law must reinforce party autonomy by requiring them to refer disputes to arbitration where they have a valid arbitration agreement which has not been mutually abandoned. Where there is a valid arbitration agreement between the parties and one party goes to the court for litigation, if the other party invokes the valid arbitration agreement to the court, the court should stay any action brought before it if the matter is subject to the arbitration agreement.

2. The balance between mandatory and default rules in arbitration

The arbitration law of every legal system features mandatory rules from which the parties may not derogate. Arbitration law must also provide default rules to support the arbitral process when the agreement of the parties breaks down, yet it is in the nature of such rules that parties are free to agree otherwise. In China, some of the provisions of the arbitration law are mandatory and the provisions of the CIETAC Rules are default rules. Thus the agreement of the parties may override the CIETAC Rules but not the arbitration law. In both the Model Law and the 1996 Act, some rules are mandatory. In this way, law supervises arbitration by forbidding parties to make the agreement which might adversely affect the integrity of the arbitral process or harm the public interest. For example, under the Chinese law, the Model Law, and the 1996 Act, provisions governing the grounds on which awards may be challenged are mandatory, and parties are not allowed to make their own agreements on this issue. This protects the finality of ar-

中英仲裁法比较研究
A Comparative Study of the Chinese Arbitration
Law and the Arbitration Laws of the UK

bitral awards and prevents unnecessary court intervention. Under the Model Law, the 1996 Act, and Chinese law, conflict with public policy is a ground for challenging an award. In this way, the public interest can be protected.

3. Judicial control over arbitration proceedings

Courts play an indispensable role in controlling the arbitral process and award. In the Model Law and the 1996 Act, the court might have procedural control over the case where it removes the arbitrators on the grounds specified therein. Moreover, under Chinese arbitration law, the Model Law and the 1996 Act, the court might have procedural control where a party applies to set aside the arbitral award on the ground that the arbitral proceedings have not been conducted according to the parties' agreement or the arbitration rules. The court might also have substantive control over arbitral award, as where a party is allowed to challenge an award on the ground of uncertainty or ambiguity as to its effect, or where a party is allowed to appeal to the court on a question of law arising out of the award.

III. The Respective Roles of the Court and Arbitral Tribunal in Arbitration

The principle that the roles of judges and arbitrators are complementary is considered to be an established fact. It suggests a certain equality between the judge and the arbitrator in their respective roles, the common object of which is to ensure the effectiveness of international commercial arbitration. Yet we shall see that such equality is not absolute. A balance between judicial intervention and arbitral autonomy should be achieved. The most important examples relate to the respective roles of the court and arbitral tribunal in determining the jurisdiction of the tribunal, and in dealing with challenges to arbitral awards.

A. Determining the Jurisdiction of the Tribunal —Competence-competence Principle

When a party challenges the competence of the arbitral tribunal, should the tribunal, the arbitration agency or the court have jurisdiction to rule on that competence? This is called the competence-competence problem. It has given rise to much controversy and misunderstanding, and behind the appearance of unanimity —most laws now recognize the principle in some form —it continues to be the subject of considerable divergence between different legal systems.[1] The competence-competence principle is now recognized by the main international conventions on arbitration.[2] The central idea is that any objection against a tribunal's jurisdiction should be dealt with, at least initially, by the tribunal itself. A statutory statement of the principle helps avoid the logical conundrum of how a tribunal, which rules that it has no jurisdiction, can be said to have jurisdiction to make such a ruling in the first place.

The underpinning of the competence-competence principle is that the tribunal's competence to rule over its own competence is the basic power for the tribunal to work properly, even though the tribunal's decision on this issue might be varied or cancelled by the court. In the 1950s, Devlin J. stated that the law does not require an arbitrator to refuse to perform his function as an arbitrator simply because his competence has been challenged. Neither does the law require an arbitrator to continue arbitration, leaving the prob-

---

① Dimolitsa, Antonias, Separability and Kompetenz-Kompetenz, in A. J. van den Berg(ed.), Improving the Efficiency of Arbitration Agreements and Awards: 40 Years of Application of the New York Convention (ICCA Congress Series No.9),1999,217; Park, William W., The Arbitrability Dicta in First Options v. Kaplan: What Sort of Kompetenz-Kompetenz Has Crossed the Atlantic, 12 Arb. Int'l, 1996,137; Park, William W., Determining Arbitral Jurisdiction: Allocation of Tasks Between Courts and Arbitrators, 8 Am. Int'l Arb.,1997,133.

② See, e. g., Article V, para. 3 of the 1961 European Convention; Article 41 of the 1965 Washington Convention.

中英仲裁法比较研究
A Comparative Study of the Chinese Arbitration
Law and the Arbitration Laws of the UK

lem of competence-competence to be solved by the court. Rather, the arbi-tral tribunal has the power to rule on its own competence. The aim of doing this is not to make a decision on the subject-matter of the dispute, but to re-solve a preliminary problem so that the parties could know whether the arbi-tration could be continued.[①] Sandrock has since stated that, as the parties wished to resolve their dispute via arbitration, the arbitral tribunal should it-self decide whether it has competence over the case. To leave the compe-tence-competence problem to be decided by the court would be a waste of time and money.[②]

Also, the fact that the most modern arbitration statutes[③] and the main institutional arbitration rules include the principle is the further evidence of its widespread recognition of the competence-competence principle. Howev-er, some scholars doubt whether recognition of the principle by the arbitral institutions is sufficient to ensure its effectiveness. Institutional arbitration rules derive their authority from the parties' agreement. The rights of arbi-

---

① Redfern, Alan & Hunter, Martin, Law and Practice of International Commercial Arbitration, London: Sweet & Maxwell,1991,276; Per Devlin J., Christopher Brown Ltd. v. Genossenschaft Oesterreichischer Waldbesitzer Holzwritschaftsbetribe Registrierte Genossenschaf Mt It Beschrankler Haftung, I Q. B. 1954,12-13.

② Sandrock, Otto, Arbitration between U. S. and West Germany Companies: An Example of Effective Dispute Resolution in International Business Transactions, 9 (1) U. Pa. J. Int'l Bus. L. 1987,22-23.

③ The Model Law provides in Article 6, paragraph 3 that the arbitral tribunal may rule on a plea that the arbitral tribunal does not have jurisdiction either as a preliminary question or in an award on the merits, and that, in the event of an action to set aside a par-tial award concerning jurisdiction, the arbitral tribunal may continue the arbitral proceed-ings and make an award. Article 186 of the 1987 Swiss Private International Law Statute and Article 8 para. 1, of the Swiss Concordat; Article 1697(1) of the Belgian Judicial Code (law of July 4,1972); Article 1052 (1) of the Netherlands Code of Civil Procedure (Law of Dec. 1,1986); Article 23 (3) of the Spanish Law 36/1988 of December 5,1988 on Arbitra-tion. Article 458 bis 7 of the Algerian Code of Civil Procedure (legislative decree No.93-09 of April 25,1993); Sec. 30 of the 1996 English Arbitration Act; Article 1040 of the Ger-man ZPO (1997).

trators given by institutional arbitration rules cannot exceed those allowed by the applicable legal systems. In other words, unlike national laws, arbitration rules are contractual in nature and therefore cannot answer why arbitrators should have power to determine their own jurisdiction, unless we adhere to an extreme contractual theory of arbitration. More fundamentally, although an arbitrator's jurisdiction to rule on his own jurisdiction is indeed one of the effects of the arbitration agreement, the basis of that power is neither the arbitration agreement itself, nor the principle of pacta sunt servanda giving the agreement binding force.[1] If that were the case, a "vicious circle" would immediately be created, raising the question how can an arbitrator, solely on the basis of an arbitration agreement, declare that an arbitration agreement is void or even hear a claim to that effect?

Thus the answer is simple: the basis for the competence-competence principle cannot lie in the arbitration agreement, but in the arbitration laws of the country where the arbitration is held and, more generally, in the laws of all countries liable to recognize the arbitral award.[2] If a country does not recognize competence-competence principle, this principle has no basis to exist. For example, at this stage, the Chinese arbitration law does not recognize competence-competence principle, and as a result, the parties are not allowed to agree that the arbitral tribunal should have the competence to rule on its own jurisdiction. Yet, while the power of an arbitral tribunal to rule

---

① Savage, John, Goldman, Emmanuel, Fouchard Gaillard Goldman on International Commercial Arbitration, New York: ASPEN Publishers, Inc., 1999, 29; Mustill, Michael J. & Boyd, Stewart C., Commercial Arbitration, 2nd ed., London: Butterworths Law, 1989, 41; Han, Depei (ed.), Current Issues of Private International Law, Wuhan: Publishing House of Wuhan University, 2004, 396.

② Savage, John, Goldman, Emmanuel, Fouchard Gaillard Goldman on International Commercial Arbitration, New York: ASPEN Publishers, Inc., 1999, 29; Mustill, Michael J. & Boyd, Stewart C., Commercial Arbitration, 2nd ed., London: Butterworths Law, 1989, 41; Han, Depei (ed.), Current Issues of Private International Law, Wuhan: Publishing House of Wuhan University, 2004, 399.

中英仲裁法比较研究
A Comparative Study of the Chinese Arbitration
Law and the Arbitration Laws of the UK

on its own jurisdiction may effectively prevent specious jurisdictional objections from being resorted to obstructing the proceedings, if the tribunal's determination of this issue were unreviewable, the potential for abuse would be immense. No serious legal system could permit an arbitral tribunal be the final determiner of its own jurisdiction. Thus in every system any jurisdictional ruling, whether a separate ruling or as part of an award on the merits of the dispute, may be appealed to the courts. The system under which a national court is involved in the question of jurisdiction before the arbitral tribunal has issued a final award on the merits is known as "concurrent control".[1] In most systems the tribunal may rule on jurisdictional issues as a preliminary award or as part of the final award. The advantage of ruling on jurisdictional issues as a preliminary award is that it enables the parties to know relatively quickly where they stand; and they will save time and money if the arbitration proceedings prove to be groundless. Only if the tribunal has confidence in its jurisdiction over the case would it decide to rule on jurisdictional issues as part of the final award.

B. Dealing with Arbitral Awards —the Comprehensive Supervision Theory Versus the Procedural Supervision Theory

After an arbitral award is made, either party may challenge the award in court. The issue thus arises whether the court should review both procedural and substantive issues, or simply the former. There are two theories on this issue in China: the comprehensive supervision theory and the procedural supervision theory. The former theory, advanced by Professor Chen An claims that the standard of supervision of foreign-related and domestic awards should be the same, embracing both procedural and substantive issues. Firstly, its theoretical base is that differential supervision of foreign-related and domestic awards is not common internationally.

---

① Redfern, Alan & Hunter, Martin, Law and Practice of International Commercial Arbitration 2nd ed., London: Sweet & Maxwell, 1991, 365.

Secondly, justice is deemed to be more important than efficiency, and the legality and impartiality of an award more important than its finality. Professor Chen An argues that where the parties agree to refer disputes to arbitration, they have abandoned the right to litigate. Through abandoning this right, the dispute can be resolved by a single determination. Yet what the parties have abandoned is the right to litigate, rather than the right to appeal to the courts, unless they have explicitly agreed to abandon this right also. Thus, it cannot be assumed that, as the parties have chosen arbitration, they have abandoned the right to ask the court to exercise a supervisory role and correct errors, especially where a foreign-related award is improper or illegal. It is an essential legal principle that violation of the law must be investigated and dealt with.[1]

Thirdly, the system of challenging arbitrators provided by Articles 34 and 38 of the PRC Arbitration Law 2017 only supervise their personal behavior, and is not enough to protect the correctness of awards.

The procedural supervision theory, advanced by Professor Xiao Yongping suggests that foreign-related and domestic awards should be supervised in different ways —the former only procedurally, the latter both procedurally and substantively. The advocates of this theory attack the theoretical basis of the comprehensive supervision theory as follows. Firstly, it is commonplace internationally to distinguish foreign-related awards from domestic awards, and this trend is gaining momentum. Professor Xiao Yongping points out that, compared with domestic arbitration, the rules regarding international arbitration are more flexible, and international arbitration is subject to

---

[1]   Chen An, Discussion on the System Supervising Chinese Foreign-Related Arbitration, 2 Social Science of China, 1998, 101-102.

中英仲裁法比较研究
A Comparative Study of the Chinese Arbitration
Law and the Arbitration Laws of the UK

minimal court supervision.① Secondly, the trend is towards decreasing court supervision of foreign-related awards.② Thirdly, the aim of court supervision is to strike a balance between finality of awards and the need for judicial review, in other words between the efficiency of arbitration system and justice. Professor Xiao Yongping claims that the goal of court supervision is to correct the potential mistakes of arbitrators, so that a fair award can be achieved, whereas if the scope of supervision is too large, time and energy would be unnecessarily wasted. It can be seen from legal practice that the reason why the parties choose arbitration to resolve disputes is that they want to achieve a final award, avoiding fussy and lengthy legal proceedings. Although the finality of awards may result in a party losing the right of appeal against potential errors, that finality is of greater benefit. The law should protect the reasonable expectations of the parties regarding the finality of awards. The task of law is to balance the autonomy of the parties and proper legal supervision. If Chinese law allows the court to supervise the substance of foreign-related awards, the arbitral process could be threatened by legal proceedings, which would adversely affect the finality of awards.③ Fourthly, since the PRC has been constituted, the Chinese arbitration sys-

---

① Xiao Yongping, Discussion about the Scope of the Court's Supervision on Arbitration in China, 1 Law Review of Wuhan University,1998,42; Xiao, Yongping, Opinions on the System of the Supervision upon Domestic Arbitration and Foreign-related Arbitration, 2 Social Science in China,1998,94.

② Xiao Yongping, Opinions on the System of the Supervision upon Domestic Arbitration and Foreign-Related Arbitration, 2 Social Science in China,1998,94.

③ Professor Xiao Yongping has also pointed out that, considering contractual essence of arbitration and the principle of autonomy of the parties, the parties may be allowed to make their own agreement to choose between finality of awards and supervision on substantial problems, i. e., the parties may be allowed to give the court the power to supervise on substantial problems. Xiao Yongping, Discussion about the Scope of the Court's Supervision on Arbitration in China, 1 Law Review of Wuhan University 1998,45; Xiao Yongping, Opinions on the System of the Supervision upon Domestic Arbitration and Foreign-Related Arbitration, 2 Social Science in China,1998,95-96.

tem has been divided into two parts —domestic and foreign-related arbitration. Nowadays, the supervision of foreign-related arbitration only on procedural issues is better suited to the practice of China.[①]

The supporters of this theory also point out that, arbitration is composed of the arbitral proceedings and arbitral award, so that arbitral justice should include just arbitral proceedings and a just award. However, since substantive justice is difficult to achieve and assess, an arbitral award should be deemed just if the principle of party autonomy has been obeyed, the arbitral proceedings have been conducted according to the agreement of the parties, during the process of arbitration the parties have been treated equally and have been given a adequate opportunity to make representations and to provide evidence, and the arbitrators have heard the case cautiously. In my opinion, the procedural supervision theory is more sensible than the comprehensive supervision theory.

Ⅳ. Conclusion

Arbitration has both a contractual nature and an adjudicatory character. The powers of arbitrators derive from the agreement between the parties, rather than being conferred by the state, but the courts may often have to employ their inherent powers to fill the inevitable gaps so that the integrity of the arbitral process and the public interest may be protected. Issues are likely to arise in relation to judicial intervention in various areas, such as party autonomy in making and enforcing arbitration agreements, striking a balance between mandatory and default rules in arbitration, control over the

---

① Xiao Yongping, Discussion about the Scope of the Court's Supervision on Arbitration in China, 1 Law Review of Wuhan University, 1998, 42; Xiao Yongping, Opinions on the System of the Supervision upon Domestic Arbitration and Foreign-Related Arbitration, 2 Social Science in China, 1998, 94.

中英仲裁法比较研究
A Comparative Study of the Chinese Arbitration
Law and the Arbitration Laws of the UK

arbitral proceedings, control over the substantive issues. Although court supervision is necessary, the level of that supervision should not be too high, otherwise the autonomy of the arbitral process will be damaged. Thus a careful balance should be made between court intervention and arbitral autonomy. To achieve that balance, the court intervention should be restricted. For example, an arbitral tribunal should have competence to rule on its own jurisdiction, at least initially, while arbitral awards should be subject to procedural but not substantive supervision. As discussed in Chapter 2, Chinese arbitration law has a very specific culture, tradition and historical background. As a result, the state plays a significantly different role in supervising arbitration under Chinese law as compared with either the Model Law or the 1996 Act, while different roles are conceived for the court and arbitral tribunal. Those differences will be compared and analyzed so as to find out whether the level of court support and supervision in Chinese arbitration law is rational. If the answer is negative it will be considered how to improve Chinese law so that a balance between judicial intervention and arbitral autonomy can be achieved.

CHAPTER 4

THE ARBITRATION AGREEMENT AND ITS FORM

Ⅰ. Introduction

A valid arbitration agreement is the basis on which a party may refer a dispute to arbitration, and on which the arbitration agency and arbitral tribunal can accept a case. To make an arbitration agreement valid, is the consent of the parties enough? Or must arbitration agreements adopt a particular form and content? If the law permits different forms of arbitration agreements, do consequences flow from the different forms? This chapter aims to consider the Chinese approach as to the above questions, and compare it with the approach of the law of Scotland and England.

中英仲裁法比较研究
A Comparative Study of the Chinese Arbitration
Law and the Arbitration Laws of the UK

Ⅱ. The Chinese Approach to Arbitration Agreements

A. Definition and Form

The general definition of arbitration agreement given by Article 16 of the PRC Arbitration Law 2017 is "a written agreement to submit present or future differences to arbitration"[①]. Article 3 of the CIETAC Rules Claims that an arbitration agreement can be made to resolve disputes concerning economic relations and trade bounded or not bounded by contracts.[②] An agreement to arbitrate may, therefore, either be contained in a contract to be activated where a dispute arises under that contract (an arbitration clause), or it may be reached after a dispute has arisen between the parties (a submission agreement).[③] Generally, a submission agreement is a separate contract; while an arbitration clause is usually contained in a principal contract. Since an arbitration clause is a part of the principal contract, in most cases, it is made before the dispute arises, although it would be possible for the parties to agree to add such a clause once a dispute has arisen. A submission arbitration agreement can only be made after the dispute arises.[④] Under the Chinese legal system, the parties are permitted to refer either existing or future disputes to arbitration. The PRC Arbitration Law 2017 states that, upon written application by one of the parties, the Arbitration Commission

---

① Article 16 of the PRC Arbitration Law 2017.

② Article 3 of the CIETAC Arbitration Rules (2015).

③ Lew, Julian D. M., Arbitration Agreements: Form and Character, in Peter Sarceviced, Essays on International Commercial Arbitration, London: Graham & Trotman/Martinus Nijhoff, 1989,52; Redfern, Alan & Hunter, Martin, Law and Practice of International Commercial Arbitration 2nd ed., London: Sweet & Maxwell,1991,130.

④ Han Jian, Theory and Practice on Modern International Commercial Law, Beijing: Law Press,2000,43.

takes cognizance of cases in accordance with an agreement between the parties to refer their disputes to the Arbitration Commission for arbitration, which agreement may be concluded before or after the occurrence of the disputes.① CIETAC has accepted a similar regulation in the amendment of its arbitration rules.② The arbitration agreement is the basis on which a party may refer a dispute to arbitration, and on which the arbitration agency and arbitral tribunal can accept a case.③ A valid arbitration agreement ousts the jurisdiction of the courts and is the basis on which the award can be enforced.④

B. The Content of Arbitration Agreements

According to the arbitration law, an arbitration agreement shall contain the following: (1) The expression of an application for arbitration. (2) The matters to be arbitrated. (3) The arbitration commission chosen.⑤ This can create obvious problems when the agreement takes the form of an arbitration clause, driving the parties to give such clauses the widest possible scope. If an agreement for arbitration fails to specify any of these matters, the parties may conclude a supplementary agreement, but if a supplementary agreement cannot be reached, the agreement is invalid.⑥ When the parties have chosen CIETAC to arbitrate, they are not required to choose subcommittee to actually deal with disputes. The parties concerned may reach an agreement to have their disputes arbitrated by the arbitration committee in Beijing or by the subcommittees of the arbitration committee in Shenzhen or Shanghai. In the absence of an agreement the claimant shall decide where the case should

① Article 2 of the PRC Arbitration Law 2017.
② Article 3 of the CIETAC Arbitration Rules (2015).
③ Article 4 of the PRC Arbitration Law 2017.
④ Article 5 of the PRC Arbitration Law 2017.
⑤ Article 16(2) of the PRC Arbitration Law 2017.
⑥ Article 18 of the PRC Arbitration Law 2017.

中英仲裁法比较研究
A Comparative Study of the Chinese Arbitration
Law and the Arbitration Laws of the UK

be arbitrated, in Beijing, Shenzhen or Shanghai. The first choice of the site shall be the final. Should any dispute arise in regard to the place of arbitration, the arbitration committee shall make the decision[①]. It should be noted that CIETAC was formerly called the Foreign Trade Arbitration Committee of the Chinese Council for the Promotion of International Trade, which was later renamed as the Foreign Economic Relations and Trade Arbitration Committee of the Chinese Council for the Promotion of International Trade. Article 2(4) of the CIETAC Rules(2015) provides that if the arbitration agreement or arbitration clause in a contract specifies that the arbitration shall be conducted by the arbitration committee or its subcommittees or by the former Foreign Trade Arbitration Committee of the Chinese Council for the Promotion of International Trade or the Foreign Economic and Trade Arbitration Committee, it shall be deemed that the parties have agreed to have the case arbitrated by the arbitration committee or its subcommittees.

Since the legal requirements regarding the content of arbitration agreements are so demanding, the courts, especially the Supreme People's Court (hereinafter referred to as "the SPC"), the Beijing High Court and the Beijing Second Intermediate Court, have adopted an extremely flexible view of those requirements in order to render apparently defective arbitration agreements effective. The SPC recognizes that in international arbitrations the parties may agree to ad hoc arbitration abroad. In Fujian Company of Raw Material for Production v. Jin Ge Merchant Shipping Limited Company, it held that, since the parties had agreed to ad hoc arbitration abroad, the court had no jurisdiction, as if parties have agreed on the place of arbitration, that arbitration agreement should be deemed valid unless ad hoc arbi-

---

① Article 7(2) of the CIETAC Arbitration Rules (2015).

tration is forbidden in the place of arbitration.① Obviously, in an ad hoc arbitration, the arbitration agreement would not nominate an arbitration commission.

C. The Requirement of Writing

The Chinese law of arbitration takes the view that the need for writing should not be abandoned. Arbitration agreements have to be in writing, and an oral arbitration agreement would be deemed invalid. The rules of CIETAC provide that the arbitration committee shall accept a case upon a written application by a party for the arbitration of a dispute pursuant to an arbitration agreement between the parties concluded before or after the dispute arises.② They continue that an arbitration agreement means an arbitration clause stipulated by the parties in their contract, or any other written agreement concluded by the parties to submit their dispute for arbitration.③ Article 16 of the the PRC Arbitration Law 2017 defines an arbitration agreement as a written agreement to submit present or future differences to arbitration. Article 11 of the PRC Contract Law offers a modern and flexible definition of writing, which mirrors the development of science and commercial practice, by providing that written form means any form which can show the described contents visibly, such as written contractual agreement letters, and data-telex(including telegram, telex, fax, EDI and e-mail). It can be seen that the legislative requirement for writing is flexible.

It is also clear that the highest courts interpret the requirement of writing very flexibly. For example, in one case, the SPC confirmed the validity

---

①　See the "Reply by Letter on the Validity of Arbitration Agreement Contained in the Bill of Lading of the International Shipping Dispute Case between General Company of Raw Materials of Fujian Province and Jin Ge Shipping Ltd." by the SPC, Law Letter No. 135,Oct.20,1995.

②　Article 3 of the CIETAC Arbitration Rules (2015).

③　Article 5(2) and (3) of the CIETAC Arbitration Rules (2015).

中英仲裁法比较研究
A Comparative Study of the Chinese Arbitration
Law and the Arbitration Laws of the UK

of arbitration clause, even though there was no actual arbitration clause in the principal contract. The parties had agreed that the common terms of delivery between China and Mongolia should apply to all unsettled matters, and these common terms included an arbitration clause. The SPC held that[1] as the parties had agreed to be bound by these terms, and since they stipulated that any dispute arising from the contract "which cannot be resolved by consultation, shall be referred to arbitration", the parties were deemed voluntarily to have chosen arbitration to resolve their disputes. Thus the court was not entitled to hear the case. This decision of the highest court demonstrates commendable flexibility and is in accordance with international legal practice.[2]

Ⅲ. Disadvantages of the Chinese System

Firstly, since the parties are required to choose an arbitration agency, ad hoc arbitration is definitely rejected, even though the parties are permitted to agree to ad hoc arbitration abroad by the decision of the SPC. An ad hoc arbitration may arise when an arbitration clause provided for arbitration, without agreeing upon a particular arbitral body, or invoking a set of institutional rules. The Commission of Legal Affairs of Standing Committee of the National People's Congress explains why there are only provisions about institutional arbitration: "There are two main reasons. Firstly, ad hoc arbitration appeared earlier than institutional arbitration. Ad hoc arbitration is going to disappear. Secondly, the history of arbitration in China is relatively

---

① See "Reply by Letter to How to Determine Jurisdiction Where an Arbitration Agreement Is not Included in an Economic Contract Concerning Mongolia" by the SPC, Law Letter No.177 (1996), Dec.14,1996.

② Zhao Jian, Judicial Supervision of International Commercial Arbitration, Beijing: Law Press,2000,75.

short. There is only institutional arbitration, rather than ad hoc arbitration."

This explanation is questionable. Firstly, although ad hoc arbitration appeared earlier than institutional arbitration, it is hard to say which is better and hard to predict how they will fare in the future. It cannot be decided that ad hoc arbitration will just disappear. On the contrary, nowadays, most of the disputes in the world are decided by ad hoc arbitration.[1] One can be sure that ad hoc arbitration will not disappear in the near future. Secondly, the mere fact that institutional arbitration came into being later than ad hoc arbitration cannot be a reason that ad hoc arbitration should not be recognized.

Ad hoc arbitration needs to be recognized by Chinese law. First of all, it has merits, such as high efficiency, low costs and flexibility. That is why parties generally prefer it to institutional arbitration. If ad hoc arbitration cannot be recognized, the will of parties to have ad hoc arbitration in China will not be achieved, to the detriment of the development of the Chinese arbitration system. Secondly, the rejection of ad hoc arbitration causes an imbalance between the obligations and rights of China under the 1958 New York Convention on the Recognition and Enforcement of Foreign Arbitral Awards. Under the 1958 New York Convention, the courts of China have to recognize and enforce foreign awards, whether made by ad hoc or institutional arbitration. However, awards of ad hoc arbitration in Chinese arbitrations would not be recognized and enforced by foreign courts because they are not valid in China. It is obvious that this is unfair for China and the par-

---

[1]   Nowadays, there are large numbers of arbitration cases in the world each year, but the main arbitration institutions only deal with no more than 4000 cases (International Chamber of Commerce Arbitration Agency deals with 400 cases at most, CIETAC deals with 900 cases at most, Hongkong International Arbitration Centre deals with 100 cases, USA Arbitration Institute deals with 100 international arbitration cases). Most of cases have been dealt with through ad hoc arbitration.

中英仲裁法比较研究
A Comparative Study of the Chinese Arbitration
Law and the Arbitration Laws of the UK

ties to such arbitrations.[1] Yet it is the rejection to ad hoc arbitration by Chinese law which causes the unfairness, rather than 1958 New York Convention or foreign countries.

Secondly, the requirement of choosing an arbitration agency may give the arbitral tribunal, or in some circumstances the People's Court, the burden of examining whether the parties have chosen an arbitration agency effectively. The common understanding, as to effectiveness of a choice of arbitration agency in an arbitration agreement, was achieved in an "arbitration business coordination conference" (a meeting in which scholars discuss legal problems). Although this common understanding cannot be used as law when the tribunal or the court deals with disputes, it shows that China had been trying quite hard to produce clear rules to determine the effectiveness of a choice of an arbitration agency. The common understanding was that the courts would hold the following arbitration agreements valid:[2]

a. an arbitration agreement which nominates two or more arbitration agencies.

b. an arbitration agreement in which the parties use the former name of an agency.

c. an arbitration agreement which contains a clerical error, but where the arbitration agency chosen can be discerned.

---

[1] Han Jian, Agreement about Arbitration Institution in Arbitration Agreement — Discussion of Related Provision of the PRC Arbitration Law, 4 Law Review of Wuhan University,1997,31.

[2] See Cai Xinyu, Validity and Improvement of Agreement with Defects, 64(4) Journal of Carder Institute of Politics and Management in Hubei Province, 1999, 58-59; Li Denghua, Discussion on the Validity and Improvement of Arbitration Agreement with Defects, 9 Lawyer's World,1997,20-21; Lin You, Study on Several Problems Arising from Implementation of Arbitration Law,Politics and Law,1996,68; Feng Jun, On Legal Matters Regarding Arbitration Agreement in Chinese Arbitration Law, Law and Science,1996, 23-25; Liu Lu, Research on Un-normal Arbitration Agreement, 6 Politics and Law Review,2004,72-75.

(i) an arbitration agreement which contains an arbitration agency which does not exist.[1] (For example, CIETAC does not have subcommission in Wuhan. If the parties agree to submit the dispute to the subcommission in Wuhan, the agreement is still valid. In these circumstances, the parties are deemed to have chosen CIETAC arbitration with the arbitral proceedings merely being located in Wuhan.)

(ii) an arbitration agreement in which the parties have not specified an arbitration agency, if only one agency can possibly be chosen.

To provide exhaustive rules regarding arbitration agreements which contain an effective choice of arbitration agency, is not the greatest way to resolve the problem. It might be asked whether the situation would be better if the parties are not required to make a choice of arbitration agency. Moreover, if there is no need to make such a choice in an arbitration agreement, no practical problem will arise since the parties may make that choice once the dispute has arisen.

Thirdly, Article 16 of the PRC Arbitration Law 2017 defines an arbitration agreement as a written agreement to submit present or future differences to arbitration. It is not clear what "written" means. Although the PRC Contract Law and the views of the SPC give some clues as to what the term means, if the arbitration law and the CIETAC Rules themselves do not deal with the matter, Chinese arbitration law is incomplete. Furthermore, whether the provisions of the contract law and the judicial interpretation thereof are adequate is itself an issue.

Chinese arbitration law needs to be improved in this area. How that might happen and whether China should adopt rules from more developed le-

---

[1]   The Supreme Court considers the following arbitration agreements invalid: (1) the arbitration agreement stipulates that the disputes can be solved by arbitration or litigation, or that if the parties are not satisfied with the award, they could appeal to the court; (2) the arbitration agreements which are obviously unfair. See the Supreme Court Law Reply(96), No.26.

中英仲裁法比较研究
A Comparative Study of the Chinese Arbitration
Law and the Arbitration Laws of the UK

gal systems is the question which the next section will attempt to answer.

Ⅳ. The Approach of the Law Operating in the UK

It is submitted that it is useful to look to the United Kingdom for a paradigm which may be followed, as it offers two models for consideration — the Arbitration Act 1996 in England (the 1996 Act), and the UNCITRAL Model Law on International Commercial Arbitration (the Model Law), which has been adopted in Scotland. The 1996 Act can deal with a number of issues not addressed by the Model Law or deal with issues more specifically than the Model Law.

A. Definition and Form

Article 7(1) of the Model Law provides,

"An arbitration agreement is an agreement by the parties to submit to arbitration all or certain disputes which have arisen or which may arise between them in respect of a defined legal relationship whether contractual or not. An arbitration agreement may be in the form of an arbitration clause in a contract or in the form of a separate agreement."

Thus under Article 7(1) the arbitration agreement may call for the submission to arbitration of both existing and future disputes including disputes arising out of contract, quasi-contract and tort.①

Equally Section 6(1) of the 1996 Act② defines an arbitration agreement

---

① See the Analytical Commentary, Doc. A/CN. 9/264, p.21." It is submitted that the expression 'defined legal relationship' should be given a wide interpretation so as to cover all non-contractual commercial cases occurring in practice (e. g., third party interfering with contractual relations, infringement of trademark or other unfair competition)".

② This is the effect of the 1996 Act, Section 100 (2), which extends the general definition in Section 6 to 1958 New York Convention cases.

as "an agreement to submit to arbitration present or future disputes (whether they are contractual or not)". By virtue of section 82(1)①, "dispute" includes "any difference" between the parties and there is authority to suggest that this inclusion embrace in particular a failure to agree.② It is suggested that China adopt this rule.

An agreement to arbitration may either be contained in an agreement to be activated where a dispute arises under the main contract③(an arbitration clause), or may be reached independently after a dispute has arisen between the parties (a submission agreement). The line between these two types of arbitration agreement is not always clear cut. Pursuant to Article 7(1), an arbitration agreement may be in the form of an arbitration clause in a contract or in the form of a separate agreement. Both forms are comprised in the term "arbitration agreement" and a model law state which accepts this provision without change is bound to recognize either.④ Equally, the 1996 Act recognizes the distinction between an arbitration clause and a submission agreement, but does not afford it very significant consequences. Since whether an arbitration agreement is a submission arbitration agreement or an arbitration clause, it shows the consent of the parties to arbitration, there is no need to treat them differently. Moreover, if some rules of the arbitration law do not apply to deal with an arbitration clause, some parties may choose not to make an arbitration clause in their contract, or even not to go to arbitration at all. It is not helpful to attract international arbitrations to China.

---

① Section 82 of the 1996 Act provides that "... 'dispute' includes any difference..."

② F. & G. Skyes (Wessex)Ltd. v. Fine Fare Ltd [1967] 1 Lloyd's Rep.53. "Arbitration Law", Lloyd's of London Press Ltd, pp.1-2.

③ Disputes may be referred serially, as and when they arise: Compagnie Grani re SA v. Fritz Kopp AG [1980] 1 Lloyd's Law Reports, 463.

④ Broches, Aron, Commentary on the Model Law on International Commercial Arbitration, Boston: Kluwer Law and Taxation Publishers,1990,40.

中英仲裁法比较研究
A Comparative Study of the Chinese Arbitration
Law and the Arbitration Laws of the UK

B. The Content of Arbitration Agreements

Neither the 1996 Act nor the Model Law prescribes the content of an arbitration agreement. The parties are free to decide matters such as the number of arbitrators and the applicable arbitration rules (if any). Neither of the measures provide default rules which apply in the absence of agreement on vital issues. Since the parties are not required to choose an arbitration agency, ad hoc arbitration is permitted under both the 1996 Act and the Model Law. Under the guise of a definition, UNCITRAL inserted a statement in Article 2(a) of the Model Law that "arbitration" means "any arbitration whether or not administered by a permanent arbitral institution". [1] By virtue of this article, arbitration covers "pure" ad hoc arbitration as well as all forms of administered arbitration, whether by private national or international institutions, or by the courts of arbitration attached to chambers of commerce for foreign trade in socialist countries.[2] The 1996 Act does not explicitly provide that ad hoc arbitration is permitted, but such is the case.

It is suggested that China delete the requirement that arbitration agreements must nominate an arbitration agency and ad hoc arbitration should be explicitly permitted. The reason why the parties who apply the 1996 Act know ad hoc arbitration is permitted is because there is such a tradition in England, and English law has a long history of ad hoc arbitration. Therefore it is not quite necessary for the 1996 Act to give a clear rule to permit ad hoc arbitration. The situation in China is completely different. China does not have a history or a tradition of ad hoc arbitration. If the Chinese arbitration law does not recognize ad hoc arbitration literally, the parties and the arbi-

---

[1] Cf. 1958 New York Convention, Article I(2): "The term 'arbitral awards' shall include not only awards made by arbitrators appointed for each case but also those made by permanent arbitral bodies to which the parties have submitted."

[2] Broches, Aron, Commentary on the Model Law on International Commercial Arbitration, Boston: Kluwer Law and Taxation Publishers, 1990, 39.

tral tribunal would have no idea whether ad hoc arbitration is permitted or not. Where the other party makes a challenge that ad hoc arbitration is not permitted, the arbitral tribunal would find no legal rule to support ad hoc arbitration. To avoid the problems which might be raised, it is better for Chinese arbitration law to state clearly that ad hoc arbitration is permitted.

C. The Requirement of Writing

Article 7(2) of the Model Law provides that the arbitration agreement shall be in writing. The drafters of the Model Law pointed out that if the law required the arbitration agreements to be signed in order to be effective, many problems would arise. Accordingly, there is no requirement of signature in Article 7(2) with regard to agreements arising from exchanges of letters, telexes or telegrams. As far as formal arbitration agreements are concerned, it is not clear whether there is a requirement of signature or not. Article 7(2) refers to the agreement being "contained in a document signed by the parties", so it is certainly arguable that, to make a formal agreement valid, the signature of the parties is required. Traditionally, an arbitration agreement is recognized by English legislation only if it has been reduced to writing. Currently Section 5 of the 1996 Act confirms the established English principle by stating that an arbitration agreement must be in writing in order for Part I of the 1996 Act to apply. Indeed all agreements between the parties concerning an arbitration, such as variations to the arbitration agreement, agreements as to procedural matters, agreements to opt out of non-mandatory provisions[1], and so on, must be in writing if they are to be effective for the purpose of the 1996 Act. The only exception to the requirement of writing concerns agreements to terminate an arbitration[2]. The exception exists in this case because of the impracticality of imposing a require-

---

① Section 4(2) of the 1996 Act.
② Section 23(4) of the 1996 Act.

中英仲裁法比较研究
A Comparative Study of the Chinese Arbitration
Law and the Arbitration Laws of the UK

ment of writing in certain of the circumstances in which an arbitration may be mutually allowed to terminate, for example where both parties simply abandon proceedings, or allow them to lapse.① The view of the 1996 Departmental Advisory Committee on Arbitration Law (hereinafter "the DAC") on this point was that a signature requirement did not fit the established procedures of many of the trades in which arbitration is commonly used, and they pointed out that signature would pose particular problems in the export trade, which operated under unsigned bills of lading, and for corporate articles of association which generally contain arbitration clauses but are obviously not signed by shareholders.② The 1996 Act provides that an agreement in writing is binding whether or not the parties have signed it, as long as an intention to be bound can be ascertained from the surrounding circumstances.

At first sight, it is reasonable for the Model Law to require an arbitration agreement "contained in a document" to be "signed by the parties", as it is practically possible to sign a document, while it is more inconvenient to sign letters, telexes or telegrams. However, it might be asked why a more formal agreement, such as a paper document, needs to be signed, while a less formal agreement, such as a letter, telex or telegram, needs not. From my point of view, since a signature would pose problems in the commercial trade, the best way is not to ask for a signature, therefore, the approach of the 1996 Act is more recommendable.

Although the Model Law does not clearly deal with the question whether an oral or partly oral arbitration agreement is valid, its drafters did recognize that the requirement of writing would exclude many familiar types of commercial contracts which were oral or partly oral, such as bills of lading,

---

① Harris, Bruce, Planterose, Rowan & Tecks, Jonathan, The Arbitration Act 1996: A Commentary, 3rd ed., Malden: Blackwell Publishing, Inc., 2003,61.

② Merkin, Robert & Lyde, Barlow & Gilbert, Arbitration Law, London, Hong Kong: LLP Professional Publishing,1991,2-6.

reinsurance contracts, certain types of commodity contract. ① It is suggested that the logic of the Model Law be that an agreement which is not in writing is simply not recognized by the Model Law. The question whether that a-greement may have legal consequences outwith the framework of the Model Law then becomes a matter for the domestic law of the adopting state.

It should nonetheless be emphasized that under the 1996 Act, the requirement of writing is not a precondition to the validity of the agreement to go to arbitration, but rather to the applicability of Part Ⅰ, as the common law applying to such agreements is expressly preserved by section 81(1) (b)②, which provides a saving for oral agreements. There was some conflict in the earlier authorities as to whether an agreement had to be reduced to writing in its entirety, so that oral evidence was inadmissible in so far as it was to be used to resolve any ambiguity, ③ or whether it was enough that the agreement's salient features had been reduced to writing. The 1996 Act provides a more generous approach that the 1996 Act can be applied to a partly written and partly oral agreement, because such an agreement is either made in writing, or at least evidenced in writing, as permitted by Section 5(2) (c), or referring to writing, as permitted by Section 5(3). Section 5(3) is also mainly designed to give effect to many types of agreements which are purely oral. Oral or partly oral agreements are permitted under the 1996 Act, while the Model Law does not clearly provide so. The 1996 Act gives clear answer to the problem, and therefore, if China wants to adopt the Model Law, it should states clearly oral or partly oral agreements are permitted.

An agreement may be made — that is to say itself embodied — in writ-

---

① U. N. doe A/40/17, para.84.

② Section 81(b) of the 1996 Act provides that nothing in this Part shall be construed as excluding the operation of any rule of law consistent with the provisions of this Part, in particular, any rule of law as to... (b) the effect of an oral arbitration agreement...

③ Aughton Ltd. VMF Kent Services Ltd. [1992] ADRLJ 83.

中英仲裁法比较研究
A Comparative Study of the Chinese Arbitration
Law and the Arbitration Laws of the UK

ing, in which case its form will probably be a document. This is provided by Section 5(2)(a) of the 1996 Act, and, as noted earlier, signature is not required. It will be recalled that Article 7(2) of the Model Law also provides that an agreement is in writing if it is contained in a document signed by the parties.

The 1996 Act Section 5(2)(b), in providing that an agreement may be made by the exchange of communications in writing, is a more general version of Section 7 of the Arbitration Act 1979, which referred to "an exchange of letters and telegrams". By contrast, the Model Law, Article 7(2), is rather more elaborate in providing that an agreement is in writing if "it is contained... in an exchange of letters, telexes, telegrams or other means of telecommunication which provide a record of the agreement".① Earlier versions of the Bill which became the 1996 Act referred to any letter, telemessage, telex, fax or any other means of communication providing a record of the agreement, wording almost identical to that in Article 7(2) of the Model Law. However, the final version of Section 5(2)(b) takes the line that the general phrase "exchange of communications" covers all eventualities, and sees no need to spell any of them out. Indeed, it is made clear by Paragraph 34 of the 1996 DAC Report that the purpose of generalization was to widen rather than to narrow the scope for a finding of an agreement under these circumstances②. It is also to be noted that the requirement that an exchange of communications is to provide "a record of the agreement" in Article 7(2) of the Model Law does not appear in Section 5(2)(b) of the 1996 Act. This omission is a strong indication that, under the 1996 Act, it is sufficient for

---

① For illustrations of this provision, see: Pacific International Lines (Pte) v. Tsinlien Metals and Minerals Co. Ltd. [1992] ADRLJ 240. Oonc Lines Ltd. v. Sino-American Trade Advancement Co. Ltd. [1994] ADRLJ 291. LG Caltex Gas Co. Ltd. and Contigroup Companies Inc. v. China National Petroleum Co. and China Petroleum Technology and Development Corporation [2001] BLR 235, reversed on other grounds, [2001] BLR 325.

② Para.3(4) of the DAC's Februrary 1996 Report.

consensus on the principle of arbitration to appear in the exchange of communications.[1]

Section 5(5) of the 1996 Act states: "An exchange of written submissions in arbitral or legal proceedings in which the existence of an agreement otherwise than in writing is alleged by one party against another party and not denied by the other party in his response constitutes as between those parties an agreement in writing to the effect alleged." This subsection is taken from Article 7(2) of the Model Law, which provides that an agreement is in writing if it is "in an exchange of statements of claim and defence in which the existence of an agreement is alleged by one party and not denied by another". The position under earlier English legislation was probably the same,[2] and indeed there are cases in which an exchange of submissions accepting the existence of an arbitration agreement was sufficient to create an ad hoc submission to arbitration where none previously existed, e. g., because the express arbitration clause was ineffective.[3] The mere allegation of an oral agreement made by one party in an exchange of written submissions in an arbitration or an action will suffice to make an agreement in writing if the other party responds, but does not controvert the allegation. This only applies between the parties to the exchange, and to the effect alleged.[4] Un-

[1]   Merkin, Robert & Lyde, Barlow & Gilbert, Arbitration Law, London, Hong Kong: LLP Professional Publishing,1991,2-6.

[2]   Roper v. Levy (1851) 7 Exch 55. Lievesley v. Gilmore (1866) LR I CP 570; Jones Engineering Services Ltd. v. Balfour Beatty Building Ltd. [1994] ADRLJ 133. Earlier English authorities had treated endorsement on the brief submitted to counsel as sufficient written evidence of an agreement to arbitrate: Aitken v. Bachelor (1893) LJQB 193; Brandon v. Smith (1853) LJQB 321.

[3]   The Amazonia [1990] 1 Lloyd's Law Reports 236; For the creation of ad hoc agreements generally, and for problems which the absence of writing creates where the agreement is ad hoc.

[4]   Harris, Bruce, Planterose, Rowan & Tecks, Jonathan, The Arbitration Act 1996: A Commentary, 3rd ed., Malden: Blackwell Publishing, Inc.,2003,61.

中英仲裁法比较研究
A Comparative Study of the Chinese Arbitration
Law and the Arbitration Laws of the UK

der the 1996 Act, an allegation must be made by one party which is "*not denied by the other in his response*". The italicized words mean that if the other party does not respond at all, the subsection cannot apply. In other words, there is no estoppel by complete silence, but there is an estoppel where a response is made in the form of submission which does not deny the existence of the agreement.① The Model Law has omitted that restriction by stating that the failure by the respondent to deny the existence of the arbitration agreement can be ascertained either by complete silence or by silence on the particular point in a response.② Care must also be taken as to the meaning of the word "submission" in Section 5(5) of the 1996 Act, as not every written response is a submission. The DAC in its February 1996 Report, Paragraph 39, makes it clear that informal written communications between the parties do not suffice to create a Section 5(5) estoppel, and that formal submissions are required.③Since the precise scope of the phrase "statements of claim and defence" in Article 7(2) of the Model Law is unclear, it is difficult to say whether an informal statement of claim and defence suffices to create an estoppel or not. Some doubt whether an uncontradicted statement concerning the alleged existence of an arbitration agreement in a letter simply relates to an appointment would amount to a "written submission", but such an uncontradicted statement in a letter seeking a direction, to which the other party responds, could be covered.④ Once again, it is arguable whether the scope of "in arbitral and legal proceedings"(under the 1996 Act) is bigger than the scope of "contained in an exchange of statement of claim and defence"(under the Model Law). From my point of view, the former is big-

---

① This is expressly stated to be the case by the DAC in its February 1996 Report, para.38.

② See, however, H. Small Ltd. v. Goldroyce Garment Ltd. [1994] ADRLJ 298.

③ The DAC in its February 1996 Report, para.39.

④ Harris, Bruce, Planterose, Rowan & Tecks, Jonathan, The Arbitration Act 1996: A Commentary, 3rd, ed., Malden: Blackwell Publishing, Inc.,2003,61.

ger, since there could be some other documents transferred in the arbitral and legal proceedings, besides the statements of claim and defence. The 1996 Act requires the submission to be a formal written one, while the Model Law is not clear about this issue. Under the 1996 Act, a party would not be regarded as failing to deny the existence of an agreement if he does not respond at all. By contrast, complete silence under the Model Law may impliedly create an agreement. Thus the Model Law would appear more generous. However, the phrase under the 1996 Act "in arbitral and legal proceedings" is wider than the phrase in the Model Law "in an exchange of statements of claim and defence". Consequently, it is better for Chinese law to make a rule which says that an exchange of written submissions in arbitral or legal proceedings in which the existence of an agreement otherwise than writing is alleged by one party against another party and not denied by the other party constitutes an agreement in writing.

In light of Section 5(3) of the 1996 Act, a non-written agreement that incorporates by reference the terms of a written agreement containing an arbitration clause constitutes an arbitration agreement in writing. It is obvious where parties agree by reference to an oral agreement, the agreement they make is not in writing. Moreover, to incorporate the written terms the reference must be sufficient. Section 6(2) requires the reference must be such as to make that clause part of the agreement. The "terms which are in writing" could include, for example, a standard form of agreement containing an arbitration clause, or a specific written agreement containing such a clause, or a set of written arbitration rules.[1]

Section 5(3) provides support for the proposition that a partly oral agreement is within the phrase "agreement... made in writing" under Section 5(2), by stating that "where the parties agree otherwise than in writing by reference to terms which are in writing, they make an agreement in writ-

---

[1]   Section 6(2) of the 1996 Act.

中英仲裁法比较研究
A Comparative Study of the Chinese Arbitration
Law and the Arbitration Laws of the UK

ing." Section 5(3) is also primarily designed to give effect to many types of agreements which are purely oral, but which refer to the terms of a written agreement containing an arbitration clause, e. g. oral sale of goods contracts which may be taken to have incorporated standard commodity arbitration rules, on the basis of the fact that the seller has performed the contract. Section 5(3) will operate to full effect only when the oral agreement is confined to the incorporation of arbitration terms only. It may also cover an agreement by conduct, which is plainly referable to a written document containing an arbitration clause, as where a party proposes to contract on written terms, and the other accepts them by performing the contract in accordance with them. Thus where an offer document, containing an arbitration clause, is issued to the public at large, the terms of which may be accepted by conduct, any person who accepts the offer by conduct is bound by the arbitration clause, on the basis that the agreement refers to terms which are in writing in accordance with Section 5(3) of the 1996 Act.[①] Article 7(2) of the Model Law provides that "the reference in a contract to a document containing an arbitration clause constitutes an arbitration agreement provided that the contract is in writing and the reference is such as to make that clause part of the contract". It is obvious that a reference to an oral agreement is insufficient and when the reference is to a document, the reference must be so sufficient to make that clause part of the contract. The Working Group pointed out that this language should not be understood as requiring an explicit reference to the arbitration clause in the other document.[②] I cannot see any reason why an agreement by conduct should not be covered. When a party performs according to a written clause, he should be regarded to agree with the clause by his conduct. Although the provisions in the 1996 Act and

---

① National Boat Shows Ltd. v. Tameside Marine, July 2001, unreported (invitation to take up display space at a boat show).

② And its national law did not recognize arbitration agreements so evidenced[1958 New York Convention, Article Ⅶ(1)].

the Model Law do not recognize literally the effect of agreements by conduct, agreements by conduct are covered under the two laws. When a party proposes to contract on written terms, and the other accepts them by performing the contract in accordance with them, that performance is plainly referable to a written document containing an arbitration clause, and could constitute an agreement referring to writing in accordance with Section 5(3) of the 1996 Act.[1] The approaches of the two laws are basically similar, and the Chinese law could adopt either of them.

Section 5(2)(c) of the 1996 Act allows a single party to record a binding arbitration agreement by some form of writing, and the arbitration agreement is then effective, without more. This subsection is best regarded as safety net provision, for it catches those agreements not committed to writing but for which there is some evidence in other documentation. The subsection is amplified by Section 5(4), under which it is also possible for one of the parties, or a third party to make such a record. In either case the recording must have the authority of both parties. The authority can presumably be given orally.[2] The purpose of the subsection is explained by the DAC in its February 1995 Report, paragraph 37, to incidentally facilitate flexibility during hearing, promoting flexibility in determining whether or not an agreement exists.[3] Variations to the arbitration agreement or agreements as to procedural matters which are made orally will still be effective for the purposes of this part of the 1996 Act if they have been duly recorded, with authority. It is also admissible for the tribunal to carry out the recording as the authorized third party. It is plainly open to a court to conclude there is an agreement evidenced in writing in a case where there is some oral and some

---

[1]   National Boat Shows Ltd. v. Tameside Marine, July 2001, unreported (invitation to take up display space at a boat show).

[2]   Harris, Bruce/Planterose, Rowan & Tecks, Jonathan, The Arbitration Act 1996: A Commentary, 3rd ed. Malden: Blackwell Publishing, Inc.,2003,61.

[3]   The DAC in its February 1995 Report, para.37.

中英仲裁法比较研究
A Comparative Study of the Chinese Arbitration
Law and the Arbitration Laws of the UK

written evidence. It is to be noted that the subsection has no temporal limits. In practice, the need for authorization of the recording may prove to be of little significance. Thus, if one party makes a contemporary attendance note of telephone or other conversation, that note amounts to written evidence only when the other party has authorized the recording to be made. Yet as the authorization is required by the wording of the section to apply to the recording, rather than to the information contained in the recording, it would seem to follow that if one party makes an attendance note to the knowledge of the other party, it is admissible, even if the other party may subsequently take issue with the content of that note.[1] Under the Model Law, there is not an independent provision about an agreement evidenced in writing. But it indicates that an exchange of letters, telexes, telegrams or other means of telecommunication constitutes an agreement in writing only if they provide a record of the agreement. It can be seen from that that, under the Model Law the scope of exchange of communication is smaller than that under the 1996 Act, since the latter does not require the exchange of communication to be a record of the agreement. It also obvious that the scope of agreements evidenced in writing is smaller than that under the 1996 Act, since the latter does not require the evidence to be an exchange of letters, telexes, telegrams or other means of telecommunication which provides a record of the agreement. Under the Model Law, to be an agreement in writing, an exchange of communication must be a record of the agreement, and there is no independent provision about agreements evidenced in writing. The 1996 Act indicates that both agreements made in exchange of communication and agreements evidenced in writing constitute agreements in writing. The approach of the 1996 Act is preferable, and so Chinese law should adopt it.

---

[1]   Merkin, Robert & Lyde, Barlow & Gilbert, Arbitration Law, London, Hong Kong: LLP Professional Publishing, 1991, 2-6.

V. Conclusion

The requirement of choice of arbitration agency under Chinese arbitration law has two main disadvantages. First of all, the requirement of choice of arbitration agency rejects ad hoc arbitration, which has lots of merits that institutional arbitration does not have. If ad hoc arbitration is rejected, the will of parties to have ad hoc arbitration in China will not be achieved, and an imbalance between obligations and rights of China under the 1958 New York Convention would be caused. Secondly, the requirement gives the arbitral tribunal and the court a heavier burden to examine the validity of arbitration agreements. Therefore, it is suggested that Chinese arbitration law adopt the approach of either the Model Law or the 1996 Act, which has no requirement for the parties to choose an arbitration agency. Chinese arbitration law requires arbitration agreements to be in writing, not recognizing oral agreements, but it does not give clear rules as to what constitutes "in writing". It is suggested that China adopt the 1996 Act which permits oral agreements literally and gives relatively comprehensive interpretation as to "in writing".

中英仲裁法比较研究
A Comparative Study of the Chinese Arbitration
Law and the Arbitration Laws of the UK

CHAPTER 5

THE STAYING OF LEGAL PROCEEDINGS

Ⅰ. Introduction

Where the parties have entered into an arbitration agreement, either before or after a dispute has arisen, if a party considers it is more beneficial to go to court, it is possible that he would choose to do so without showing the arbitration agreement to the court. When the other party comes to aware of the litigation brought by that party, he may invoke the arbitration agreement before the court, asserting that the dispute should be dealt with by arbitration. In these circumstances, must the court stay the legal proceedings, or does it have discretion, and if so within what parameters? This chapter aims to consider how Chinese law directs a court to deal with such cases, and compares this with position under the 1996 Act and the Model Law.

II. The Chinese Approach to Staying Legal Proceedings

A. Before the Arbitration Law

Before 1994 when the PRC Arbitration Law was promulgated, the Chinese law of arbitration stated that arbitration agreements could overcome the jurisdiction of the courts. For example, Article 271 of the PRC Civil Procedure Law 1991 provided that, with respect to contractual disputes arising from the foreign economic, trade, transport or maritime activities in China, if the parties included an arbitration clause in the contract, or subsequently reached a written agreement on arbitration, they must submit any dispute to arbitration by the foreign affairs arbitration agency of China, and might not bring a suit in a people's court.

This provision is quite different from corresponding laws in most other countries. Most countries require courts to refuse to accept cases concerning a dispute which is within the scope of an arbitration agreement, or to stay the proceedings so that the arbitration agreement may be supported. By contrast, article 257 imposes a requirement upon the parties, rather than the courts. In light of this rule, the parties lose the right to go to the court as soon as they make an arbitration agreement. Obviously, the provision not only diminishes the legal effect of arbitration agreements upon the courts, since the court is not expressly forbidden from accepting the case, but also adversely affects the flexibility of arbitration and the autonomy of the parties, in that the wording of the provision seems to prevent the parties abandoning the arbitration agreement by mutual consent. Furthermore, it is not clearly provided that whether a court should stay the proceedings when the respondent party to litigation invokes an arbitration agreement.

In 1992, the SPC published "Opinions of the SPC on the Several Mat-

中英仲裁法比较研究
A Comparative Study of the Chinese Arbitration
Law and the Arbitration Laws of the UK

ters of the Application of the Civil Procedure Law", which gives an answer to the problem that whether the court should stay when an arbitration agreement is invoked. Section 148 of the Opinion indicates that when a party goes to the court without reference to an arbitration agreement, if the other party responds to the action, the court would have jurisdiction over the case. It can thus be seen that even after making an arbitration agreement, the parties still have right to go to the court. The court may accept the case, if the party initiating legal action does not state that there is an arbitration agreement. Once the court has accepted the case, if the other party does not challenge its jurisdiction, the court would then have jurisdiction. Nonetheless, the Opinion does not make the following problems clear:

a. whether the court should stay proceedings if the other party challenges its jurisdiction, or simply does not respond to the action.

b. whether the court should stay proceedings of its own motion.

c. whether the court has the right to force the parties to arbitrate.[1]

Another problem is the relationship between the validity of arbitration agreements and the exclusive jurisdiction of the courts. Article 33 and Article 34 of the PRC Civil Procedure Law 1991 confines the scope of exclusive jurisdiction of the courts, by providing that lawsuits concerning real estate, harbor operations, inheritance disputes arising from the performance of contracts for Chinese-foreign equity joint ventures, or Chinese-foreign contractual joint ventures, or Chinese-foreign cooperative exploration and development of natural resources shall be under the jurisdiction of the people's courts of China.

Yet under Chinese law, the exclusive jurisdiction of the courts does not necessarily oust the jurisdiction of arbitral tribunals. The Law on Chinese-

---

① Deng Jie, On Staying the Court Proceedings and Enforcing the Arbitration Agreement: Discussion about the Support of the Court to the Validity of Arbitration Agreements, 57(6) Journal of Wuhan University (Philosophy and Social Science Edition), 2004, 845.

Foreign Contractual Joint Ventures and the Law on Joint Ventures using Chinese and Foreign Investment state that any disputes between the Chinese and foreign parties arising from the execution of the contract, or under the articles of association for a contractual joint venture, shall be settled through consultation or mediation. If either party is unwilling to settle the dispute through consultation or mediation, or they have failed to settle the dispute by those means, the parties may submit it to a Chinese arbitration agency or any other arbitration agency for arbitration in accordance with an arbitration clause in the original contract, or a subsequent written arbitration agreement.① The Opinion stipulates that by virtue of Articles 33 and 271 of the PRC Civil Procedure Law 1991, the parties are not entitled to make an agreement conferring jurisdiction on foreign courts to deal with matters which are within the exclusive jurisdiction of the people's courts of China, but they are entitled to agree to refer such cases to arbitration.② That Chinese law admits that the exclusive jurisdiction of the court which might yet yield to an agreement to arbitrate is not illogical, as arbitration and litigation are different ways of resolving disputes, and if an arbitration agreement could not oust the jurisdiction of the court, whether domestic or foreign, international arbitration could hardly operate.

B. After the Arbitration Law

The PRC Arbitration Law 1994 deals comparatively clearly with the problems which were not resolved by the Opinion, and makes the relationship between the validity of arbitration agreements and the jurisdiction of the courts more explicit. Article 5 provides that if the parties have agreed to ar-

---

①   Article 24 of the Law of the PRC on Chinese-Foreign Contractual Joint Ventures, Article 15 of the Law of the PRC on Joint Ventures Using Chinese and Foreign Investment 2001,81.

②   Article 305 of the "Opinions of the SPC on the Several Matters of the Application of the PRC Contract Law", Law Issue No.22 (1992), July 14,1992,82.

中英仲裁法比较研究
A Comparative Study of the Chinese Arbitration
Law and the Arbitration Laws of the UK

bitrate, the court shall not accept a suit brought by a single party, unless the arbitration agreement is invalid. Article 26 provides that when the parties have agreed to arbitrate, but one brings a suit without notifying the court that there is an agreement for arbitration and, after the court has accepted the case, the other party submits the agreement for arbitration before the first hearing, the court shall reject the suit, unless the arbitration agreement is invalid. It is obvious that only the other party, i. e., the party against whom legal proceedings are brought, can apply to the court to stay. If the other party fails to raise objection to the court's acceptance of the case before the first hearing, it shall be regarded as having abandoned the agreement to arbitration, and the court shall continue the hearing. It is obvious that the time-limit set up by the PRC Arbitration Law 1994 is ineffective to safeguard the legal proceedings against dilatory tactics. Fortunately, Article 6(4) of the CIETAC Rules provides that any objection to an arbitration agreement and/or the jurisdiction over an arbitration case shall be raised in writing before the first oral hearing held by the arbitral tribunal. When a case is to be decided on the basis of documents only, such an objection shall be raised before the submission of the first substantive defense.[1] When the parties have agreed to arbitrate, yet one seeks to litigate, the court should not accept the case if it is aware of the existence of the agreement. If it is not aware of the existence of agreement, it should accept the case. The other party may invoke the arbitration agreement and challenge jurisdiction of the court, but he must make any challenge before the first hearing. If he fails to do so, he would be deemed to abandon the arbitration agreement, and the court has jurisdiction. If the party invokes the arbitration agreement after the first hearing, and challenges the jurisdiction of the court, the court should dis-

---

① Deng Jie, On Staying the Court Proceedings and Enforcing the Arbitration Agreement: Discussion about the Support of the Court to the Validity of Arbitration Agreements, 57(6) Journal of Wuhan University (Philosophy and Social Science Edition), 2004, 845.

miss the challenge.[1] If the party invokes the arbitration agreement before the first hearing, the court should stay the proceedings and dismiss the action.[2] It seems that the court should dismiss the case, rather than stay the legal proceedings, providing it considers the arbitration agreement valid. The "Notice of Several Problems of Application of the PRC Arbitration Law" provides that when the parties have made an agreement in writing to abandon the arbitration agreement, and if one party goes to the court, the court should accept the case.[3]

Can the court stay the proceedings and start to examine the validity of the arbitration agreement of its own motion? Or may it do so only if the parties apply? Does it have discretion as to whether to examine the validity of arbitration agreement or not? The court could supervise the arbitration by examining the validity of the arbitration agreement. Alternatively, it may supervise the arbitration by nullifying awards or refusing to enforce them, neither of which is possible unless a party applies the arbitration to the court. The parties have the right to choose whether to challenge jurisdiction.[4] It can be seen from those provisions that the principle that the autonomy of the parties should be protected is a basic principle of Chinese arbitration law. In light of that principle, the parties should have not only the right to choose arbitration to resolve their disputes, but also the right to abandon the arbitration agreement implicitly or explicitly, if they agree to do so.

Article 26 of the PRC Arbitration Law 2017 provides that when the parties have reached an agreement to arbitrate, but one party brings a suit in

---

[1]   "Opinion of the Shanghai High Court of Enforcement of the PRC Arbitration Law" made by the Shanghai High Court on 16th, July, 2004.

[2]   Guangli Exploitation Company v. Shenzhen New Xuguang Machine Limited Company, Cai Zi No.114, Shenzhen Intermediate People's Court, 1998.

[3]   Section 1 of "Notice of Several Problems on Application of the PRC Arbitration Law" by the SPC, Law Issue No.4 (1997), Mar. 26,1997,113.

[4]   Article 20 of the PRC Arbitration Law 2017.

中英仲裁法比较研究
A Comparative Study of the Chinese Arbitration
Law and the Arbitration Laws of the UK

the people's court without notifying the court of the existence of the agreement, and after the court has accepted the case the other party submits the agreement before the first hearing, the court shall reject the suit, unless the agreement is invalid[1]. Obviously the law does not stipulate that the court is entitled to refer the parties to arbitration. The "Opinion on the Application of Civil Procedure Law" made by the SPC states that, when the parties have agreed to arbitration in a written contract, or have agreed in writing to arbitrate after the dispute arises, and if one party goes to the court, the court shall reject the suit and instruct the plaintiff to go to arbitration, unless the arbitration agreement is invalid or unenforceable because of the ambiguity of its content[2]. The "Notice of Several Problems in the Application of the Arbitration Law" indicates that arbitration agreements made before the promulgation of the arbitration law continue to be valid. If one party goes to the court, the court should decline to accept the case and advise the party to go to arbitration[3]. It can be seen from these decisions that, when the arbitration agreement is valid, the court should not only refuse to accept the case, but also advise the parties to go to arbitration. However, it is not clear whether the court will actually refer the parties to arbitration. In practice, in most cases the courts simply dismiss the suit, without referring the parties to arbitration, nor even advising them to refer the dispute to arbitration.[4]

In terms of the legislation, when the arbitration agreement is invalid,

---

① Article 26 of the PRC Arbitration Law 2017.

② Article 145 of the "Opinions of the SPC on the Several Matters of the Application of the PRC Civil Procedure Law", Law Issue No.22 (1992),July 14,1992.

③ Section 1 of "Notice of Several Problems on Application of the PRC Arbitration Law" by the SPC, Law Issue No.4 (1997), Mar. 26,1997,85.

④ Hong Kong Zhen Lian International Limited Company, Du Stock Limited Company of Xiang Zhou, Zhu Hai v. Jian Yuan Engineering Limited Company of Zhu Hai Economic Especially District (1998) Zhu Civil Chu Zi No.45. Hu Bei Press Import and Export Company v. Hu Bei Dong Hu Compact Disc Technology Limited Company. (2004) Wu Civil Commercial Foreign Chu Zi No.9.

the court has jurisdiction. Thus the court should examine whether an arbitration agreement is valid or not. The court may not rule the matter at its discretion. The SPC definitely requires that the court not accept a case when an objection on the validity of arbitration agreement is filed to the court after the first hearing at the arbitration tribunal or a petition for confirming the validity of arbitration agreement is presented to the court after the arbitration agency makes a decision. Besides, a petition for setting aside a decision made by arbitration agency on the validity of arbitration agreement may not be accepted by the court.[1] As regards the determination of the validity of arbitration agreements, there are three basic kinds of situation: first of all, the parties have doubts as to the validity of an arbitration agreement: one asks the arbitration agency for a decision while the other asks the court for a ruling. If the agency makes a decision before the court accepts the request, the court may not accept the request. If at that point the agency has not made a decision, the court shall accept the request and instruct the agency to stay its proceedings. If, after the arbitration agency makes its decision on jurisdiction, a party appeals to arbitration, while the other party requests the court for a ruling regarding the validity of the arbitration agreement, the court shall accept the case and instruct the arbitral institution to stay its proceedings.[2] Secondly, when a party refers the dispute to arbitration, and the other party asks the court to make a determination that the arbitration agreement is invalid, the court should accept the application, rather than stay. Article 6(2) of the CIETAC Rules(2015) provides that a jurisdictional challenge should not affect the arbitration proceedings. "Challenge" under this article includes challenges made to the arbitral tribunal and the court. Therefore, when a party applies to the court to determine the validity of the

---

[1]　Article 13, Interpretation on the Application of the PRC Arbitration Law by the SPC, 86.

[2]　The "Official and Written Reply to the Questions about Affirming the Validity of Arbitration Agreement" by the SPC, Law Interpretation, No.27 (1998), October 21, 1998.

中英仲裁法比较研究
A Comparative Study of the Chinese Arbitration
Law and the Arbitration Laws of the UK

arbitration agreement, the tribunal doesn't need to suspend the arbitration proceedings. Under this circumstance, after the party applies to the court to determine the validity of the arbitration agreement, if the party who refers the dispute to arbitration applies to the arbitration agency to make a determination that the arbitration is valid, the court should stay its proceedings. Thirdly, when a party refers a dispute to arbitration, and the other brings legal proceedings, the court should examine the validity of the arbitration agreement. The tribunal doesn't need to suspend its proceedings. Under this circumstance, if after the court begins to examine the validity of the arbitration agreement, the party who refers the dispute to arbitration goes to arbitration agency for a determination on the validity of the arbitration agreement, again the court should stay its proceedings. If, after examining the validity of the arbitration agreement, the court considers it valid, it should stay its proceedings. If the court considers the arbitration agreement invalid, it should refuse to stay and have the jurisdiction over the case[1]. Article 145 of the "Opinion on the Application of the Civil Procedure Law" indicates that when the parties have reached an agreement for arbitration, but one party brings a suit in the court without notifying the court that there is an agreement for arbitration, and, after the court has accepted the case, the other party submits the agreement for arbitration before the first hearing, the court shall reject the suit, unless the arbitration agreement is invalid or unenforceable[2]. Therefore, by virtue of this Opinion, the court may refuse to stay legal proceedings if it considers the arbitration agreement is invalid, or unenforceable. The "Opinion of the Shanghai High Court on the enforcement of the PRC Arbitration Law" states that if the arbitration agreement is found to be invalid or unenforceable, the court should treat domestic disputes and foreign-related disputes differently. When the dispute is domestic, the court

---

① Article 5 and Article 26 of the PRC Arbitration Law 2017.

② Article 145 of the "Opinions of the SPC on the Several Matters of the Application of the PRC Civil Procedure Law", Law Issue, No.22 (1992), July 14,1992,88.

should dismiss any jurisdictional challenge, and assume jurisdiction over the case, while foreign-related disputes must be referred to a higher court[1]. If the appeal court holds the arbitration agreement to be invalid or unenforceable, it should refer the case to the SPC. Until the SPC makes its decision, no court should make a jurisdictional ruling.[2]

Generally, the court should examine only formalities. There are five aspects thereof: (1) Is the arbitration agreement in writing? (2) Have the parties agreed to refer disputes to arbitration? (3) Do the parties have capacity to agree? (4) Is the dispute arbitrable? (5) Is the will of the parties to arbitrate genuine?

Ⅲ. Disadvantages of the Chinese System

Firstly, there is a conflict in the application of the law.

The arbitration law requires the parties to raise a jurisdictional challenge before the first hearing, otherwise they are deemed to abandon the right to arbitration[3]. Yet the PRC Civil Procedure Law 2017 sets up a different time-limit —Article 127 provides that a party must raise a jurisdictional objection after the court has accepted a case, during the term for filing the bill of defence. Article 167 of the PRC Civil Procedure Law 2017 provides that the defendant shall file a bill of defence within 15 days from his receipt of the copy of the bill of complaint. If a defendant has no domicile in China, the court

---

① Section 1 of "Notice of Several Problems on Application of the PRC Arbitration Law" by the SPC, Law Issue No.4 (1997), Mar. 26,1997.

② "Opinion of the Shanghai High Court of Enforcement of the PRC Arbitration Law" by the Shanghai High Court on July 16,2004.

③ Article 26 of the PRC Arbitration Law 2017; Article 145 of the "Opinions of the SPC on the Several Matters of the Application of the PRC Civil Procedure Law", Law Issue, No.22 (1992), July 14,1992.

中英仲裁法比较研究
A Comparative Study of the Chinese Arbitration
Law and the Arbitration Laws of the UK

shall serve a copy of the bill of complaint on the defendant and notify him to forward his bill of defence within 30 days after he receives the copy of the bill of complaint. In light of these provisions, parties domiciled in China must make a challenge within 15 days of the defendant receiving the counterpart of the bill of complaint, and those who are not domiciled in China must object within 30 days of the defendant receiving the counterpart of the bill of complaint. As the PRC Civil Procedure Law 1991 was made earlier than the PRC Arbitration Law 1994, the latter should prevail in light of the principle that later law derogates earlier law and that special law derogates general law. So the PRC Arbitration Law 1994, rather than the PRC Civil Procedure Law 1991, would apply as to the time-limit for raising a jurisdictional challenge, as the unity of Chinese law would be damaged, if Article 127 of the PRC Civil Procedure Law 1991 set up a different time-limit.[1] Therefore, it is recommended that an amendment should be made to the PRC Civil Procedure Law 1991 so that the integrity of Chinese law could be preserved.

Secondly, Chinese arbitration law only permits the party against whom legal proceedings are brought to apply to the court to stay.

Yet the party who brought the proceedings may change his mind, and agree to refer the dispute to arbitration, or in very rare cases may discover the arbitration agreement after bringing the legal proceedings. The party who brought the proceedings may simply withdraw his claim. Article 154 of the PRC Civil Procedure Law 2017 provides that an appeal may be lodged against an order applied to rejection of a lawsuit, objection to the jurisdiction of a court, dismissal of an action.[2] "The SPC's Opinions on the Matters concerning the Application of the Civil Procedure Law" provides that after the court dismisses the action, where the plaintiff brings an action against the dispute again, if the requirements to commence an action are satisfied, the

---

[1] Qing Xucai, Discussion about Article 26 of the PRC Arbitration Law, in Translation of the University of Zhongnan Finance and Economics, No.1. (1999).

[2] Article 154 of the PRC Civil Procedure Law 2017.

people's court should accept the case.① However, the only case in which the requirements can be satisfied after the dismissal of the court is, after the dismissal the plaintiff persuades the defendant to abandon the arbitration agreement in writing and the defendant agrees to litigation. In practice, this kind of thing never happens in China. Therefore, after the court dismisses the action, the plaintiff cannot bring the action again, and the plaintiff is permitted to appeal against the dismissal of the court. Article 144 of the Opinion provides that after the party withdraws his claim, if the party brings the action against the same dispute, the court should accept the case.② Since the legal results of dismissing the action by the court and withdrawing the claim by the party are different, and it is possible that a party does not want to withdraw his claim, but wants to apply to the court to dismiss the action. In that case, if that party does not have the right to apply to the court to stay, it seems that autonomy of the parties would be destroyed.

In this area, the main disadvantages of Chinese arbitration law are the conflict of applicable laws, and the limits on who can apply. The first can be resolved simply by changing the rules of the civil procedure law. To resolve the latter problem, one might have reference to more developed laws. More importantly, the Chinese law system of staying legal proceedings is based on the fact that the Chinese arbitration law does not adopt the beneficial principle of competence-competence. If the principle of competence-competence were adopted by China, the system of staying legal proceedings would change accordingly. The next section will attempt to deal with the problems which may arise if China adopts the principle of competence-competence.

---

① Article 142 of the "Opinions of the SPC on the Several Matters of the Application of the PRC Civil Procedure Law", Law Issue, No.22 (1992), July 14,1992.

② Article 144 of the "Opinions of the SPC on the Several Matters of the Application of the PRC Civil Procedure Law", Law Issue, No.22 (1992), July 14,1992.

中英仲裁法比较研究
A Comparative Study of the Chinese Arbitration
Law and the Arbitration Laws of the UK

Ⅳ. The Approach of the Laws Operating in the UK

As ever we refer to the United Kingdom for a paradigm which may be-followed, looking at the 1996 Act and the Model Law. Article 8 of the Model Law provides that a court before which an action is brought in a matter which is the subject of an arbitration agreement shall, if a party so requests not later than when submitting his first statement on the substance of the dispute, refer the parties to arbitration unless it finds that the agreement is null and void, inoperative or incapable of being performed. In terms of this provision, any party could make such a request. Permitting any party, rather than only the party against whom legal proceedings are brought, to apply for a stay effectively protects the autonomy of the parties. Under the 1996 Act, only the party against whom legal proceedings are brought may apply to the court to stay the proceedings.[①] Chinese arbitration law should adopt the stance of the Model Law in this regard. The time-limit for making such a request set up under the Model Law is "not later than when submitting his first statement on the substance of the dispute". It does not preclude an application being made simultaneously with a step which would otherwise be inconsistent with the request for a stay. Equally Section 9 of the 1996 Act provides that an application may not be made by the party before taking the appropriate procedural step to acknowledge the legal proceedings against him or after he has taken any step in those proceedings to answer the substantive claim.[②] The chance of a party using recourse to arbitration as a dilatory tactic is thus enormously reduced. It is contemplated by the Model Law and the 1996 Act that a party may make an application co-incidentally with his first

---

① Section 9(1) of the 1996 Act.
② Section 9(3) of the 1996 Act.

statement on the substance of the dispute, and Chinese arbitration law boasts a similar provision.

It can be seen from Article 8(1) of the Model Law that the court will only grant a stay when the relevant conditions are fulfilled. One of the conditions is a timeous request by a party.[1] Therefore the court may not stay its proceedings of its own motion.[2] Under the 1996 Act, the court has no power to grant a stay of legal proceedings, unless a party makes such an application.[3] The reason why the Chinese arbitration law, the Model Law, and the 1996 Act all forbid the court to stay its proceedings of its own motion is that a party going to court regardless of an arbitration agreement shows his will to abandon that agreement. In this case, if the other party does not challenge the jurisdiction of the court, instead defends himself or even counterclaims, that defence or counterclaim means he abandons the arbitration agreement too. Since both parties have abandoned the arbitration agreement, the court should respect their wishes and deal with the case. If the court refuses to accept the case, the parties may neither go to court nor refer the dispute to arbitration. Therefore, they have the right to decide whether to apply to the court to examine the validity of the arbitration agreement, and the court

---

[1]   Broches, Aron, The 1985 UNCITRAL Model Law on International Commercial Arbitration: An Exercise in International Legislation, 18 N. Y. I. L. 1987, 43.

[2]   During the discussion in the Working Group of what became Article 8(1), some support was expressed for a proposal to delete the requirement of the request of a party. The proposal was rejected and the requirement maintained in order to be consistent with the 1958 New York Convention text, an argument frequently indiscriminately used, rather than for the compelling reason that a court should not be permitted to enforce an arbitration agreement against the will of the parties.

[3]   Tweeddale, Keren & Tweeddale, Andrew, A Practical Approach to Arbitration Law, London: Blackstone Press Limited, 1998, 57.

中英仲裁法比较研究
A Comparative Study of the Chinese Arbitration
Law and the Arbitration Laws of the UK

should not stay the proceedings of its own motion.[①]

The Model Law does not say whether the court shall stay the proceedings or dismiss the action. The Working Group decided that this matter should be determined by the procedural law of the adopting state.[②] If China wants to adopt this rule, it has to consider whether to require the court to stay or to dismiss. The 1996 Act provides that the court should stay its proceedings, rather than dismiss the case. Under Chinese arbitration law, the court is required to dismiss the suit. Which approach is more beneficial for China? Under the 1996 Act, the court has discretion as to whether to examine validity of the arbitration agreement, and as discussed later, it may stay its proceedings until the tribunal (or even the court in Section 32[③]) makes a decision. Therefore by requiring the court to stay its proceedings rather than dismiss the action the 1996 Act takes an appropriate course. As far as Chinese arbitration law is concerned, the court should examine validity of the arbitration agreement without any discretion. After the court makes a decision on the validity of the arbitration agreement, if it considers the arbitration agreement valid, it could simply dismiss the legal action. There is no need for the court to stay the proceedings as it would not continue the proceedings later on. However, it might be asked whether Chinese arbitration law should give the court discretion to examine the validity of the arbitration agreement in the future. If that is the case, Chinese arbitration law should require the court to stay legal proceedings rather than dismiss the action.

---

① Deng Jie, On Staying the Court Proceedings and Enforcing the Arbitration Agreement: Discussion about the Support of the Court to the Validity of Arbitration Agreements, 57(6) Journal of Wuhan University (Philosophy and Social Science Edition), 2004, 845.

② See, for details, Broches, Aron, The 1985 UNCITRAL Model Law on International Commercial Arbitration: An Exercise in International Legislation, 18 N. Y. I. L. 1987, 19-22.

③ This contemplates that in certain circumstances a party may directly request the court to determine a preliminary point of jurisdiction.

The Article 8(1) of the Model Law directs the court to "refer the parties to arbitration", which phrase is borrowed from the 1958 New York Convention and originally the 1923 Geneva Protocol on Arbitration Clauses.① It is suitable for a treaty to use this phrase to make it clear that courts should refrain from hearing and determining the merits of disputes, leaving it to implementing legislation to translate this objective into the procedural laws of the adopting states.② But it is not useful for national procedural law to adopt this requirement. I have two main reasons for saying this. Firstly, when a court rules that it has no jurisdiction because a valid arbitration agreement exists; the only way of resolving the dispute is arbitration. So if the parties want to resolve the dispute, they must go to arbitration, even if the court does not order them to do so. If the party who goes to the court in the first place wants to resolve the dispute, he has to go to arbitration, and the other party is not likely to refuse to do so, as he has challenged the jurisdiction of the court on the ground that a valid arbitration agreement exists. Should the party who has challenged the jurisdiction of the court seek to go to arbitration in order to make a counterclaim? It is possible that the other party will refuse to arbitrate. In this circumstance, the former party may inform the arbitration agency of the ruling of court on the validity of the arbitration agreement and question of the jurisdiction. Moreover, if the parties do not want to resolve the dispute any more, or have decided to resolve the dispute themselves, the court has no right to force them to arbitrate. Secondly, the court does not have any practical means of forcing the parties to arbitrate, as it could neither send the parties under escort to arbitration, nor impose a fine upon them if they do not go. Consequently, it would be pointless for the law to provide that the court should refer the parties to arbitration. Neither the Chinese arbitration law nor the 1996 Act includes the phrase "refer the par-

---

① League of Nations Treaty Series, Vol. XXVII, p.158, No.678, Article 4.

② Broches, Aron, Commentary on the Model Law on International Commercial Arbitration, Boston: Kluwer Law and Taxation Publishers, 1990, 43.

中英仲裁法比较研究
A Comparative Study of the Chinese Arbitration
Law and the Arbitration Laws of the UK

ties to the arbitration".

Under both the Model Law and the 1996 Act, the court will not stay its proceedings when the validity of the arbitration agreement is in question①. In such a case the court will determine whether there is a valid arbitration agreement or not, and only if it concludes that there is a valid agreement will it then stay the proceedings②. Under Article 8(1) of the Model Law, when a arbitral tribunal is dealing with an issue and a party asks the court to consider the issue, arguing that the arbitral tribunal has no jurisdiction over it, the court might, but need not, suspend its proceedings if the tribunal is dealing with the issue. The court is not bound by the decision of the arbitral tribunal.③ It can be seen that the court has the discretion on whether to examine the validity of the arbitration agreement. It is allowed to rule at any time that the arbitration agreement is "null and void, inoperative or incapable of being performed."

Article 8(2) provides that the arbitral proceedings may be commenced or continued when a jurisdictional issue is brought before a court. This provision is in accordance with the power of the arbitral tribunal to determine its own jurisdiction, i. e., the principle of competence-competence, and aims to protect the arbitral process against dilatory tactics. ④Therefore it is clear that the court and the arbitral tribunal can proceed concurrently. The Model Law does not determine which of the two proceedings will in fact move first to a decision, and thus a conflict of decision might arise. The conflict might arise when the tribunal decides to rule on the plea as a preliminary question

① Article 16 of the Model Law and Section 32 of the 1996 Act.

② Brise Construction Ltd. v St. David Ltd. [1999] 1 BLR 194. See Tweeddale, Keren & Tweeddale, Andrew, A Practical Approach to Arbitration Law, London: Blackstone Press Limited, 1998, 57.

③ Broches, Aron, Commentary on the Model Law on International Commercial Arbitration, Boston: Kluwer Law and Taxation Publishers, 1990, 43.

④ Broches, Aron, Commentary on the Model Law on International Commercial Arbitration, Boston: Kluwer Law and Taxation Publishers, 1990, 48.

and decides that it has jurisdiction①. If that decision precedes the ruling of the court, any party may appeal against the tribunal's ruling to the court specified in Article 6, whose decision shall not be subject to appeal②. It would appear that the court before which the jurisdictional issue is pending should be bound by the decision of the court in Article 6. To avoid this conflict, it is suggested that the former court suspend its proceedings until the arbitral tribunal has determined its own jurisdiction as a preliminary question. Alternatively, the Model Law should require the court in Article 6 to dismiss any request for a decision if at that time the court in Article 8 has already made a decision upon the validity of the arbitration agreement.③

Under the 1996 Act, if in an application for a stay a question arises as to whether there is a concluded arbitration agreement between the parties or whether the dispute falls within the terms of the arbitration agreement, the court may decide that question or give directions to enable it to be decided and may order the proceedings to be stayed pending its decision.④It can be seen that the court under the 1996 Act also has discretion as to whether examine the validity of the arbitration agreement. When the issue is pending before the court, the arbitral tribunal should not be precluded from initiating or continuing the arbitral proceedings, in accordance with the competence-competence principle⑤. The tribunal may either rule the issue of validity of the arbitration agreement as a preliminary question⑥ or on a challenge to the award⑦. After the tribunal has made a decision, whether or not it is in fa-

---

① Pursuant to Article 16(3), the arbitral tribunal may rule on the plea either as a preliminary question or in an award on the merits.

② Article 16(3) of the Model Law.

③ Broches, Aron, Commentary on the Model Law on International Commercial Arbitration, Boston: Kluwer Law and Taxation Publishers,1990,50.

④ Article 62.8(3) of the Civil Procedure Rules in England.

⑤ Section 32(4) of the 1996 Act.

⑥ Section 32 of the 1996 Act.

⑦ Section 67 of the 1996 Act.

中英仲裁法比较研究
A Comparative Study of the Chinese Arbitration
Law and the Arbitration Laws of the UK

vour of its jurisdiction, the party may apply to the court specified in Section 32 to determine the validity of the arbitration agreement under Section 32.[①] The decision of the court in Section 32 should be subject to no appeal. If the decision of the court in Section 32 is different from the decision of the court in Section 9, a conflict could arise. To avoid this conflict, it could be recommended that the court in Section 9 suspends its proceedings until the arbitral tribunal has determined its own jurisdiction as a preliminary question, or, if the party asks the court in Section 32 to make the decision, until that court has made its decision. Again I leave open the question whether the 1996 Act could require the court in Section 32 to dismiss a request for a decision if at that time the court in Section 9 had already made a decision upon the validity of the arbitration agreement. As will be recalled, Chinese arbitration law does not have this potential conflict of decisions of different courts, since Chinese arbitration law does not adopt the principle of competence-competence adopted by the Model Law and the 1996 Act. The other reason is the "Official and Written Reply to Questions about Validity of Arbitration Agreement made by the SPC on October 21st, 1998". However, as mentioned in Chapter 9 (concerning jurisdictional matters and the doctrine of separability), it is beneficial for China to adopt the principle of competence-competence. If China adopts the principle of competence-competence, the "Official and Written Reply to Questions about Validity of Arbitration Agreement made by the SPC on October 21st, 1998" will lose its usefulness in practice. In that case, the Chinese arbitration law would probably be faced with the problem of conflict of decisions, which faces the Model Law and the 1996 Act. The recommendation given above to avoid the conflict in the Model Law and the 1996 Act could also be used to resolve any conflict in Chinese arbitration law. The Model Law permits the court not to suspend legal proceedings if it finds that the agreement is null and void, inoperative or incapable

---

① Section 32 of the 1996 Act.

of being performed. This can effectively protect legal proceedings against dilatory tactics. The Chinese arbitration law and the 1996 Act have the similar rules[①].

V. Conclusion

To resolve the problems existing in the Chinese arbitration law and the problems which might arise if the principle of competence-competence is adopted, it is useful to look to the Model Law and the 1996 Act. Chinese arbitration law may adopt the position of the Model Law permitting any party to apply to the court to stay proceedings. If China adopts the principle of competence-competence someday, many rules in the Chinese arbitration law need to be changed. In that case, the Chinese arbitration law should adopt the approach in the 1996 Act and require the court to stay its proceedings, rather than dismiss the action, as the legal proceedings might be continued later. The courts in China should have discretion on whether to examine the validity of the arbitration agreement, adopting the approach of either the Model Law or the 1996 Act.

---

① Section 9(4) of the 1996 Act.

中英仲裁法比较研究
A Comparative Study of the Chinese Arbitration
Law and the Arbitration Laws of the UK

CHAPTER 6

THE CREATION OF THE ARBITRAL TRIBUNAL

I. Introduction

In the PRC Arbitration Law the non-enforcement or revocation of an international arbitral award is subject to more stringent conditions than a purely domestic award, in that the revocation or non-enforcement of an international arbitral award is only possible on procedural grounds, while the non-enforcement or revocation of a domestic award is also possible on evidential grounds. Therefore, the principal basis for challenging an international arbitral award is the impartiality of the arbitral procedures. Undoubtedly, the composition of an arbitral tribunal and the process for appointing arbitrators are of the greatest importance in this context. As regards the creation of the arbitral tribunal, should the law have rules as to the number of arbitrators, and who should be allowed to be an arbitrator? Should the parties have the right to agree upon key specifics of the arbitral tribunal? And if so, should the law have default rules to deal with situations where the parties reach no agreement or where the procedures agreed by the parties break down? This chapter aims to consider the Chinese approach as to the above questions, and compares it with the approach taken in English Law and the Model Law.

II. The Chinese Approach to the Creation of the Arbitral Tribunal

A. Arbitration Commission

Only institutional arbitration is permitted in China. Ad hoc arbitration is not permitted under Chinese arbitration law. There are many arbitration institutions, which are in charge of accepting the parties' application, the employment and dismissal of arbitrators, creating the arbitral tribunal and protecting the arbitral process. These institutions are nongovernmental bodies, and have relatively consummate arbitration rules and lists of arbitrators.[1] The term "arbitration commission" first appeared in Article 4 of the PRC Arbitration Law 1994, which provides that in settling disputes through arbitration, an agreement to arbitrate should be voluntarily reached by the parties concerned; and without such an agreement, the arbitration commission must refuse to accept an application for arbitration by a single party.[2] This rule has three functions: firstly, it establishes the principle of autonomy of the parties; secondly, it permits institutional arbitration and implicitly forbids ad hoc arbitration; thirdly, it indicates that the function of the ar-

---

[1]   Song Xiaoli, Ma Yongshuang, Discussion on Independence of Arbitration, 6(2) Journal of Adult Education of Hebei University, 2004,65-66.

[2]   Article 4 of the PRC Arbitration Law 1994.

中英仲裁法比较研究
A Comparative Study of the Chinese Arbitration
Law and the Arbitration Laws of the UK

bitration commission is to accept cases, rather than review their merits.[①] In China, CIETAC is a major arbitration institution dealing with disputes concerning international or foreign economic and trade disputes.[②] The main functions of CIETAC are as follows:

a. accepting international arbitration cases and foreign-related arbitration cases.

b. accepting other arbitration cases with authorization of the government or other domestic or international organizations.

c. supplying other services to resolve disputes when the parties agree to do so.

d. by virtue of the agreement or application of the parties, appointing arbitrators for ad hoc arbitration abroad.[③]

e. disseminating, popularizing and researching arbitration and other resolutions of disputes.

f. taking part in the related international or domestic organizations.[④]

The PRC Arbitration Law 2017 provides that branches of the recognized arbitration commissions may be set up in municipalities under the direct jurisdiction of the central government, provinces and autonomous regions, or in other places according to need. The CIETAC Rules(2015) state that CIETAC is based in Beijing. It has sub-commissions or arbitration centers (Appendix I). The sub-commissions/arbitration centers are CIETAC's

---

① Kang Ming, How the Arbitrators/Arbitration Tribunal Play the Role in the Institutional Arbitration, 2 China's Foreign Trade — Arbitration in China,2002,44-46.

② In China, CIETAC only dealt with the disputes concerning international or foreign economic relations and trade before implementing its Rules, 2000 in which the scope of accepting cases begins to extend to the domestic disputes.

③ It shall be noted that the parties can agree to ad hoc arbitration abroad. In Fujian Company of Raw Material for Production v. Jin Ge Merchant Shipping Limited Company, the SPC held that in international arbitrations the parties are permitted to agree to ad hoc arbitration abroad.

④ Article 2 of the CIETAC Constitution Rules (2005).

branches, which accept arbitration applications and administer arbitration cases with CIETAC's authorization.① An arbitration commission must have its own name, residence, property, members and arbitrators available for appointment.②

The arbitration committee shall be composed of a chairman, a number of vice-chairmen, a secretary-general, commissioners, and a number of other employees.③ The chairman, vice-chairmen and commissioners shall be experts in law, economy and trade, with practical work experience, and must constitute at least two-thirds of the membership as a whole.④ The chairman shall perform the duties endowed by the relevant rules and the vice-chairman may take over the duties and responsibilities of the chairman if they are entrusted to him by the chairman.⑤The arbitration committee shall have a secretariat to handle routine affairs and each subcommittee shall have a secretariat to handle the routine affairs of that branch. The secretariat helps to ensure a proper procedure by handling routine affairs such as registration of cases and acceptance of arbitration fees. If a case is handled by a subcommittee, the duties and functions prescribed to be performed by the chairman and secretariat of the arbitration committee shall be performed by the chairman and secretariat of the subcommittee.⑥

B. Arbitral Tribunal

Arbitral tribunals must consider cases and make awards.⑦ Arbitrators

---

① Article 2(3) of the CIETAC Constitution Rules (2015).
② Article 11 of the PRC Arbitration Law 2017.
③ Article 3, Article 4 of the CIETAC Constitution Rules (2005).
④ Article 12 of the PRC Arbitration Law 2017; Article 3 of the CIETAC Constitution Rules (2005).
⑤ Article 2(1) of the CIETAC Arbitration Rules (2015).
⑥ Article 2(5) of the CIETAC Arbitration Rules (2015).
⑦ Song Xiaoli, Ma Yongshuang, Discussion on Independence of Arbitration, 6(2) Journal of Adult Education of Hebei University,2004,65-66.

中英仲裁法比较研究
A Comparative Study of the Chinese Arbitration
Law and the Arbitration Laws of the UK

are not representatives of the parties, and must treat the parties equally.[1] The PRC Arbitration Law 2017 provides that the arbitral tribunal can be composed of one or three arbitrators.[2] The PRC Arbitration Law 2017 does not prevent the parties from making their own agreement on the number of the arbitrators. It can be seen from the CIETAC Rules(2015) that if the parties have agreed to vary the rules, they can act according to their agreement, unless it is not capable of being implemented, or it is forbidden by the mandatory rules of the place of arbitration. It can also be seen that the parties are free to agree on the number of arbitrators. If there is no such agreement, or the procedures agreed by the parties break down, the PRC Arbitration Law 2017 and the CIETAC Rules provide default rules. The PRC Arbitration Law 2017 provides that an arbitral tribunal shall be composed of one or three arbitrators, and in the latter case there must be a chief arbitrator.[3] The CIETAC Rules(2015) also state that an arbitral tribunal shall be composed of one or three arbitrators, continuing that an arbitral tribunal shall be composed of three arbitrators, unless the parties otherwise agree or the CIETAC Rules otherwise provide.[4]

CIETAC has a list of the panel of arbitrators.[5]The panel is drawn from arbitrators appointed by the China Council for the Promotion of International Trade (China International Chamber of Commerce) from among Chinese and foreigners who have the knowledge and practical experience in law, economic relation or trade, science and technology. An arbitrator must meet one of the following requirements:

a. at least eight years experience in the field of arbitration.

b. at least eight years of experience as a lawyer.

---

[1] Article 24 of the CIETAC Arbitration Rules (2015).

[2] Article 31 of the CIETAC Arbitration Law 2017.

[3] Article 30 of the CIETAC Arbitration Law 2017.

[4] Article 20 of the CIETAC Arbitration Rules (2015).

[5] Article 26(1) of the CIETAC Arbitration Rules (2015).

c. at least eight years of experience as a judge, or

d. engaging in law research and teaching, with a senior academic title.

e. having begal knowledge, engaging in economic and trade and other professional work, and having a senior title or the same professional level.

An arbitration commission shall prepare a list of arbitrators according to different specialities.[1] It can be seen that the qualifications required of arbitrators are quite demanding. The secretariats of CIETAC and its subcommissions may make a list of arbitrators. The Commission of Examining Qualification of the Arbitrators of CIETAC (CEQ) will examine the ability of the arbitrators whose names are in the list, and CIETAC will then employ any arbitrators who satisfy the CEQ of their ability, and will report to the China Council for the Promotion of International Trade. That body then puts the list on record.[2] The strict requirements regarding the qualifications of arbitrators and the strict regulation of the process of admitting arbitrators to the list ensure that all arbitrators in the list are qualified. "The Notice that Incumbent Judges cannot be Chosen as Arbitrators" of the SPC (July 13th, 2004) provides that in light of the judicial law and the arbitration law, if judges could be chosen to be arbitrators, the relative rules will be broken and legal rights of parties to litigation would not be protected. Being an arbitrator is inconsistent with the role of a judge. Therefore, judges cannot be arbitrators, and judges already chosen as arbitrators had to resign the latter occupation within a month after the publication of the Notice. Therefore judges cannot be admitted to the list of arbitrators.

The parties may choose arbitrators from the list or outwith.[3] The CIETAC Rules(2015) state that when the parties have agreed to appoint arbitrators from outside the list, those arbitrators can only act after being affirmed by the chairman of CIETAC. If the parties' agreement is breached by

---

① Article 13 of the PRC Arbitration Law 2017.
② Article 14 of the CIETAC Constitution Rules (2005).
③ Article 21 of the CIETAC Arbitration Rules (2015).

中英仲裁法比较研究
A Comparative Study of the Chinese Arbitration
Law and the Arbitration Laws of the UK

the arbitration commission, the awards shall not be enforceable[1]. In most cases, the chairman will affirm the choice of the parties, as their autonomy must be protected and very few parties will choose arbitrators who are obviously unqualified to deal with the case. But there are some cases in which the chairman will disaffirm the parties' choice. In light of CIETAC's regulation on the behaviour of arbitrators, if an arbitrator in the list has discussed the case with either party, or has given advice about the case to either party, he cannot be chosen as an arbitrator in that case[2]. It may be supposed that if the parties choose such a person or a judge[3], the chairman will disaffirm their choice.

A controversial issue is the existence of "in-house arbitrators". In CIETAC, it is common for the chairman, vice-chairman, secretary-general, and other full-time managers to be arbitrators. The advantage of such "in-house arbitrators" is that they are more familiar with the arbitration process. Working full-time in CIETAC they have enough time to devote to cases. They are more likely to be experts in arbitration, so that arbitrations may proceed faster and the justice of the process could be ensured[4]. Yet certain scholars doubt their independence and impartiality. They argue that, if those who have the right to employ arbitrators and to make the list of arbitrators, are themselves arbitrators, who can supervise them? They also point out that there is a risk that other arbitrators may be unwilling to express opin-

---

① Article 7(4) of "Arrangement of Mutual Enforcement of Awards between Mainland and Hong Kong SAR", Law Interpretation, No.3 (2000), Feb. 2, 2000.

② Zhang Meicheng, On the Legal Status of Arbitration System and the Liability of Arbitration Institutions in China, 3(2) Journal of Jiangsu Polytechnic University (Social Science Edition), June 2002, 13-16.

③ "Notice that Incumbent Judges Shall Not Be Chosen as Arbitrators" by the SPC, Law Issue, No.129 (2004), July 13, 2004.

④ Song Lianbing, Approaches to the Several Issues on Amending the PRC Arbitration Law 1994, 4 Journal of International Economic Law Discussion of Reform of System of Arbitrators, 2001, 615.

ions which are different from those of the "in-house arbitrators", considering the relationship between the "in-house arbitrators" and CIETAC.

In my opinion, concerns regarding "in-house arbitrators" are unfounded. The PRC Arbitration Law 2017 sets up demanding qualifications required of arbitrators.[1] There is strict regulation of the process of admitting arbitrators to the list, and the decision as to whether a person is qualified to be an arbitrator is not made by one person, but by the Commission of Examining Qualification of the Arbitrators of CIETAC (CEQ). Thus "in-house arbitrators" are supervised by the law and the CEQ. The risk mentioned above is unlikely to materialize in practice. Since arbitrators are experts in law, economy and trade, mostly coming from universities and academic research institutions, they have no real incentive to agree with "in-house arbitrators", and no disincentive to disagree with them. Thus they would surely not be afraid to air their own opinions. If the arbitrator is a lawyer, it is possible that he may fear that an "in-house arbitrator" may have a bias against him in the future, should he appear as counsel in a case heard by an "in-house arbitrator"? Yet that situation might arise whether or not the arbitrator with whom he disagrees is an "in-house arbitrator", and it is surely unlikely that any arbitrator will bias against such a lawyer-arbitrator simply because their opinions differ in a previous case. However, parties may sometimes have similar concerns. When an "in-house arbitrators" is chosen by one party, the other may be doubtful as to his impartiality, and may refuse to cooperate with the tribunal and decline to abide by the award. In that case, the arbitration may be delayed or even completely undone. To avoid this happening, the "Regulation of Examination of Arbitrators" provides that if the chairman, vice-chairman, or any other arbitrator who works in CIETAC is appointed by one party to be an arbitrator, that person shall refuse the appointment.[2] By con-

---

① Article 13 of the PRC Arbitration Law 2017.
② Article 5(7) of the "Regulation of Examination of Arbitrators" of CIETAC.

中英仲裁法比较研究
A Comparative Study of the Chinese Arbitration
Law and the Arbitration Laws of the UK

trast, if such a person is appointed by the chairman of CIETAC, he can accept the appointment, as the parties would have no reason to doubt his independence and impartiality.

Permitting the parties to choose arbitrators has two main advantages. First of all, the autonomy of the parties is protected, and secondly, the parties will always try to appoint arbitrators who are high-minded and well qualified. Thus arbitrators will view cases impartially to ensure they have a good reputation. When the parties want to choose arbitrators from the list, they can be secure in the knowledge that they have chosen an appropriate person. If they want to choose arbitrators outside the list, supervision is provided by the Chairman of CIETAC. Considering arbitration does not have a very long history in China and arbitration is not well known by the public, that support and supervision are needed.

The parties also have the right to agree on the appointment procedure, including the waiting periods within which the parties must attempt to reach agreement. The CIETAC Rules(2015) allow the parties to agree to vary it, unless the agreement is not capable of implementing or is forbidden by the mandatory rules of the place of arbitration.[①] If there is no such agreement, or the procedures agreed by the parties break down, the arbitration law and arbitration rules would provide default rules. The PRC Arbitration Law 2017 states that when the parties agree that the arbitration tribunal is to be composed of three arbitrators, each shall choose one arbitrator or entrust the appointment to the chairman of the arbitration commission, while the third arbitrator will be jointly chosen by the parties or by the chairman of the arbitration commission when jointly entrusted with this task by the parties. The third arbitrator shall be the chief arbitrator.[②] When the parties agree to have a single, they shall jointly choose the arbitrator or entrust the choice to the

---

① Article 4(3) of the CIETAC Arbitration Rules (2015).
② Article 31, para.1 of the PRC Arbitration Law 2017.

chairman.① When the parties fail to decide on the composition of the arbitral tribunal or fail to choose arbitrators within the time limit prescribed in the arbitration rules, the chairman shall make the decision.②

The CIETAC Rules(2015) go into more details: When the parties agree that the arbitral tribunal is composed of three arbitrators, each of them shall, within 15 days after receiving the notice of arbitration, choose one arbitrator or entrust the appointment to the chairman of the arbitration commission. If the parties fail to choose an arbitrator or entrust the appointment to the chairman, the chairman shall choose the arbitrators. The chief arbitrator, within 15 days after receiving the notice of arbitration, shall be jointly chosen by the parties, or appointed by the chairman if jointly entrusted by the two parties.③ As regards choosing the chief arbitrator, each party may recommend up to three arbitrators as candidates, and shall submit that recommendation to CIETAC within 15 days after receiving the notice of arbitration. If the name of one arbitrator appears in both of recommendations, he will be appointed chief arbitrator. If the names of more than one arbitrator appear in both recommendations, the Chairman of CIETAC shall choose one. If no name is recommended by both parties, the chairman shall appoint a chief arbitrator from outwith the recommendations.④ The functions of the arbitrators can be agreed by the parties. If there is no such agreement, the legal status of all three arbitrators is the same, each having only one vote. However, Article 49(6) of CIETAC Rules(2015) provides that if a majority vote cannot be reached, the award shall be decided on the basis of the opinion of the chief arbitrator. The views of other arbitrators can be written down in the record, but do not constitute part of the award. This is echoed in Article 53 of the PRC Arbitration Law 2017, which also states that an ar-

---

① Article 31, para.2 of the PRC Arbitration Law 2017.
② Article 32 of the PRC Arbitration Law 2017.
③ Article 27 of the CIETAC Arbitration Rules (2015).
④ Article 27 of the CIETAC Arbitration Rules (2015).

中英仲裁法比较研究
A Comparative Study of the Chinese Arbitration
Law and the Arbitration Laws of the UK

bitral award shall be decided by the majority, and the views of the minority can be written down in the record. Thus when a majority vote cannot be achieved, the view of the chief arbitrator is crucial.

Since the chief arbitrator plays a more important role in the arbitration, more attention shall be paid to that appointment. Scholars have suggested that a chief arbitrator: (1) be impartial and have good moral character, (2) be an expert in the sort of case concerned, (3) be familiar with the arbitral process, (4) be good at speaking and speak steadily, (5) master the technology of hearing, (6) have enough time to deal with the case, (7) be fluent of foreign languages, if there are foreign arbitrators.[1]

When the parties agree that the tribunal should be composed of one arbitrator, the parties may choose the sole arbitrator in accordance with Article 22(2) and (3) of the CIETAC Rules(2015)[2]. According to Article 22(2) and (3), the sole arbitrator shall, within 15 days after receiving the notice of arbitration, be jointly chosen by the parties concerned or appointed by the chairman of the arbitration commission jointly entrusted by the two parties. Each party may recommend up to three arbitrators, and shall submit the recommendations to CIETAC within 15 days after receiving the notice of arbitration. If the name of one arbitrator appears in both recommendations, he becomes the sole arbitrator. If the names of more than one arbitrator appear in both recommendations, the Chairman of CIETAC shall choose one taking into account the nature of the dispute. If no name is recommended by both parties, the Chairman of CIETAC shall appoint the sole arbitrator from outwith those recommendations[3]. In practice, the parties rarely agree to choose a sole arbitrator before a dispute arises, while the choice of a sole arbitrator after a dispute arises is more rarely still.

---

[1]   Kang Ming, How the Arbitrators/Arbitration Tribunal Play the Role in the Institutional Arbitration, 2 China's Foreign Trade — Arbitration in China,2002,44-46.

[2]   Article 28 of the CIETAC Arbitration Rules (2015).

[3]   In light of Article 22(2)(3) of the CIETAC Arbitration Rules (2015).

Since an arbitral tribunal must be composed of one or three arbitrators[1], if there are two or more parties involved, it is not possible for each party to appoint an arbitrator. In such cases, the claimants' side and the respondents' side shall, through consultation, each appoint one arbitrator from among the panel of arbitrators of the Arbitration Commission, or entrust the chairman of the commission to make that appointment. If, within 15 days from the date on which the respondents' side receives the notice of arbitration, either side fails so to appoint or entrust, the appointment will be made by the chairman[2]. The parties may choose the chief arbitrator or the sole arbitrator in accordance with Article 27 and 28 of CIETAC Rules (2015)[3]. Requiring the claimants' side and the respondents' side each to appoint one arbitrator can effectively prevent the arbitral tribunal from becoming cumbersome. Some scholars consider that not permitting each claimant and respondent to appoint an arbitrator damages the principle of "equitable treatment". But from my point of view, although the principle of "equitable treatment" is an important basic principle, it should not be "treated as sacrosanct"[4]. It is not right to say that if each party cannot appoint an arbitrator the justice of arbitration will be damaged. Substantially, equitable treatment in appointing arbitrators means that every party has the same legal rights regarding appointment. It does not mean every party must have the right to choose an arbitrator. Obviously, if the arbitral tribunal permits only certain parties to be involved in the choice, the principle of "equitable treatment" will be damaged[5]. But if all parties are forbidden to choose arbitra-

---

① Article 25 of the CIETAC Arbitration Rules (2015).

② Article 27 and Article 28 of the CIETAC Arbitration Rules (2015).

③ Article 27 and Article 28 of the CIETAC Arbitration Rules (2015).

④ Christopher, Stippl, International Multiparty Arbitration: The Role of Party Autonomy, 7 Am. Rev. Int'l Arb.,1996,52.

⑤ See, e. g., Thomas, J. Stipanowich, Arbitration and Multiparty Disputes: The Search for Workable Solutions, 72 Iowa L. Rev.1987,473,523.

中英仲裁法比较研究
A Comparative Study of the Chinese Arbitration
Law and the Arbitration Laws of the UK

tors of their own motion and are required to choose arbitrators jointly, the principle of "equitable treatment" is not damaged.[1] It would be more unjust if, for example, there were 3 claimants and 1 respondent, and each could appoint an arbitrator.

Moreover, in most cases, arbitrators are persons who have professional knowledge and are high-minded. They will view the case and make awards on the basis of the facts of the case and the relevant legal rules. Therefore, there is no reason to suppose that the arbitrator chosen by a party will favor that party. The CIETAC Rules(2015) contain provisions as to the requirement of impartiality and independence of arbitrators[2]. These provisions require arbitrators to ensure their impartiality and independence; while a party who doubts the impartiality or independence of any arbitrator, may raise an objection to that appointment. It can be seen that even if a party has no right to choose his own arbitrator, he still can play a role in appointing arbitrators.

It should be noted that, if the parties are from different countries, the CIETAC Rules do not require that the chief arbitrator be from a third country. Yet this does not mean CIETAC never appoints a person from a third country to be the chief arbitrator, even though it appoints Chinese as chief arbitrators more often than persons from third countries. There are several reasons why CIETAC appoints Chinese individuals as chief arbitrators more often than foreigners. The fees of foreign arbitrators are high, and arbitral remuneration is modest in China. Equally, often parties are not willing to pay such travel costs. Moreover, few foreigners would be satisfied with the payment on offer, and thus few are willing to become chief arbitrators.[3] Furthermore, the CIETAC Rules require arbitrators to treat the parties eq-

---

① Martin, Platte, When Should an Arbitrator Join Cases, 18 (1) Arb. Int'l 2002, 75.

② Article 31 of the CIETAC Arbitration Rules (2015).

③ Gao Fei, If the Chief Arbitrator Is Not from a Third Country, Will the Injustice of Arbitration Be Damaged, 8 China's Foreign Trade — Arbitration in China, 2001, 17.

uitably [1]. They must be impartial regardless of their nationality. Therefore, if the parties have agreed to appoint a person from a third country as chief arbitrator, CIETAC shall behave accordingly. When parties have no such agreement, it is unreasonable to doubt the integrity of the arbitral tribunal simply because the chief arbitrator is not from a third country. So far no award has been deemed unenforceable simply because the chief arbitrator is not from a third country.[2] Yet while the rules do not produce problems in practice, in order to make them more developed, it is recommended they require that when the two parties are from two different countries, the third arbitrator or the sole arbitrator shall be from a third country.

III. The Disadvantages of the Chinese Approach

CIETAC's list of arbitrators is too simple. The PRC Arbitration Law 2017 only requires the arbitration commission to make a list of arbitrators in accordance with different professional specialities, without requiring the list to contain the contact and other details of arbitrators. The list simply records the arbitrators' names, academic attainments, titles and professional specialities. The list was made so simple because its makers thought this would prevent parties contacting arbitrators in an unlawful way.[3] However, in practice, parties who want to contact arbitrators, easily find other ways to discover their details. Moreover, since the list is so basic, it is quite difficult for the parties to gauge the professional ability of arbitrators, or to know whether the arbitrators have enough time to deal with the case.

---

① Article 24 of the CIETAC Arbitration Rules (2015).

② Gao Fei, If the Chief Arbitrator Is Not from a Third Country, Will the Injustice of Arbitration Be Damaged, 8 China's Foreign Trade —Arbitration in China,2001,17.

③ Kou Liyun, Main Problems of Chinese System of Arbitrators and Suggestions about Reform, 6 Arbitration and Law,2002,16-28.

中英仲裁法比较研究
A Comparative Study of the Chinese Arbitration
Law and the Arbitration Laws of the UK

IV. The Approach of the Laws Operating in the UK

As ever we refer to the United Kingdom for a paradigm which offers two models for consideration —the 1996 Act and the Model Law. Chinese arbitration law, the Model Law, and the 1996 Act all permit the parties to agree on the number of arbitrators and the appointment procedure. When there is no such an agreement or the agreement made by the parties break down, each law provides default rules. Permitting the parties to agree on these issues protects the autonomy of the parties, and providing default rules ensures the arbitration proceedings being conducted successfully. Since there are differences in culture and tradition, there are differences between the three laws as to the details of the rights of the parties and the default rules. The main difference is that in Chinese arbitration law, the court is never asked to appoint arbitrators, whereas under the 1996 Act and the Model Law, the court can play a role in the appointment procedure. As regards whether judges can be arbitrators, the attitude of Chinese arbitration law again differs from that of the 1996 Act and the Model Law.

Article 10(1) of the Model Law gives the parties the right to determine the number of arbitrators, as the Working Group believed that the Model Law should not contain mandatory requirements as to the number of arbitrators, and the parties should be free to agree on the matter.[①] Equally, Section 15(1) of the 1996 Act permits the parties to agree on the number of arbitrators, and whether there is to be a chairman or umpire. The agreement of the parties as to the structure of the tribunal may well arise by reference

---

① Broches, Aron, Commentary on the Model Law on International Commercial Arbitration, Boston: Kluwer Law and Taxation Publishers, 1990, 53.

to institutional rules.① If the parties do not specify the number of arbitrators, but simply agree that the dispute shall be resolved by "arbitrators", there is a presumption that the tribunal shall consist of two arbitrators, unless there is contrary evidence.② In light of Section 15(2), an agreement that there shall be two arbitrators (or any other even number) shall be understood as requiring the appointment of an additional arbitrator as chairman of the tribunal. Yet when the parties specifically agree that the arbitral tribunal shall consist of an even number of arbitrators and an umpire, or an even number of arbitrators alone, the tribunal shall be composed accordingly. If there is no such specific agreement, the tribunal shall be composed of an even number of arbitrators and a chairman.③

When there is no agreement as to the number of arbitrators, the Model Law and the 1996 Act both provide default rules. Under the Model Law, the tribunal shall consist of three arbitrators (or one in Scotland).④ This number follows Article 5 of the UNCITRAL Arbitration Rules⑤, and reflects common practice in international commercial arbitration. By contrast, under the 1996 Act the default rule is that tribunal shall consist of a sole arbitrator.⑥ The DAC considered that the cost of three arbitrators was likely to be three times of that of a sole arbitrator, and that this burden should not be imposed on the parties unless they so chose. In Chinese practice, the parties

---

① Harris, Bruce, Planterose, Rowan & Tecks, Jonathan, The Arbitration Act 1996: A Commentary, 3rd ed., Malden: Blackwell Publishing, Inc.,2003,87.

② Fletamentos Maritimos SA v. Effjonhn International BV [1995] 1 Lloyd's Law Reports 311. See Tweeddale, Keren & Tweeddale, Andrew, A Practical Approach to Arbitration Law, London: Blackstone Press Limited,1998,103.

③ Tweeddale, Keren & Tweeddale, Andrew, A Practical Approach to Arbitration Law, London:Blackstone Press Limited,1998,103.

④ Article 10(2) of the Model Law.

⑤ If the parties have not previously agreed on the number of arbitrators (i. e., one or three)... three arbitrators shall be appointed.

⑥ Section 15(3) of the 1996 Act.

中英仲裁法比较研究
A Comparative Study of the Chinese Arbitration
Law and the Arbitration Laws of the UK

rarely agree to choose a sole arbitrator. Therefore the default rule provided by the 1996 Act would not suit practice in China.

In practice arbitration agreements often demand that arbitrators have certain qualifications. Under the Model Law the parties may apply to the court to remove an arbitrator on the ground that he does not possess the qualifications required by the arbitration agreement, or may challenge the arbitral award on that ground.① Under the 1996 Act, a party to arbitral proceedings may apply to the court to remove an arbitrator if he does not possess the qualifications required by the arbitration agreement.② If there is no express agreement as to the qualifications of arbitrators, there is no basis for the removal of an arbitrator who does not possess the qualifications anticipated by one of the parties.③ In Chinese arbitration law, the parties may also demand qualifications of arbitrators. The PRC Arbitration Law 2017 lays down grounds on which an arbitrator can be removed and on which the

---

① Articles 12 and 34 of the Model Law.

② Section 24(1)(b) of the 1996 Act.

③ Merkin, Robert & Lyde, Barlow & Gilbert. Arbitration Law, London, Hong Kong: LLP Professional Publishing, 1991, 8-10.

award shall be set aside①. Failure by arbitrators to fulfill the qualifications agreed by the parties is included in neither set of grounds. In my view, the Chinese arbitration law should permit parties to apply to the court to remove an arbitrator on the ground that he does not possess the qualifications required by the arbitration agreement, and make this a ground of challenge of the arbitral award.

Neither the Model Law nor the 1996 Act contains restrictions on the persons who are allowed to be arbitrators.② Yet if the court is to appoint an arbitrator, Article 11(5) of the Model Law directs that it shall have due regard to any qualifications required of the arbitrator by the agreement of the

---

① Article 34 of the Arbitration Law of the PRC 2017: An arbitrator shall be withdrawn and the parties concerned have the right to request withdrawal, whereas: (1) The arbitrator is a party involved in the case or a blood relation or relative of the parties concerned or their attorneys. (2) the arbitrator has vital personal interests in the case. (3) the arbitrator has other relations with the parties or their attorneys involved in the case that might effect the fair ruling of the case. (4) the arbitrator meets the parties concerned or their attorneys in private or has accepted gifts or attended banquets hosted by the parties concerned or their attorneys.

Article 58 of the PRC Arbitration Law 2017: If parties concerned have evidences to substantiate one of the followings, they may apply for the cancellation of arbitral award with the intermediate people's court at the place where the arbitration commission resides. (1) There is no agreement for arbitration. (2) The matters ruled are out of the scope of the agreement for arbitration or the limits of authority of an arbitration commission. (3) The composition of the arbitration tribunal or the arbitration proceedings violate the legal proceedings. (4) The evidences on which the ruling is based are forged. (5) Things that have an impact on the impartiality of ruling have been discovered concealed by the opposite party. (6) Arbitrators have accepted bribes, resorted to deception for personal gains or perverted the law in the ruling. The people's court shall form a collegial bench to verify the case. Whereas one of the aforesaid cases should be found, the arbitral award should be ordered to be cancelled by the court. Whereas the people's court establishes that an arbitral award goes against the public interests, the award should be cancelled by the court.

② Merkin, Robert & Lyde, Barlow & Gilbert, Arbitration Law, London, Hong Kong: LLP Professional Publishing, 1991, 8-10; F. Davidson, Arbitration, W. Green, para.6.22 (14 Dec. 2000).

中英仲裁法比较研究
A Comparative Study of the Chinese Arbitration
Law and the Arbitration Laws of the UK

parties and to such considerations as are likely to secure the appointment of an independent and impartial arbitrator. The parties are free to specify directly, or through the incorporation of institutional rules, that nationals of certain states may, or may not be appointed as arbitrators.① But when there is no such specification, no person shall be precluded by reason of his nationality from acting as an arbitrator.② The Model Law does not require that a sole arbitrator should have a nationality other than those of the parties, unless the parties so specify.③ But when the court is to make the appointment, it shall take into account the advisability of appointing an arbitrator of a nationality other than those of the parties.④ The 1996 Act gives no such guidance when the court is to make the appointment. Nor does it make clear whether any person shall be precluded by reason of his nationality from acting as an arbitrator. It is to be supposed that no person shall be precluded by reason of his nationality from being an arbitrator, unless the parties have so specified. There is certainly no requirement that a sole arbitrator or chairman shall have a nationality other than those of the parties. Chinese arbitration law does not require that the chief arbitrator be from a third country. Yet while the rules do not produce problems in practice, in order to make them more developed, it is beneficial for the Chinese arbitration law to adopt the stance of the Model Law. Under the Model Law, the court shall take into account the advisability of appointing an arbitrator from a third country. Of course in China the court does not appoint arbitrators, so if Chinese arbitration law adopts the stance of the Model Law, it would be for the Chairman of CIETAC to take into account the advisability of appointing an arbitrator from a third country.

---

① Doc. A/CN. 9/264, p.28, para.1.

② Article 11(1) of the Model Law.

③ A proposal for an explicit provision to this effect was made in the written observation of Sudan on the Working Group draft. (Doc. A/CN. 9/263/Add. 1, p.9).

④ Article 11(5) of the Model Law.

Section 93 of the 1996 Act provides that a judge of the commercial court or an official referee[1] may, if in all the circumstances he thinks fit, accept appointment as a sole arbitrator or as umpire by virtue of an arbitration agreement[2], but he shall not do so unless the Lord Chief Justice has informed him that, having regard to the state of business in the High Court and the Crown Court (or the state of official referees' business), he can be made available[3]. An application that a judge at the trial of an action sit in the dual capacity of judge and arbitrator was refused on the basis that no one person can fulfill both functions at the same time.[4] In practice appointments of judges as arbitrators are very rare, partly no doubt due to their heavy workload. The Model Law does not say whether judges can be appointed as arbitrators. The Chinese arbitration law forbids judges to be arbitrators. The approach of both Chinese arbitration law and the 1996 Act is effectively to ensure that a judge cannot rule on a challenge to any award which he himself has made.

Article 11(2) of the Model Law provides that the parties are free to agree on a procedure for appointing the arbitrator or arbitrators. Their freedom is not unlimited, since their agreement may not run counter to Article 11(4) (which provides for recourse to the court in defined circumstances), nor to Article 11(5) (which provides criteria to be observed by the court in appointing arbitrators).[5] Failing such agreement, the default rules provided

---

[1]   Section 93(5): In this section, "arbitration agreement" has the same meaning as in Part I. and "official referee" means a person nominated under Section 68(1)(a) of the SPC Act 1981 to deal with official referees' business.

[2]   Section 93(1) of the 1996 Act.

[3]   Section 93(2),(3) of the 1996 Act.

[4]   Wilson v. Keen, unreported, Court of Appeal, June 25,1991. See Sutton, David St. John & Gill, Judith, Russell on Arbitration, 22nd ed., London: Sweet & Maxwell, 2003,455.

[5]   Broches, Aron, Commentary on the Model Law on International Commercial Arbitration, Boston: Kluwer Law and Taxation Publishers,1990,56.

中英仲裁法比较研究
A Comparative Study of the Chinese Arbitration
Law and the Arbitration Laws of the UK

by the Law apply. Article 11(3) provides that if the arbitral tribunal is to consist of three arbitrators, each party shall appoint one arbitrator within 30 days of receipt of a request to do so from the other party, and the two arbitrators thus appointed shall appoint the third arbitrator within 30 days of their appointment. If the tribunal is to consist of a sole arbitrator, the parties shall agree on the appointment. There is no period specified for the appointment of the sole arbitrator. Section 16(1) of the 1996 Act also gives the parties autonomy to agree on a procedure for appointing the arbitrator(s), including a procedure for appointing any chairman or umpire. The parties may also agree that a particular body should appoint the arbitrators. Examples of such appointing bodies are the Chartered Institute of Arbitrators, the London Court of International Arbitration, the Royal Institute of British Architects and the Royal Institute of Chartered Surveyors.[1] If or to the extent that there is no such agreement, the default rules provided by the 1996 Act apply. If the tribunal is to consist of a sole arbitrator, the parties shall jointly appoint the arbitrator not later than 28 days after service of a request in writing by either party to do so.[2] If the tribunal is to consist of two arbitrators, each party shall appoint one arbitrator not later than 14 days after service of a request in writing by either party to do so.[3] If the tribunal is to consist of three arbitrators, each party shall appoint one arbitrator not later than 14 days after service of a request in writing by either party to do so, and the two so appointed shall forthwith appoint a third arbitrator as the chairman of the tribunal.[4] If the tribunal is to consist of two arbitrators and an umpire, each party shall appoint one arbitrator not later than 14 days after service of a request in writing by either party to do so, and the two so ap-

---

[1] Tweeddale, Keren & Tweeddale, Andrew, A Practical Approach to Arbitration Law, London: Blackstone Press Limited, 1998, 105.

[2] Section 16(3) of the 1996 Act.

[3] Section 16(4) of the 1996 Act.

[4] Section 16(5) of the 1996 Act.

pointed may appoint an umpire at any time after they themselves are appointed and shall do so before any substantive hearing or forthwith if they cannot agree on a matter relating to the arbitration.① The court has power to extend these time limits pursuant to Section 79.② It should be noted that two arbitrators must appoint an umpire before any substantive hearing, even if at that stage there is no disagreement between them.③

The Model Law, the 1996 Act and Chinese arbitration law all give the parties freedom to agree on the appointment procedure, including the periods within which the parties must attempt to reach an agreement. Yet there are differences in these default rules. First of all, the periods within which the parties must attempt to reach agreements are different in the three laws. The period in Chinese arbitration law is 15 days, as against 30 days in the Model Law, and 14 or 28 days in the 1996 Act. The reason why time limits imposed by the default rules in the 1996 Act are expressed in multiples of seven days is because that DAC considered that the possibility of their expiring on a weekend could be avoided in this way. In Chinese practice, where a

---

① Section 16(5) of the 1996 Act.

② Section 79 of the 1996 Act: (1) Unless the parties otherwise agree, the court may by order extend any time limit agreed by them in relation to any matter relating to the arbitral proceedings or specified in any provision of this part having effect in default of such agreement. This section does not apply to a time limit to which section 12 applies (power of court to extend time for beginning arbitral proceedings. (2) An application for an order may be made — (a) by any party to the arbitral proceedings (upon notice to the other parties and to the tribunal), or(b) by the arbitral tribunal (upon notice to the parties). (3)The court shall not exercise its power to extend a time limit unless it is satisfied — (a) that any available recourse to the tribunal, or to any arbitral or other institution or person vested by the parties with power in that regard, has first been exhausted, and(b) that a substantial injustice would otherwise be done. (4) The court's power under this section may be exercised whether or not the time has already expired. (5) An order under this section may be made on such terms as the court thinks fit. (6) The leave of the court is required for any appeal from a decision of the court under this section.

③ Harris, Bruce, Planterose, Rowan & Tecks, Jonathan, The Arbitration Act 1996: A Commentary, 3rd ed., Malden: Blackwell Publishing, Inc.,2003,90.

中英仲裁法比较研究
A Comparative Study of the Chinese Arbitration
Law and the Arbitration Laws of the UK

time limit expires on a weekend or a public holiday, the arbitration commission or the arbitral tribunal permits the period to extend to the next working day. Therefore, the time limit in the Chinese arbitration law does not produce problems. There is no need for Chinese arbitration law to adopt the time limit imposed by the Model Law and the 1996 Act. Secondly, the 1996 Act and the Chinese arbitration law both contain the rules concerning with the period within which a sole arbitrator shall be appointed, while the Model Law does not.

Article 11(4) of the Model Law provides that, when the arbitrators cannot be chosen under an appointment procedure agreed upon by the parties, any party may request the court to take the necessary measure, unless their agreement provides other means for securing the appointment. It can be seen that preeminence is given to the right of the parties to agree on the means for securing the appointment. Article 11(4) also specifies the situations in which the parties may request the court to act. Those situations are: where a party fails to act as required under the agreed procedure; where the parties or two arbitrators, are unable to reach an agreement expected of them under the procedure; where a third party, including an institution, fails to perform any function entrusted to it under such procedure. It is noted that Article 11(4) is a mandatory provision from which the parties may not derogate, i. e., they may not exclude appointment by the court as a last resort.[1] As mentioned above, if the parties have reached no agreement on an appointment procedure, the default provisions of the Model Law apply. If the parties fail to appoint arbitrators, Article 11(3) enables a party to request the court to make the appointment. Article 11(5) indicates that this decision shall be subject to no appeal.

Under Section 17(1) of the 1996 Act, the parties are free to agree how

---

① Broches, Aron, Commentary on the Model Law on International Commercial Arbitration, Boston: Kluwer Law and Taxation Publishers,1990,57.

to deal with the situation in which each party is to appoint an arbitrator and one party refuses to do so or fails to do so within the time specified. If the parties have not made such an agreement, Section 17(1) states that the other party, having duly appointed his arbitrator, may give notice in writing to the party in default that he proposes to appoint his arbitrator to act as sole arbitrator. Section 17(2) then requires the party in default to make the required appointment and notify the other party that he has done so, within 7 clear days of that notice being given. If he fails to do so, the other party may appoint his arbitrator as sole arbitrator, whose award shall be binding on both parties as if he had been so appointed by agreement. The court has the power to extend the 7 day time limit.[1] When a sole arbitrator has been appointed under Section 17(2), the party in default may, upon notice to the appointing party, apply to the court to set aside the appointment.[2] The 1996 Act does not prescribe any grounds on which the court might do so. Therefore, the court seems to have unfettered discretion as to whether to set aside the appointment of the sole arbitrator. But that discretion is subject to the general principles expressed in Section 1.[3] The leave of the court is required for any appeal from its decision under this section.[4] By virtue of Section 18 (1), the parties are free to agree what is to happen in the event of a failure of the procedure for the appointment of the arbitral tribunal. There is no failure if an appointment is duly made under Section 17, unless that appointment is set aside. Section 16(7) provides that in any other case, particularly

---

[1]   Section 79 of the 1996 Act.
[2]   Section 17(3) of the 1996 Act.
[3]   Section 1 of the 1996 Act provides: The provisions of this part are founded on the following principles, and shall be construed accordingly — (a) the object of arbitration is to obtain the fair resolution of disputes by an impartial tribunal without unnecessary delay or expense. (b) the parties should be free to agree how their disputes are resolved, subject only to such safeguards as are necessary in the public interest. (c) in matters governed by this part the court should not intervene except as provided by this part.
[4]   Section 17(4) of the 1996 Act.

中英仲裁法比较研究
A Comparative Study of the Chinese Arbitration
Law and the Arbitration Laws of the UK

if there is a multiparty arbitration, the procedure stated in Section 18 applies, and the parties are free to agree as to how to deal with the situation where the arbitrators cannot be appointed in a multiparty arbitration. To the extent that there is no such agreement, any party may apply to the court to exercise its powers, which include giving directions as to the making of any necessary appointments, directing that the tribunal shall be constituted by such appointments (or any one or more of them) as have been made, revoking any appointments already made, and making any necessary appointments itself. Any application must be made upon notice to the other parties.[1] In considering whether, and if so how, to exercise its powers, the court is required to have due regard to any agreement of the parties as to the qualifications required of arbitrators,[2] unless the agreement expresses that certain qualifications are not required if the appointment is made by the court under Section 18.[3] The court can either direct one of the parties to initiate some process for making an appropriate appointment, or make any appointment that he failed to make. When the tribunal is to consist of more than one arbitrator, one party fails to appoint an arbitrator, Section 17 will apply, and the arbitrator chosen will be the sole arbitrator. Therefore, the court will direct that the tribunal shall be constituted by such appointments as have been made only if there are more than one arbitrator. This power is also likely to be exercised where, for instance, two arbitrators have failed to appoint a third arbitrator or umpire, or where there are more than two parties, and one has failed to make an appointment. As far as choosing an umpire is concerned, if the arbitrators cannot agree but fail to give notice of that fact, or if any of them fails to join in the giving of notice, any party to the arbitral

---

① Section 18(2), (3) of the 1996 Act.

② Harris, Bruce, Planterose, Rowan & Tecks, Jonathan, The Arbitration Act 1996: A Commentary, 3rd ed., Malden: Blackwell Publishing, Inc.,2003,95.

③ Harris, Bruce/Planterose, Rowan & Tecks, Jonathan, The Arbitration Act 1996: A Commentary, 3rd ed., Malden: Blackwell Publishing, Inc.,2003,98.

proceedings may (upon notice to the other parties and to the tribunal) apply to the court, which may order that the umpire shall replace the other arbitrators as the tribunal with power to make decisions, orders and awards as if he were sole arbitrator. The leave of the court is required for any appeal from its decision under this section.[1] The court's power to revoke appointments made allows it to redress the balance, since where one party chooses his own arbitrator and the other party has an arbitrator imposed by the court, there may be unfair.[2] Similarly, this power can only be used where there are a number of arbitrators, or two arbitrators have failed to appoint a third arbitrator or umpire, or where there are more than two parties, and one has failed to make an appointment. Moreover, the power can only be invoked where there is a failure in appointment, and not by a mischievous party seeking the removal of an arbitrator when the appointment procedure had otherwise been successfully implemented.[3] The court will make an appointment itself as a last resort. It would be important to obtain an indication of willingness to act from the potential arbitrators whose names are put forward, and a further indication of their ability and suitability. The court also must take into account the agreement of the parties as to the qualifications required of the arbitrators.[4] When the court makes an appointment under Section 18(3) of the 1996 Act, it is treated as having the same effect as if it had been made by the agreement of the parties.[5] The leave of the court is required for any appeal from its decision under this section.[6]

---

[1]   Section 21(5), (6) of the 1996 Act.
[2]   Harris, Bruce, Planterose, Rowan &. Tecks, Jonathan, The Arbitration Act 1996: A Commentary, 3rd ed., Malden: Blackwell Publishing, Inc.,2003,95.
[3]   Harris, Bruce, Planterose, Rowan &. Tecks, Jonathan, The Arbitration Act 1996: A Commentary, 3rd ed., Malden: Blackwell Publishing, Inc.,2003,95.
[4]   Harris, Bruce, Planterose, Rowan &. Tecks, Jonathan, The Arbitration Act 1996: A Commentary, 3rd ed., Malden: Blackwell Publishing, Inc.,2003,96.
[5]   Section 18(4) of the 1996 Act.
[6]   Section 18(5) of the 1996 Act.

中英仲裁法比较研究
A Comparative Study of the Chinese Arbitration
Law and the Arbitration Laws of the UK

It can be seen that under the Model Law and the 1996 Act the court plays a role in appointment procedure where the parties themselves cannot appoint arbitrators, while under Chinese arbitration law, only the arbitration commission will play such a role. Since the decision made by the arbitration commission in this regard under Chinese arbitration law has the same legal effect as the decision made by the court under the Model Law and the 1996 Act, it is not necessary for the Chinese court to intervene in the appointment procedure. In China, when parties fail to make an appointment within an agreed time limit, the arbitration commission will appoint arbitrators, but has no power to give any direction as to the making of any necessary appointments prior to making an appointment itself. Since a main principle of the Modern Law is that the court shall not intervene too much in arbitration, Chinese arbitration law could be modernized if the arbitration commission was given the power to give directions to the parties as to appointment of arbitrators prior to making an appointment itself.

Furthermore, when there are more than two parties, Chinese arbitration law requires each side to appoint one arbitrator. When one side has chosen its own arbitrator, but the other side has an arbitrator imposed upon by the arbitration commission, it may be said unfair. Therefore, it is beneficial for the Chinese arbitration law to adopt the stance of the 1996 Act and give the arbitration commission power to revoke any appointments already made. It is noted that the Model Law deals separately with the situation where the parties have no appointing agreement and fail to choose arbitrators according to the default rules of the Model Law, and the situation where the parties fail to act according to their agreed appointment procedure. In my view, there is no need to regulate the two situations separately, as the resolutions provided by the Model Law to deal with them are the same. The 1996 Act and the Chinese arbitration law do not separate the two situations. Under the Model Law, the parties are at liberty to agree on the means for securing the appointment in their agreement on the appointment procedure. It is possible that the parties, who have no agreement on the appointment procedure, want to agree on the means for securing the appointment after the failure of appointment arises. It seems that this situation is omitted and the Model Law does not say in that case whether the parties could agree on the means for securing the appointment. By contrast, the 1996 Act, by providing that the parties are free to agree on what is to happen in the event of a failure of the procedure for the appointment of the arbitral tribunal, permits the parties to agree on how to secure the appointment procedure, whether or not the parties have made their agreement on the appointment procedure. Chinese arbitration law, the parties can agree on the means of securing the appointment procedure and an agreement on the appointment procedure is not required.

The functions of the arbitrators can be agreed by the parties. If there is no such agreement, where there is unanimity or a majority, the decision shall be made by unanimity or the majority, and the chairman's view has no more weight than that of any other arbitrator. Where there is no unanimity or a majority, the chairman's view would prevail. One difference is that the 1996 Act contains the concept of "umpire" which does not exist in the other two laws. The use of an umpire in arbitral proceedings is a peculiarly English concept (although Scots law features a similar idea in the institution of oversman), of no interest to other systems, and rare in practice even in England.

V. Conclusion

To resolve the problems existing in Chinese arbitration law, it is useful to look to the Model Law and the 1996 Act. Chinese arbitration law does not regard an arbitrator's lack of agreed qualifications as a ground for removing him or challenging the award. Thus the parties have no recourse when arbi-

中英仲裁法比较研究
A Comparative Study of the Chinese Arbitration
Law and the Arbitration Laws of the UK

trators do not possess the qualifications agreed by the parties. Chinese arbitration law might usefully adopt the approach either of the Model Law or the 1996 Act and make this a ground for both removing arbitrators and challenging awards. Where there are more than two parties, Chinese arbitration law requires each side to appoint one arbitrator. When one side chooses an arbitrator, and the other side has an arbitrator imposed by the arbitration commission, it may be said unfair. In the 1996 Act, the court has the power to revoke appointments already made by the parties to redress the balance. The Chinese arbitration law may adopt the stance of the 1996 Act and give the arbitration commission the power to revoke the appointments already made.

CHAPTER 7

REVOCATION OF AR-
BITRAL AUTHORITY AND ITS CON-
SEQUENCES

I. Introduction

As we know, it is very important to have appropriate arbitrators. If they are not qualified or do not conduct the proceedings impartially and independently, their awards will not be just or impartial. Although it is important that the parties have the right to appoint arbitrators, it is possible that the arbitrators chosen are disqualified or inequitable. Thus the power to supervise arbitrators after their appointment is vital. In particular, it is important to be able to revoke the authority of arbitrators, whom the parties consider to be unqualified or to be conducting the proceedings less than impartially. This chapter aims to discuss the revocation of arbitral authority and its consequences, including the process of disqualification and challenge, removal of arbitrators by the court, time limits for challenges and responses to challenges. As ever, the Chinese approach to the above questions will be

中英仲裁法比较研究
A Comparative Study of the Chinese Arbitration
Law and the Arbitration Laws of the UK

compared with the approach taken in English law and the Model Law.

II. The Chinese Approach to the Revocation of Arbitral Authority

By virtue of Article 4(2) of the CIETAC Rules(2015), the parties are free to agree on grounds for challenge and whether arbitrators have a duty to disclose any circumstance, unless their agreement is inoperative or in conflict with a mandatory provision of the law of the place of arbitration. The reason why the parties' agreement should not conflict with a mandatory provision of the law of the place of arbitration is because if that is the case, the arbitral award may not be recognized or enforced by the court of the place of arbitration. The mandatory rules of the PRC Arbitration Law 2017 regarding the grounds for challenge are found in Article 34 which provides that the authority of an arbitrator shall be revoked and the parties shall have the right to challenge, where:

(a) the arbitrator is a party involved in the case or a blood relation of any party or the attorney of a party.

(b) the arbitrator has a vital personal interest in the case.

(c) the arbitrator has other relations with any party or the attorney of a party which might affect the fair ruling of the case.

(d) the arbitrator has met any party or the attorney of a party in private, or has accepted gifts from or attended banquets hosted by such a person.

In a broad sense, situations (1), (3) and (4) may fall within situation (2), since in each case it might be argued that the arbitrator has a vital personal interest in the case,[1] albeit that the PRC Arbitration Law 2017 does

---

① Wen Jie, Discussion on the Withdrawal of the Arbitrators Who Are in Special Status, 2 China Foreign Trade Arbitration in China,2003,48-50.

not give a clear definition of vital personal interests. There is no requirement in the PRC Arbitration Law 2017 for arbitrators to disclose relevant circumstances. Thus the parties can agree to release the arbitrator from the duty of disclosure. If there is no such agreement, the CIETAC Rules(2015) provide default rules regarding the grounds for challenge and the duty of disclosure. Article 25(1) of those rules provides that any arbitrator appointed by the parties or the arbitration commission shall give a written statement of any fact that might produce reasonable doubt as to his independence or impartiality. Article 25(2) further requires that an arbitrator, throughout the arbitral proceedings, shall without delay disclose to CIETAC any circumstance that may produce reasonable doubt as to his independence or impartiality. Article 26(2) provides that a party who has justifiable doubts as to the impartiality or independence of an appointed arbitrator may make a request in writing to CIETAC for that arbitrator's removal. In such a request, the facts and reasons on which it is based must be stated, along with supporting evidence. (It should be noted that neither the PRC Arbitration Law 2017 nor these CIETAC Rules regards the fact that the arbitrators do not achieve the qualifications required by the law or agreed by the parties as a ground of challenge.) These provisions indicate two things. First of all, the ground provided by the CIETAC Rules is that circumstances exist that may produce reasonable doubt as to an arbitrator's independence or impartiality. Secondly, arbitrators must disclose relevant circumstances to CIETAC, and the duty is a continuing one. In light of Article 25(3) of the CIETAC Rules, where an arbitrator discloses circumstances producing justifiable doubts as to his independence or impartiality, CIETAC will then forward any such statement and/or any information disclosed to the parties.[1]

Article 4(2) of the CIETAC Rules enables the parties to agree on a challenge procedure. Nonetheless, their agreement should not be inconsis-

---

[1]   Article 31(3) of the CIETAC Arbitration Rules (2015).

中英仲裁法比较研究
A Comparative Study of the Chinese Arbitration
Law and the Arbitration Laws of the UK

tent with Articles 35 and 36 of the PRC Arbitration Law 2017. Article 35 provides that in requesting removal, the parties must state reasons before the first hearing of the tribunal. If such reasons become known only after the first hearing, they may be stated at any time before the end of the last hearing. Article 36 provides that the removal of an arbitrator shall be decided upon by the chairman of the arbitration commission, or where the chairman actually serves as an arbitrator, by the arbitration commission acting collectively. If there is no such agreement, when an arbitrator discloses circumstances that may produce justifiable doubts as to his impartiality and independence, a party who intends to challenge the arbitrator on the basis of the information disclosed, shall, within ten days of receiving the announcement and/or disclosure, send a challenge to CIETAC in writing.① Where an arbitrator is released from the duty of disclosure or a party has discovered relevant circumstances which have not been disclosed, if the party becomes aware of a factor indicating a potential ground of challenge before receiving the notice of constitution of arbitral tribunal, he shall, within fifteen days after receiving the notice of constitution of arbitral tribunal, intimate that challenge to CIETAC in writing. If a party becomes aware of any circumstance giving rise to justifiable doubts as to the arbitrator's impartiality or independence after receiving the notice of constitution of arbitral tribunal, he shall make any challenge in writing within fifteen days after becoming aware of the circumstance. No challenge shall be made after the last arbitral hearing.②

Article 29(2) of the CIETAC Rules indicates that when both of the parties and the arbitral tribunal consider that there is no need for a hearing, the tribunal may adjudicate the case by written record. There is no rule in the CIETAC Rules as to time limits for such adjudication, although in practice,

---

① Article 32(1) of the CIETAC Arbitration Rules (2015).
② Article 32(3) of the CIETAC Arbitration Rules (2015).

parties are required to issue any challenge before the statement of a substantive defence. Under the PRC Arbitration Law 2017, where the facts fall within the grounds for revocation provided by the law, revocation is automatic, although the party also has the right to challenge. Under the CIETAC Rules(2015), revocation is not automatic, but depends on a challenge being made. Some scholars argue that the CIETAC Rules should follow the line of the PRC Arbitration Law 2017 providing that revocation is automatic in such circumstances. Yet I would argue that the revocation should not be automatic, otherwise the autonomy of the parties would be damaged. Rather, the PRC Arbitration Law 2017 should adopt the stance of the CIETAC Rules, and provides that the revocation should depend on challenge by a party.

By virtue of Article 26(4) of its rules, CIETAC shall, without delay, deliver in writing any challenge to the other party, the challenged arbitrator, and any other arbitrators. The other party and the challenged arbitrator are entitled to respond to the challenge. Article 26(5) provides that when one party challenges the authority of the arbitrator, and the other party agrees with the challenge, or the challenged arbitrator resigns of his own motion, the arbitrator's authority ceases. Neither case implies that the challenge made by the party is sustainable. Article 26(6) provides that when a controversy remains as to the ground for challenge, the Chairman of CIETAC shall make a final decision on the challenge, with or without stating his reasons. The arbitrator may continue the arbitral proceedings and make an award while the Chairman's decision is pending.[1]

Although Article 4(2) of the CIETAC Rules gives the parties the right to modify them, Article 37 of the PRC Arbitration Law 2017 provides that when an arbitrator is removed or is otherwise unable to perform his duty, another arbitrator shall be chosen or appointed according to the relevant pro-

---

[1]   Article 32(7) of the CIETAC Arbitration Rules (2015).

中英仲裁法比较研究
A Comparative Study of the Chinese Arbitration
Law and the Arbitration Laws of the UK

visions of the law. Therefore, although the parties may agree upon the procedure for appointing a substitute arbitrator and whether the previous proceedings should stand, they are not at liberty to agree not to appoint a substitute arbitrator. If there is no such agreement, Article 33(1) of the CIETAC Rules provides that if an arbitrator is prevented de jure or de facto from fulfilling his functions, or has failed to fulfill his functions in accordance with the requirements of the rules within the time period specified in the rules, the Chairman of CIETAC has the power to decide whether the arbitrator should be replaced. It should be noted that the last sentence of Article 33(1) states "The arbitrator may also withdraw from office." This is confusing. Since Article 33 deals with replacement of arbitrators, it has nothing to do with the withdrawal of arbitrators. Article 33(2) of the CIETAC Rules provides that the Chairman of CIETAC shall make a final decision on whether an arbitrator should be replaced or not, with or without stating the reasons. Article 27(2) states that Articles 26, 27, 28 and 29 (procedure for appointing arbitrators and failure of appointment procedure) apply in relation to the filling of the vacancy as in relation to an original appointment. It is for the new arbitral tribunal to decide whether, and if so to what extent, the previous proceedings should stand.① It should be noted that the Chairman of CIETAC may decide whether an arbitrator should be replaced of its own motion, and the application of the parties is not needed.

The terms of Article 28 are very confusing. It provides that if, after the conclusion of the last oral hearing, an arbitrator in a three-member arbitral tribunal is unable to participate in the deliberations and/or render the award owing to his demise or removal from the CIETAC's panel of arbitrators, the other two arbitrators may request the Chairman of CIETAC to replace the arbitrator pursuant to Article 33. After consulting with the parties and upon the approval of the Chairman, the other two arbitrators may continue the ar-

① Article 33 of the CIETAC Arbitration Rules (2015).

bitration and make decisions, rulings or the award. The Secretariat of CI-
ETAC shall notify the parties of the above circumstances. This creates problems. First, in my view, there is no need to provide separately for the above
situation. The question whether to fill the vacancy should not be affected by
the time when the arbitrator ceases to hold office. The whole arbitral proceedings should not be cut into two stages —before and after the last arbitral
hearing. Second, the essence of the provision contains nothing different from
Article 33, as under this provision the Chairman of CIETAC still must decide whether to appoint a substitute arbitrator. Third, it is not clear what
the phrase "after consulting with the parties" means. Does it mean "upon
notifying the parties" or "with the permission of the parties"? There is no
decisive answer. Fourth, the last sentence of the provision, "the Secretariat
of CIETAC shall notify the parties of the above circumstances", is otiose.
As, the two remaining arbitrators must consult the parties, the parties will
thus be fully informed about the situation. There is no need for the Secretariat to notify the two parties again. It is suggested that Article 28 usefully be
deleted.

III. The Disadvantages of the Chinese Approach

(1) Chinese arbitration law provides that only if a party has reasonable
doubt regarding an arbitrator's independence or impartiality, may he apply
to the arbitration commission to remove the arbitrator.① It does not permit a
party to apply to remove the arbitrator if the latter does not possess the
qualifications required by the law or by the agreement of the parties. If a party finds that the arbitrator is disqualified, he has no recourse. (Obviously, if
both parties have an issue with the fact that the arbitrator is disqualified,

---

① Article 32(1),(2) of the CIETAC Arbitration Rules (2015).

中英仲裁法比较研究
A Comparative Study of the Chinese Arbitration
Law and the Arbitration Laws of the UK

they can simply agree to remove the arbitrator.)

(2) Unless the other party agrees with a challenge, or the challenged arbitrator resigns, it is for the Chairman of CIETAC to decide whether to remove the arbitrator at the first stage, and his decision is final.[①] It is arguable that it is sensible not to give the parties the chance to challenge the Chairman's decision.

(3) The PRC Arbitration Law 2017 does not contain mandatory rules requiring arbitrators to disclose facts or circumstances likely to give rise to justifiable doubts as to their impartiality or independence. Article 4(2) of the CIETAC Rules enables the parties to agree not to require the arbitrators to disclose such facts or circumstances. In my view, the freedom of the parties in this regard should be qualified. If the arbitrators do not disclose such facts and circumstances, and the parties find out at a later stage and then challenge the arbitrator's authority, time and energy will be wasted. Moreover, without a duty of disclosure, it is more difficult for the parties and the arbitration commission to become aware of facts or circumstances likely to give rise to justifiable doubts as to an arbitrator's impartiality or independence.

(4) Article 26(6) provides that the Chairman of CIETAC shall make a final decision on any challenge, while Article 27(1) provides that he shall have the power to decide whether the arbitrator should be replaced. Article 27(3) states that the arbitral tribunal shall decide whether the whole or part of the previous proceedings shall be repeated, and Article 27(4) states that the Chairman shall make a final decision on whether an arbitrator should be replaced or not. [Although Articles 27(1) and 27(4) seem to have identical content, the latter makes it clear that the decision of the Chairman is final. It might be better if Article 27(1) took that form, so that Article 27(4) could then be deleted.] None of these provisions indicates clearly whether the decisions made by the Chairman or the tribunal shall be subject to appeal. Since

---

① Article 32(6) of the CIETAC Arbitration Rules (2015).

these decisions are not subject to appeal, their characterization as "final" should be amended to read "subject to no appeal", which is clearer and more straightforward.

(5) Article 28 of the CIETAC Rules(2015) is confusing and unnecessary. It is better to delete it.

(6) Article 29(2) of the CIETAC Rules(2015) indicates that when both of the parties and the arbitral tribunal consider that there is no need for a hearing, the tribunal may adjudicate the case by written record. Neither the PRC Arbitration Law 2017 nor the CIETAC Rules(2015) contains time limits regarding adjudication by written record. Such a time limit should be added to the CIETAC Rules(2015), and there is no reason why it should be different from the time limit in adjudication by hearing.

(7) Article 36 of the PRC Arbitration Law 2017 provides that the removal of an arbitrator shall be decided upon by the chairman of the arbitration commission. When the chairman of the arbitration commission serves as an arbitrator, the withdrawal shall be decided upon collectively by the arbitration commission. The Law does not give any clue as to how this collective decision should be made. It is not clear whether the decision should be made by the unanimity, or by a majority, or by some particular person in the arbitration commission. Practical problems are created in making this decision by the lack of detailed regulation.

(8) Article 37 of the PRC Arbitration Law 2017 breaches the autonomy of the parties, as it prevents them agreeing whether to replace an arbitrator who is unable to perform his duty. Moreover, its requirement that the arbitrator concerned shall be replaced even deprives the Chairman of the CIETAC of his right to make the decision whether to replace the arbitrator. The decision whether an arbitrator who is unable to perform his functions should be replaced should be made on a case to case basis concerned, and should not be decided by a provision of a mandatory law. Therefore, Article 37 should be deleted. The parties should have the freedom to agree whether

中英仲裁法比较研究
A Comparative Study of the Chinese Arbitration
Law and the Arbitration Laws of the UK

an arbitrator should be replaced, and if so, how.

Ⅳ. The Approach of the Laws Operating in the UK

As ever we refer to the United Kingdom for a paradigm which offers two models for consideration —the 1996 Act and the Model Law. Chinese arbitration law, the Model Law, and the 1996 Act all permit the parties to challenge arbitrators, and if the parties' challenge is successful, the authority of the challenged arbitrator will be revoked. Since there are differences in culture and tradition, there are differences between the three laws as to the details of grounds of challenge, the challenge procedure, and the consequences of a successful challenge. The main difference is that in Chinese arbitration law, the court is never asked to remove arbitrators, whereas under the 1996 Act and the Model Law, the court can play a role in the challenge procedure. There is also a difference between the role of court under the 1996 Act and under the Model Law. The 1996 Act does not lay down a time limit for making a challenge, whereas under Chinese arbitration law and the Model Law, a party is required to make a challenge within a certain period of time, and if he fails to do so, he will be deemed to have abandoned his right to challenge the arbitrator's authority.

A. Imposing a Duty of Disclosure

Model Law: Article 12(1) of the Model Law provides that when a person is approached in connection with his possible appointment as an arbitrator, he shall disclose any circumstance likely to give rise to justifiable doubts as to his impartiality or independence. An arbitrator, from the time of his appointment and throughout the arbitral proceedings, shall without delay disclose any such circumstance to the parties unless they have already been informed of them by him. This provision is designed to avoid the appointment of an unacceptable candidate. It is clarified and strengthened by stipulating that the duty of disclosure is a continuing one and must be carried out promptly.

The 1996 Act: it does not explicitly impose a duty of disclosure of such facts or circumstances. But certain commentators suggest that such a duty be implicit,[1] without properly indicating the basis of that view and the consequences thereof.

Chinese Arbitration Law: under Chinese arbitration law, the parties may by agreement absolve arbitrators of their duty of disclosure. In the absence of such an agreement, the arbitrators are subject to a duty of disclosure. I suggest that no benefit derive from giving this freedom to the parties, as arbitrators are given a chance to conceal facts or circumstances which are grounds for challenge. In the absence of a duty of disclosure, the parties will find more difficult to discover those circumstances. Therefore, Chinese arbitration law should not give parties this freedom, but simply state explicitly that an arbitrator shall disclose any circumstances likely to give rise to justifiable doubts as to his impartiality or independence.

B. Grounds for Revoking Authority

The Model Law: under the Model Law, the parties are not permitted to agree as to the grounds on which arbitral authority may be revoked. Article 12(2) provides that the parties may challenge the authority of an arbitrator only if circumstances exist that give rise to justifiable doubts as to his impartiality or independence, or if he does not possess the qualifications agreed by the parties. A party may challenge an arbitrator appointed by him, or in whose appointment he has participated, only for reasons of which he becomes aware after the appointment has been made. By providing such limits

---

[1]   Harris, Bruce, Planterose, Rowan & Tecks, Jonathan, The Arbitration Act 1996: A Commentary 3rd ed., Malden: Blackwell Publishing, Inc.,2003,114.

中英仲裁法比较研究
A Comparative Study of the Chinese Arbitration
Law and the Arbitration Laws of the UK

on challenging a party's own appointee, abuse of the challenge procedure can be, to some extent, avoided. The Working Group considered it necessary to add the phrase " or in whose appointment he has participated", as the policy considerations which applied to the case of the party-appointed arbitrator were of equal force in the case where the parties jointly appointed an arbitrator.[1] The Analytical Commentary submits that "participation in the appointment" also includes a less direct involvement,[2] such as that which operates under the list procedure envisaged in the UNCITRAL Arbitration Rules.[3][The list procedure involves an appointing authority submitting a list of potential arbitrators to the parties, each party has the right to veto any name on the list. The appointing authority then selects the arbitrator(s) from the list of "approved" names.] Article 14(1) provides that any party may request the court to decide on the termination of an arbitrator's mandate if he becomes de jure or de facto unable to perform his functions, or for other reasons fails to act without undue delay. The secretariats' understanding of the phrase "fails to act" is that it includes, but is not limited to simple delay. The Analytical Commentary mentions among the relevant considerations in judging whether an arbitrator has failed to act, the question whether, in light of the arbitration agreement and the specific procedural situation, "his conduct fell clearly below the standard of what may reasonably be expected from an arbitrator".[4]

The 1996 Act: under the 1996 Act, Section 23(1) provides that the parties are free to agree in what circumstances the authority of an arbitrator may be revoked, and in the absence of such agreement they may always act

---

① Doc. A/CN. 91246, para.34.
② Doc. A/CN. 9/264, Article 12, nr.6.
③ Doc. A/CN. 9/264, Article 12, nr.6.
④ Doc. A/CN. 9/264, Article 14, p.34, para.4. See Broches, Aron, Commentary on the Model Law on International Commercial Arbitration, Boston: Kluwer Law and Taxation Publishers,1990,67.

jointly to revoke such authority. Moreover, a single party may always apply to the court to remove an arbitrator. Section 24 (1) provides that the court may remove a challenged arbitrator only on one of the following grounds: (a) that circumstances exist that give rise to justifiable doubts as to his impartiality; (b) that he does not possess the qualifications required by the arbitration agreement; (c) that he is physically or mentally incapable of conducting the proceedings or there are justifiable doubts as to his capacity to do so; (d) that he has refused or failed — (i) properly to conduct the proceedings, or (ii) to use all reasonable dispatch in conducting the proceedings or making an award, and that substantial injustice has been or will be caused to the applicant.

The first ground refers only to justifiable doubt as to the arbitrator's impartiality, without mentioning his independence. The DAC Report (para. 101) suggests that it is possible for an arbitrator to be impartial without being wholly independent; and unless an arbitrator demonstrates partiality, his lack of independence is irrelevant. Thus reference to independence is unnecessary.[1] There is a view that the internationally accepted requirement of independence aims to ensure impartiality, rather than to actually achieve it, and in that sense, the DAC was correct not to set independence as a further requirement.[2] However, an arbitrator's lack of independence is relevant if it is such as to give rise to justifiable doubt as to his impartiality. It might be argued that the lack of the requirement of independence will create no practical difficulty, since the parties can agree to make it a ground for challenge either expressly or by applying institutional rules which import the requirement of independence. However, I suggest that the requirement of independence should be enshrined in law, as lack of independence is much easier

---

[1]   Harris, Bruce, Planterose, Rowan & Tecks, Jonathan, The Arbitration Act 1996: A Commentary, 3rd ed., Malden: Blackwell Publishing, Inc., 2003, 111.

[2]   Harris, Bruce, Planterose, Rowan & Tecks, Jonathan, The Arbitration Act 1996: A Commentary, 3rd ed., Malden: Blackwell Publishing, Inc., 2003, 113.

中英仲裁法比较研究
A Comparative Study of the Chinese Arbitration
Law and the Arbitration Laws of the UK

to detect than partiality. By avoiding appointing an arbitrator who lacks independence, partiality can be, to a certain extent, avoided in the first place.

Chinese Arbitration Law: Under Chinese arbitration law, the parties are free to agree on the grounds for challenge,①but their agreement must be consistent with Article 34 of the PRC Arbitration Law 2017.② In the absence of such agreement, a party may challenge the authority of an arbitrator if he has justifiable doubts as to the arbitrator's impartiality or independence.③ I suggest that in the absence of agreement on the grounds for challenge, the law be changed so that lack of qualifications required by the agreement of the parties should be regarded as a ground for challenge.

C. Challenge Procedure

The Model Law: under the Model Law, where the ground for challenge falls within Article 12(2), i. e., circumstances exist that give rise to justifiable doubts as to his impartiality or independence, or if he does not possess qualifications agreed to by the parties,④ Article 13(1) explicitly gives the parties the freedom to agree upon a challenge procedure. Such agreement is

---

① Article 4(2) of the CIETAC Arbitration Rules (2015).

② Article 34 of the PRC Arbitration Law 2017 provides: An arbitrator shall be revoked and the parties concerned have the right to request revocation, whereas: (1) the arbitrator is a party involved in the case or a blood relation or relative of the parties concerned or their attorneys. (2) the arbitrator has vital personal interests in the case. (3) the arbitrator has other relations with the parties or their attorneys involved in the case that might affect the fair ruling of the case. (4) the arbitrator meets the parties concerned or their attorneys in private or has accepted gifts or attended banquets hosted by the parties concerned or their attorneys.

③ Article 26(2) of the CIETAC Arbitration Rules (2015).

④ Article 12(2) of the Model Law provides that an arbitrator may be challenged only if circumstances exist that give rise to justifiable doubts as to his impartiality or independence, or if he does not possess qualifications agreed to by the parties. A party may challenge an arbitrator appointed by him, or in whose appointment he has participated, only for reasons of which he becomes aware after the appointment has been made.

subject to the provisions of Article 13(3), which provides that if a challenge is not successful, the challenging party may, within 30 days of receiving notice of the rejection of the challenge, request the court to decide on the challenge. The court's decision shall be subject to no appeal.

When there is no agreed challenge procedure, Article 13(2) provides that a party who intends to challenge an arbitrator shall, within 15 days after becoming aware of either the constitution of the arbitral tribunal or the existence of a ground of challenge, send a written statement of the reasons for the challenge to the arbitral tribunal. The arbitral tribunal shall decide on the challenge. The Working Group agreed that such decision should be entrusted to all members of the arbitral tribunal, including the challenged arbitrator.[1] If a challenge is not successful, Article 13(3) provides that the challenging party may, within 30 days of receiving notice of the rejection of the challenge, request the court to decide on the challenge, the court's decision not being capable of being appealed.[2] The tribunal can continue the proceedings and even make an award, while the court's decision is pending. As regards the appropriateness of court control during the arbitral proceedings, the prevailing view was that the system adopted by the Working Group "struck an appropriate balance between the need for preventing obstruction with dilatory tactics and the desire to avoid unnecessary waste of time and money".[3] Although the possibility of the court reviewing the tribunal's decision on a challenge curbs the dangers of allowing a challenged arbitrator to participate in that decision and of course of allowing a sole arbitrator to rule on any challenge to him, I submit that it would still be better if the challenged arbitrator were excluded from the deliberations and decision on any challenge. The Law might provide that when the arbitral tribunal consists of

---

[1]   Doc. A/CN. 9/246, paras. 36 and 38.

[2]   Broches, Aron, Commentary on the Model Law on International Commercial Arbitration, Boston: Kluwer Law and Taxation Publishers,1990,65.

[3]   Commission Report, para.124.

中英仲裁法比较研究
A Comparative Study of the Chinese Arbitration
Law and the Arbitration Laws of the UK

more than one arbitrator, the other arbitrators shall make the decision. If that leads to a deadlock between an even number of arbitrators, the challenging party may refer the challenge to the court. When the arbitral tribunal consists of a sole arbitrator, the challenging party would obviously have to refer the challenge directly to the court.

The 1996 Act: Section 23(1) of the 1996 Act also gives the parties freedom to agree on a challenge procedure by providing that the parties are free to agree in what circumstances the authority of an arbitrator may be revoked. When there is no such agreement, by virtue of Section 23(3)(b), a challenging party may apply to any institution or person vested by them with powers to revoke an arbitrator's authority. If the ground for challenge is one of those specified in Section 24(1), the parties may apply to the court to remove the arbitrator. When the parties have vested any institution or person with the power in that regard, the court shall not exercise its power of removal unless satisfied that the applicant has first exhausted any available recourse to that institution or person.① The leave of the court is required for any appeal from a decision of the court under Section 24.② If the parties have vested in the arbitral tribunal the power to revoke an arbitrator's authority, they have the right to decide whether the challenged arbitrator shall be excluded from the deliberations and decision on the challenge, and how any deadlock is broken.

It can be seen that, under both of the Model Law and the 1996 Act the court may only decide on a challenge on specified grounds. There are four main differences between the court's role in the Model Law and the 1996 Act. First of all, the grounds of challenge are different. Secondly, under the Model Law, while in relation to certain grounds, the court may exercise its power only after an unsuccessful challenge to the tribunal, in relation to the

---

① Section 24(2) of the 1996 Act.
② Section 24(6) of the 1996 Act.

grounds that an arbitrator has become de lure or de facto unable to perform his functions, or for other reasons has failed to act without undue delay, the court shall itself make the primary decision. Under the 1996 Act, the court plays the same role as regards all grounds specified in it. If the parties have invested an institution or person (arbitral or otherwise) with the power to revoke an arbitrator's authority, the court may only intervene once the parties have firstly exhausted their recourse to such institution or person. Only if the parties have not vested such power, may the court make the primary decision. Thirdly, the court's decision under the Model Law shall be subject to no appeal, while under the 1996 Act there may be an appeal with the leave of the court. Fourthly, there are time limits for challenges involving the court under the Model Law, but not under the 1996 Act.

I suggest that the regime of the 1996 Act be more integrated than that of the Model Law. It is unnecessary for the court to play different roles when different grounds of challenge are involved, as every ground leads to the same outcome —the removal of the arbitrator. Yet if even after the parties have exhausted recourse to any institution or person they have empowered to remove arbitrators, the decision of the court can be appealed, the procedure for removal takes too long, and one of the main advantages of arbitration, the saving of time, is lost. Thus, I suggest that as under the Model Law, the court's decision not be subject to appeal. There is also a need to specify time limits for challenge, as this can effectively prevent abuses of challenge procedure.

Chinese Arbitration Law: under Chinese arbitration law, the court does not play a role in removing arbitrators. The Chairman of CIETAC makes the decision, which is final. (If the Chairman himself is an arbitrator, the revocation shall be decided upon collectively by the arbitration commission.) I believe that if parties cannot agree on a challenge procedure, their autonomy is damaged. So Chinese arbitration law should adopt the stance of the 1996 Act, and give the parties this freedom. Moreover, it is sensible to give the

中英仲裁法比较研究
A Comparative Study of the Chinese Arbitration
Law and the Arbitration Laws of the UK

challenging party an opportunity of appeal when he is unsatisfied with the Chairman's decision, so that I recommend that the court should be able to review the Chairman's decision and make the final decision. To prevent the court from overly interfering in the arbitral process, Chinese arbitration law should state that the court may remove the arbitrator only on the grounds specified in the law, as in the Model Law and the 1996 Act. Since the grounds specified by the 1996 Act are more integrated than under the Model Law, it is better for Chinese arbitration law to adopt the former grounds, subject to adding lack of independence as a ground. To avoid abuse of the challenge procedure, Chinese arbitration Law should also adopt the approach of the Model Law in providing that a party may only challenge an arbitrator appointed by him, or in whose appointment he has participated, for reasons of which he becomes aware after the appointment has been made.

D. Joint Termination and Resignation

The Model Law: Article 13(2) of the Model Law provides that when an arbitrator is challenged on the grounds specified in Article 12, the challenged arbitrator may withdraw from his office or the other party may agree to the challenge. Article 14(1) states that if an arbitrator becomes de lure or de facto unable to perform his functions or for other reasons fails to act without undue delay, his mandate terminates if he withdraws from his office or if the parties agree on the termination. Article 14(2) continues that if, under this article or Article 13(2), an arbitrator withdraws from his office or a party agrees to the termination of the mandate of an arbitrator, this does not imply acceptance of the validity of any ground referred to in this article or Article 12(2).

The 1996 Act: under Section 23(3) of the 1996 Act the authority of an arbitrator may be revoked by the parties acting jointly. The agreement to revoke that authority must be in writing, in line with the general requirement set out in Section 5(1).① An agreement to terminate the arbitration is an exception to the general requirement and needs not to be in writing, as it is not practical for parties who mutually want the arbitration to lapse to make such an agreement in writing. Accordingly, if the agreement to revoke the arbitrator's authority is made in the context of an agreement, to terminate the arbitration, neither of them should be in writing.② The 1996 Act does not explicitly provide that the resignation of an arbitrator will terminate his mandate, but it is considered implicitly. There is no rule as to whether the joint termination by the parties or the resignation of a challenged arbitrator implies acceptance of the validity of any ground for challenge.

Chinese Arbitration Law: under Chinese arbitration law, it is explicit that when an arbitrator is challenged by one party, and the other party agrees to the challenge, or the arbitrator being challenged withdraws from his office, such an arbitrator is no longer on the arbitral tribunal and neither case implies that the challenge made by the party is sustainable.③

E. Resigned Arbitrator's Entitlement to Fees or Expenses or Liability

The Model Law: when an arbitrator resigns, the Model Law does not give rules as to his entitlement to fees or expenses, or any liability thereby incurred by him.

The 1996 Act: by contrast, Section 25(1) of the 1996 Act provides that when an arbitrator resigns, the parties are free to reach agreement with him on these issues. It should be noted that an agreement between one party and

---

① Section 5(1) of the 1996 Act provides: The provisions of this part apply only where the arbitration agreement is in writing, and any other agreement between the parties as to any matter is effective for the purposes of this part only if in writing, the expressions "agreement", "agree", and "agreed" shall be construed accordingly.

② Harris, Bruce, Planterose, Rowan & Tecks, Jonathan, The Arbitration Act 1996: A Commentary,3rd ed., Malden: Blackwell Publishing, Inc.,2003,109.

③ Article 26(5) of the CIETAC Arbitration Rules (2015).

中英仲裁法比较研究
A Comparative Study of the Chinese Arbitration
Law and the Arbitration Laws of the UK

its own appointee would not fall within this section.① When there is no such agreement, the arbitrator who resigns his appointment may apply to the court to grant him relief from any liability thereby incurred by him, and to make such order as it thinks fit with respect to his entitlement to fees or expenses or the repayment of any fees or expenses already paid.② If the court is satisfied that in all the circumstances it was reasonable for the arbitrator to resign, it may grant such relief on such terms as it thinks fit.③ The leave of the court is required for any appeal from its decision.④ If an arbitrator is removed by the court, the court may make such order as it thinks fit with respect to the arbitrator's entitlement to fees or expenses, or the repayment of any fees or expenses already paid.⑤ The leave of the court is again required for any appeal from its decision.⑥

Chinese Arbitration Law: if Chinese arbitration law permitted the court to play a role in removing arbitrators, it may adopt the stance of the 1996 Act regarding the liabilities incurred by the arbitrator and his entitlement to fees or expenses.

F. Continuation of Arbitral Proceedings

The Model Law: Article 13(3) of the Model Law provides that when a party requests the court to decide on a challenge, while such a request is pending, the arbitral tribunal, including the challenged arbitrator, may continue the arbitral proceedings and make an award. It is not made clear whether the arbitral tribunal shall continue or stay the arbitral proceedings

---

① Harris, Brucel/Planterose, Rowan & Tecks, Jonathan, The Arbitration Act 1996: A Commentary, 3rd ed., Malden: Blackwell Publishing, Inc.,2003,116.
② Section 25(3) of the 1996 Act.
③ Section 25(4) of the 1996 Act.
④ Section 25(5) of the 1996 Act.
⑤ Section 24(4) of the 1996 Act.
⑥ Section 24(6) of the 1996 Act.

while the request is pending, when the party requests the arbitral tribunal to decide on a challenge.

The 1996 Act: under the 1996 Act, Section 24(3) similarly provides that the arbitral tribunal may continue the arbitral proceedings and make an award while an application to the court is pending. Yet once more when a party applies to an institution or person invested with the power to decide challenges, it is not clear whether the arbitral tribunal may continue or stay the arbitral proceedings while the request is pending.

Chinese Arbitration Law: under Chinese arbitration law, the parties are free to agree such matters while the request is pending. If there is no such agreement, the challenged arbitrator shall continue to fulfill the functions of arbitrator until a decision on the challenge has been made by the Chairman of CIETAC.[①] If Chinese arbitration law permits the court to play a role in the challenge procedure, it should also indicate whether a challenged arbitrator should continue to perform his function until the court makes the decision.

G. Effect of Death of an Arbitrator

The Model Law: the Model Law gives no rules regarding the situation that an arbitrator dies, or the person who appointed him dies.

The 1996 Act: under the 1996 Act, Section 26 provides that while the authority of an arbitrator is personal and ceases on his death; unless otherwise agreed by the parties, the death of the person by whom an arbitrator was appointed does not revoke his authority. It is better for Chinese arbitration law to adopt this provision.

H. Appointment of a Substitute Arbitrator

The Model Law: under the Model Law, the parties have no right to decide whether a substitute arbitrator should be appointed when an arbitrator

---

① Article 26(7) of the CIETAC Arbitration Rules (2015).

中英仲裁法比较研究
A Comparative Study of the Chinese Arbitration
Law and the Arbitration Laws of the UK

is removed. Article 15 provides that when the mandate of an arbitrator terminates under Article 13 or 14, or because of his withdrawal from office for any other reason, or because of the revocation of his mandate by agreement of the parties, or in any other case of termination of his mandate, a substitute arbitrator shall be appointed according to the rules that were applicable to the appointment of the arbitrator being replaced. The Working Group wanted to cover all cases in which a mandate has been terminated. As a result, the structure of that article is rather awkward.[1] In my view, it is unnecessary to have Article 15 say more than that a substitute must be appointed, whenever a mandate terminates.

It is not necessary to specify the cases in which the mandate of an arbitrator would terminate. The passage commencing with the words "under Article 13 or 14" and ending with the words "termination of his mandate" could be deleted, so that the content of the provision could be reduced to its essentials, namely the appointment of a substitute arbitrator to fill any vacancy. Article 15 makes it clear that a substitute arbitrator shall be appointed according to the rules that were applicable to the appointment of the arbitrator being replaced.

The 1996 Act: under the 1996 Act Section 27(1) states that when an arbitrator ceases to hold office, the parties are free to agree whether and if so how the vacancy is to be filled.[2] If or to the extent that there is no such agreement, the provisions of Sections 16 (procedure for appointment of arbitrators) and 18 (failure of appointment procedure) apply in relation to the filling of the vacancy as in relation to an original appointment.[3]

Chinese Arbitration Law: under Chinese arbitration law, Article 37 provides that the filling of a vacancy should be made according to the PRC Arbitration Law 2017, which provides that when the parties agree that the

---

[1] Doc. A/CN. 9/246, para.45.

[2] Section 27(1)(a) of the 1996 Act.

[3] Section 27(3) of the 1996 Act.

arbitration tribunal is to be composed of three arbitrators, each shall choose one arbitrator or entrust the appointment to the chairman of the arbitration commission, while the third arbitrator will be jointly chosen by the parties or by the chairman of the arbitration commission when jointly entrusted with this task by the parties. The third arbitrator shall be the chief arbitrator.[1] When the parties agree to have a single, they shall jointly choose the arbitrator or entrust the choice to the chairman.[2] If the parties fail to decide on the composition of the arbitral tribunal or fail to choose arbitrators within the time limit prescribed in the arbitration rules, the chairman shall make the decision.[3] I suggest that in line with the principle of the autonomy of the parties, they should be free to decide whether the vacancy should be filled. Chinese arbitration law should thus adopt the approach of the 1996 Act.

I. Standing of Previous Proceedings

Model Law: when a substitute arbitrator is appointed, the Model Law does not indicate whether the previous proceedings shall stand.

1996 Act: it provides that the parties are free to agree whether and if so to what extent the previous proceedings should stand. If there is no such agreement, the new tribunal shall determine whether and if so to what extent the previous proceedings should stand.

Chinese Arbitration Law: under Chinese arbitration law, it is for the new tribunal to make its own decision as to whether or not the arbitration proceedings shall stand and the parties are not at liberty to agree on this issue. Again, in line with the principle of the autonomy of the parties, Chinese arbitration law should adopt the stance of the 1996 Act on this matter.

---

[1]   Article 31, para.1 of the PRC Arbitration Law 2017.
[2]   Article 31, para.2 of the CIETAC Arbitration Law 2017.
[3]   Article 32 of the CIETAC Arbitration Law 2017.

中英仲裁法比较研究
A Comparative Study of the Chinese Arbitration
Law and the Arbitration Laws of the UK

V. Conclusion

To resolve certain problems of Chinese arbitration law, it is useful to look to the Model Law and the 1996 Act. In Chinese arbitration law, the court does not play a role in the challenge procedure and in most cases the Chairman shall make the decision in the first place and that decision is a final one. When the challenge is unsuccessful, the challenging party has no recourse. Thus Chinese arbitration law might permit the court to review the Chairman's decision and provide necessary supervision of the arbitral process, in line with the Model Law and the 1996 Act. If it permits the court to play a role in the challenge procedure, the Law should also specify grounds on which the court may remove the arbitrator, to ensure that the court would not interfere with the arbitral process too much. Chinese arbitration law might adopt the grounds laid down by the 1996 Act, subject to making lack of independence a ground of challenge. Under Chinese arbitration law, when an arbitrator ceases to hold his position, the parties have no freedom to agree whether a substitute arbitrator shall be appointed, and, where a new tribunal constitutes, whether the previous proceeding shall stand. I suggest that, like the 1996 Act, Chinese arbitration law should give the parties these powers. Chinese arbitration law might also fill obvious gaps by adopting the approach of the 1996 Act as to such matters as the liabilities and entitlement to fees of an arbitrator who resigns, the effect of the death of an arbitrator or the person who appointed him, and the effect of an arbitrator's ceasing to hold his position on any appointment made by him.

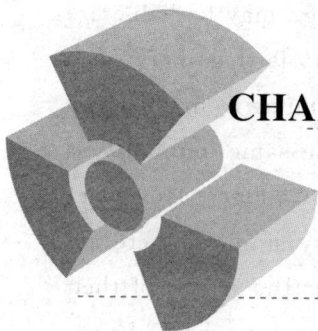

CHAPTER 8

ARBITRAL IMMUNITY

I. Introduction

Where arbitrators turn out to be disqualified or act inequitably, the parties may exercise supervisory power. In particular, a party may challenge the authority of any arbitrator, where the arbitrator has a vital personal interest in the case[①] or where the party has justifiable doubts as to the impartiality or independence of an arbitrator.[②] Damage may be brought to the parties where an arbitrator is unqualified, or has acted inequitably, or has delayed unduly. For example, delay by an arbitrator may leave a party waiting for payment which is due to him, while if an arbitrator extorts a bribe from a party, the loss of that party is obvious. Moreover, the process of revocation will cost the parties time, money and energy. Thus a crucial issue is whether arbitrators should be liable for such costs. In Chinese practice, arbitrators are not liable for acts or omissions other than those specified in those arti-

---

[①]   Article 34 of the PRC Arbitration Law 2017.
[②]   Article 32 of the CIETAC Arbitration Rules (2015).

中英仲裁法比较研究
A Comparative Study of the Chinese Arbitration
Law and the Arbitration Laws of the UK

cles. It can be seen that the matters for which arbitrators may be liable are very limited in scope. The rationale of arbitral immunity is that there is no doubt that judges acting in their judicial capacity are immune from suit, and they have therefore been presumed to be entitled to the same immunity as judges since arbitrators have long been treated as akin to judges. However, even if the functions of judges and arbitrators are very similar, there are differences between judges and arbitrators, in particular the source of their power and authority. It is worth discussing whether arbitrators should be entitled to the same immunity as judges. This chapter aims to discuss whether arbitrators should have complete immunity, and if not, for what sort of behaviour and to what extent they should be liable. As ever, the Chinese approach to the above questions will be compared with the approach taken in the English law and the Model Law.

II. The Chinese Approach to Arbitral Immunity

A. Immunity of Arbitrators

There are no clear rules as to the immunity of arbitrators. In practice, an arbitrator is not liable for anything done or omitted in the discharge or purported discharge of his functions as arbitrator unless the act or omission breaches Articles 34(4), 38 or 58(6) of the PRC Arbitration Law 2017. In effect, those articles provide that an arbitrator shall bear legal responsibility where "the arbitrator meets the parties concerned or their attorneys in private, or has accepted gifts or attended banquets hosted by the parties concerned or their attorneys", or where the parties have evidences showing that arbitrators have accepted bribes, resorted to deception for personal gain or perverted the law in their ruling.

B. To What Extent Should They Be Liable?

The circumstances in which arbitrators should be liable are discussed a-
bove. But to what extent should they be liable? Should they bear criminal,
administrative, or civil liability? In the light of Articles 10 and 14 of the
PRC Arbitration Law 2017, ① an arbitral award is not an administrative determination. Thus arbitrators cannot bear administrative liability either. Article 399 of the Criminal Law provides that, whoever, in civil or administrative proceedings, intentionally runs counter to the facts and law and twists
the law when rendering judgments or orders, shall be sentenced to fixed-
term imprisonment of not more than five years or criminal detention if the
circumstances are serious; and shall be sentenced to fixed-term imprisonment of not less than five years but not more than 10 years if the circumstances are especially serious. Consequently, under Chinese law, the arbitrators bear criminal and civil liability.

[**Civil Liability**]

The Amount of Damages: Neither the PRC Arbitration Law 2017 nor
the CIETAC Arbitration Rules prescribes the amount of damages payable by
arbitrators. In my view, to avoid making arbitrators so worried about potential awards of damages that the arbitration is adversely affected, it should be
made clear how damages will be calculated according to the types and conse-

---

① Article 10 of the PRC Arbitration Law 2017 provides: An arbitration commission
may be set up in the domicile of the people's governments of municipalities under the direct
jurisdiction of the central government (hereinafter referred to as "municipalities"), provinces and autonomous regions or in other places as requested. It shall not be set up according to administrative levels. An arbitration commission shall be set up by the relevant departments and chambers of commerce under the coordination of the people's governments
of the cities prescribed in the preceding paragraph. Article 14 of the PRC Arbitration Law
2017 provides: An arbitration commission shall be independent of any administrative organ, without any subordinate relationship with administrative organs. Neither would there
be any subordinate relations thereof.

中英仲裁法比较研究
A Comparative Study of the Chinese Arbitration
Law and the Arbitration Laws of the UK

quences of default. If an arbitrator's behaviour does not cause actual loss to the parties, he should merely be obliged to repay any remuneration he receives. If his behaviour causes delay in a party receiving due payment, the amount of his repayment should include not only his remuneration, but a sum representing the interest lost by that party. If his behaviour causes any other damage to the party, he should be also liable for that damage. If he extorts a bribe, he must return the money or other benefit to the party. If he simply receives a bribe, the money or other benefit should be confiscated by the authorities, or given to the innocent party. It is not uncommon for a party to be implicated in the arbitrator's unlawful behaviour. If that is the case, that party should also be liable to the other for the damage caused. Similarly, if the arbitration agency is implicated, it should also be liable.

Security: To avoid or reduce fraudulent or retaliatory action against arbitrators, it is suggested that an applicant shall be required to provide security before bringing an action against an arbitrator. The security includes two parts: (1) the fees and expense of the arbitrator; (2) the amount of money which will be a penalty paid by the applicant if he loses the lawsuit against the arbitrator. Before the judgment as to whether the arbitrator shall be liable for the damage or cost concerned, the fees and expenses of the arbitrator shall be paid from the security. If the arbitrator loses the lawsuit against him, he must repay his fee and expenses to the applicant. If the applicant loses the lawsuit, he shall pay an amount of money as a penalty from the security. Since there is a possibility of paying a penalty, the party will consider whether it is worth bringing an action against arbitrators, and fraudulent or retaliatory action can be effectively avoided or reduced.[①]

[**Criminal Liability**]

This crime is known as "running counter to the facts and law and twis-

---

① Ding Ying, Research on the Arbitrators, Delay of Arbitration Proceedings in International Commercial Arbitration, 6 Law Science, 2000, 69.

ting the law in arbitration". However, if the standard of "running counter to the facts and law and twisting the law in arbitration" is not strictly defined, it will make the malicious parties have the opportunity to take advantage of it. Once the losing party is unwilling, it is possible to prosecute the arbitrator involved in the crime of "running counter to the facts and law and twisting the law in arbitration." Therefore, the establishment of the criminal responsibility of "defamation law" has created a dilemma for arbitration.

Ⅲ. Disadvantages of the Chinese Approach

(1) The Chinese arbitration law does not deal adequately with the immunity of arbitrators, in that it is not clear whether arbitrators are liable for acts or omissions other than those specified in Articles 34(4), 38, and Article 58(6) of the PRC Arbitration Law 2017.

(2) There are no rules in the PRC Arbitration Law 2017 or the CIETAC Arbitration Rules regarding the extent of liability of arbitrators.

(3) There is no requirement in the PRC Arbitration Law 2017 or the CIETAC Arbitration Rules that a party bringing an action against an arbitrator should provide security.

(4) There is no solid legal basis for the establishment of criminal liability of the arbitrators, and it has no significant effect on protecting the interests of the parties and compensating the losses of the parties. Instead, it will adversely affect the enthusiasm of the arbitrators, the international image of Chinese arbitration, and the development of Chinese arbitration. In the dilemma of dealing with foreign-related arbitral awards, it is obviously more harmful than good.

中英仲裁法比较研究
A Comparative Study of the Chinese Arbitration
Law and the Arbitration Laws of the UK

Ⅳ. Approach of the Laws Operating in the UK

A. Introduction

As ever we refer to the United Kingdom for a paradigm which offers two models for consideration —the 1996 Act and the Model Law. The traditional position under English common law was that arbitrators were treated akin to the judiciary and provided with immunity from suit. However, certain doubts as to this state of absolute immunity arose from the speeches of two Law Lords in Sutcliffe v. Thackrah① and Arenson v. Arenson Casson, Beckman, Rutley Co.② The matter is now put on a statutory footing by the 1996 Act, so that arbitrators generally have immunity, but not absolute immunity. The Act provides that an arbitrator is not liable for anything done or omitted in the discharge or purported discharge of his functions as arbitrator, unless such act or omission is shown to have been in bad faith.③ By contrast, the Model Law says nothing about arbitral immunity.

B. The Traditional Position

In English law, there is no doubt that judges when acting their judicial capacity are immune from suit, whether in negligence or on the grounds that they have acted maliciously or corruptly. The reason for immunity is that the law takes the view that the system of public justice would be compromised if litigation could be brought against a judge, so that the party who has lost an action might effectively have the matter retried. Arbitrators had long been treated as akin to judges and had therefore been presumed to be entitled to

---

① ［1974］A. C. 727.

② ［1977］A. C. 405.

③ Section 29(1) of the 1996 Act.

the same immunity as judges.① As Lord Salmon observed in Sutcliffe v. Thackrah,

> It is well settled that judges, barristers, solicitors, jurors and witnesses enjoy an absolute immunity from an form of civil action being brought against them in respect of anything they say or do in court during the course of a trial. This is not because the law regards any of these with special tenderness but because the law recognizes that, on balance of convenience, public policy demands that they shall all have such an immunity... The immunity which they enjoy is vital to the efficient and speedy administration of justice.

Continuing,

> Since arbitrators are in much the same position as judges, in that they carry out more or less the same functions, the law has for generations recognized that public policy requires that they too shall be accorded the immunity of which I referred.②

There are several bases on which arbitral immunity might be justified. First of all, the doctrine of immunity of arbitrators has been in existence for many years. Secondly, it is accepted by all major industries and users of arbitration.③ There have been no cases where dissatisfied parties have sought to sue the arbitrator. Rather they have sought to have the arbitrator removed or the award overturned.④ Thirdly, if arbitrators were not immune from such actions and they were exposed to an open-ended liability to the parties,

---

① Lew, Julian D. M., The Immunity of Arbitrators, London: Lloyd's of London Press Ltd. with the School of International Arbitration, 1990, 22.

② [1974] A. C. 727 at pp.757-758.

③ For example, commodity shipping and construction arbitrations. One must distinguish here between arbitration pursuant to an arbitration agreement and the architect or surveyor issuing a certificate on a construction site and a valuer.

④ Lew, Julian D. M., The Immunity of Arbitrators, London: Lloyd's of London Press Ltd. with the School of International Arbitration, 1990, 26.

中英仲裁法比较研究
A Comparative Study of the Chinese Arbitration
Law and the Arbitration Laws of the UK

considerable harm would be done to the finality of the arbitral process, and it might be difficult to find arbitrators willing to serve at all.[1]

C. Challenge to Immunity

These certain doubts as to arbitral immunity at common law arose from the speeches of two Law Lords in Sutcliffe v. Thackrah[2] and Arenson v. Arenson Casson, Beckman, Rutley Co.[3] These two cases involved architects and auditors respectively acting as valuers, and were referred to in the speeches in the House of Lords as "quasi arbitrations". The essential issue was whether architects and auditors should be immune from suit, and the discussion was extended to the whole question of whether the previously unquestioned immunity of arbitrators was in fact justified. In Sutcliffe v. Thackrah, rejecting the architect's entitlement to immunity, Lord Reid stated:

> There is nothing judicial about an architect's function in determining whether certain work is defective. There is no dispute. He is not jointly engaged by the parties. They do not submit evidence as contentions to him. He makes his own investigations and comes to a decision.[4]

In Arenson[5], it was held that the accountants were acting as valuers and in that context were not immune from an action in negligence, Lord Simon stating,

> A person adversely affected by a negligent valuation (possibly for rich reward) is left without remedy. He is, in fact, in a worse position

---

① Harris, Bruce, Planterose, Rowan & Tecks, Jonathan, The Arbitration Act 1996: A Commentary, 3rd ed., Malden: Blackwell Publishing, Inc.,2003,128.

② [1974] A. C. 727.

③ [1977] A. C. 405.

④ Op. cit. [1974] A. C. 727, at pp.737-738. See similarly Lord Morrison of Borth-y-Gest, op. cit.,at pp.752-753.

⑤ [1977] A. C. 405.

than under a formal arbitration, where he has the right to demand a case to be stated for the opinion of the court.①

As regards the immunity of arbitrators, Lord Kilbrandon argued that he could see no difference between a valuer appointed by one person and a valuer appointed by both parties (who was considered akin to an arbitrator and therefore immune from suit). He said,

> The question which puzzled me as the argument developed was, what was the essential difference between the typical valuer (the auditor in the present case) and an arbitrator at common law or under the Arbitration Acts? It is conceded that an arbitrator is immune from suit, aside from fraud, but why? I find it impossible to put weight on such considerations as that in the case of an arbitrator (a) there is a dispute between parties, (b) he hears evidence, (c) he hears submissions from the parties, and that therefore he, unlike the valuer, is acting in a judicial capacity. As regards (a), I cannot see any judicial distinction between a dispute which has actually arisen and a situation where persons have opposed interests, if in either case an impartial person has had to be called in to make a decision which the interested parties will accept. As regards (b) and (c), these are certainly not necessary activities of an arbiter. Once the nature and the limits of the submission to him have been defined, it could well be that he would go down at his own convenience to a warehouse, inspect a sample of merchandise displayed to him by the foreman and return his opinion on its quality or value. I have come to be of the opinion that it is a necessary conclusion to be drawn from Sutcliffe v. Thackrah... and from the instant decision that an arbitrator at common law or under the Acts is indeed a person selected by the parties for his expertise thereof and that if he is negligent in that ex-

---

① Op. cit. [1974] A. C. 405, at p.421. This argument may be weakened by the abolition of the case stated system by the 1979 Act but the appeal procedure, though narrower, will be equally appropriate where it applies and questions of law are in issue.

中英仲裁法比较研究
A Comparative Study of the Chinese Arbitration
Law and the Arbitration Laws of the UK

ercise he will be liable in damages. If this conclusion were to be established by law, I do not think the consequences would be dramatic or even noticeable. It would become a generally accepted term of reference to arbitration — because the referee would insist on it — that he be given by the parties immunity from suit for negligence at the instance of either of them.①

Lord Fraser contrasted arbitrators and valuers and concluded:

The main difference between them is that the arbitrator, like the judge, has to decide a dispute that has already arisen, and he usually has rival contentions before him, while the mutual valuer is called in before a dispute has arisen, in order to avoid it. He may be employed by parties who have little or no idea of the value of the property to be valued and who rely entirely on his skill and judgment as an expert. In that respect he differs from some arbitrators. But many arbitrators are chosen for their expert knowledge of the subject of the arbitration, and many others are chosen from the legal profession for their expert knowledge of the law or perhaps because they are credited with an expertise in holding the balance fairly between parties. It does not seem possible, therefore, to distinguish between mutual valuers and arbitrators on the ground that the former are experts and the latter are not. I share the difficulty of my noble and learned friend, Lord Kilbrandon, in seeing why arbitrators as a class should have immunity from suit if mutual valuers do not.②

D. Current State of English Law

If certain speeches in Sutcliffe and Arenson had left arbitral immunity in doubt, the issue was soon overtaken by the passing of the 1996 Act. Thus

① Op. cit. [1974] A. C. 405, pp.432-433.
② Op. cit. [1974] A. C. 405, at p.442.

Section 29(1) provides that an arbitrator is not liable for anything done or o-
mitted in the discharge or purported discharge of his functions as arbitrators
unless the act or omission is shown to have been in bad faith. Section 29(2)
continues that Subsection (1) applies to an employee or agent of an arbitrator as it applies to the arbitrator himself. These provisions resolve the previous uncertainty. It can be seen that an arbitrator's immunity does not extend
to acts or omissions that are shown to have been in bad faith. The term "bad
faith" is not further defined, and may have a variety of meanings in different
contexts. It remains to be seen whether, in the context of the 1996 Act, the
courts will decide that bad faith must have a moral ingredient, and connotes,
for example, malice or dishonesty, or whether it will bear a wider interpretation. It is notable that Section 29 has mandatory status, so that the parties
are not able to agree to deprive an arbitrator of this protection.

E. My Opinion

Under the Chinese arbitration law, the situations where arbitrators
should be liable are exhaustive. My opinion is that it is not sensible to enu-
merate the situations where arbitrators should be liable, as the range of
potential cases is too complex and multifarious. Therefore, I suggest that it
is preferable for the Chinese arbitration law to recognize and adopt the concept of bad faith. Here I would like to divide the problem of arbitral immunity into two separate problems: first, whether arbitrators shall be liable for
damage caused by action or omission which is shown to have been in bad
faith; second, whether arbitrators shall be liable for damage caused by negligence.

[Bad faith]

There is no doubt that judges are absolutely immune from any action,
whether in negligence or on the grounds that they have acted maliciously or
corruptly. This practice is not intended to exclude the judge from any sort of
supervision. Judges are appointed by the state and exercise their powers on

中英仲裁法比较研究
A Comparative Study of the Chinese Arbitration
Law and the Arbitration Laws of the UK

its behalf. A judge owes a duty to the state to uphold the law and administer justice accordingly. Therefore, the State would supervise the action of a judge by requiring him to be answerable to his peer group, by removing or "impeaching" him in certain circumstances and by making his decision subject to review by a court of higher jurisdiction. The absolute immunity of a judge only means that a party is not entitled to bring any action against him regarding his actions in the discharge of his judicial function. In other words, a judge is not liable for loss caused by his actions. The reason for such immunity is to prevent litigation being brought against a judge with a view to having a matter retried by a dissatisfied and litigious party who has lost an action.[1]

Even if the functions of judges and arbitrators are the same or very similar, the source of their power and authority is fundamentally different. An arbitrator is appointed by the parties, directly or indirectly, and owes his duties to them. An arbitrator has no duty other than to perform the task with which the parties have entrusted him[2]; i. e., to hear their arguments, weigh up the evidence and render an award on their respective rights and obligations under the arbitration agreement.[3] Furthermore, in performing the task with which the parties have entrusted him, although an arbitrator must apply the mandatory rules of arbitration law, where there is no mandatory rule in that respect, an arbitrator shall perform his task according to the par-

---

① Lew, Julian D. M., The Immunity of Arbitrators, London: Lloyd's of London Press Ltd. with the School of International Arbitration,1990,21.

② This author has elsewhere argued that in international commercial arbitration, arbitrators are the guardians of the international commercial order, and have a duty to uphold the fundamental standards of international trade, customs of international trade and the fundamental moral and ethical values which underlie every level of commercial activity, i. e. international public policy: see Lew, Julian D. M., Applicable Law in International Commercial Arbitration. New York: Oceana Publications, Inc., 1978, para.413.

③ Lew, Julian D. M., The Immunity of Arbitrators, London: Lloyd's of London Press Ltd. with the School of International Arbitration,1990,22.

ties' own agreement. As a matter of fact, most of the rules of arbitration law are non-mandatory, and therefore, in most cases, an arbitrator would perform his task in accordance with the parties' own agreement. Since the power of an arbitrator is given by the parties, and the arbitrator owns a duty to perform the task with which the parties have entrusted him, the parties have the right to supervise the action of an arbitrator, e. g., the parties are entitled to challenge the authority of an arbitrator and apply to revoke that authority in certain circumstances. Similarly, a party has the right to demand compensation from an arbitrator for any loss the arbitrator causes for him. It is admitted that if arbitrators were not immune from suit, and were exposed to an open-ended liability to the parties, some harm would be done to the finality of the arbitral process and the enthusiasm of arbitrators would be adversely affected. However, the problem could be resolved by limiting the scope of the situations in which arbitrators shall be liable for damage. To be specific, it is preferable to provide that an arbitrator shall be liable for loss caused by any action, which is shown to have been in bad faith. Arbitrators can effectively avoid being sued and can protect the finality of the arbitral process by not acting in bad faith. It is not difficult for arbitrators to avoid acting in bad faith.

[Negligence]

As discussed above, theoretically, since the power of an arbitrator is conferred by the parties and he owes duties to them, an arbitrator should be liable for loss caused by him. However, if an arbitrator were liable for loss caused by his negligence, it might be difficult to find arbitrators willing to serve, as it is difficult to completely avoid negligence in performing the arbitral function. It might be helpful to permit arbitrators and parties to confer immunity for negligence on arbitrators by agreement. However, if that were the case, most arbitrators would make such an agreement with the parties. Therefore, it might be more convenient to give such immunity to arbitrators directly in the law.

中英仲裁法比较研究
A Comparative Study of the Chinese Arbitration
Law and the Arbitration Laws of the UK

Ⅴ. Conclusion

Under the 1996 Act, arbitrators are immune from suit unless the act or omission is shown to have been in bad faith. The term "bad faith" may have a variety of meanings in different contexts. In the Chinese law, the situations in which arbitrators may be liable for damage are enumerated. In my view, in this regard the approach of the 1996 Act is more sensible than that of that Chinese law. However, considering the fundamental differences between arbitrators and judges, I don't think that arbitrators should be entitled to the same immunity as judges. Rather, arbitrators should be liable for damages in negligence like other providers of professional services. To protect the finality of arbitral awards and to avoid or reduce fraudulent or retaliatory action against arbitrators, it should be possible for arbitrators to be granted immunity from suit by agreement with the parties. In the situations where there is no such agreement, a party should be obliged to provide security before bringing an action against an arbitrator. Moreover, the Chinese Criminal Law provides that the arbitrator shall be liable if he intentionally runs counter to the facts and law and twists the law when rendering an award. It is recommended to replace the "running counter to the facts and law and twisting the law in arbitration" with the "arbitrator's acceptance of bribes".

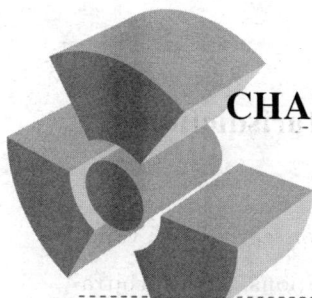

CHAPTER 9

QUESTIONS OF JURISDICTION

I. Introduction

In practically every legal system, the determination of contractual disputes is, prima facie, entrusted to the courts. Yet most legal systems nowadays concede the possibility that the parties may agree to achieve a binding resolution of their dispute through the institution of arbitration. Still, while the jurisdiction of the court is inherent and fundamental, the jurisdiction of an arbitral tribunal is rooted in and limited by the agreement of the parties. This means that it is by no means uncommon for a tribunal to be faced with a party suggesting that it has no jurisdiction, or that, it has exceeded its jurisdiction. Thus the law must feature mechanisms for dealing with such jurisdictional challenges. This chapter aims to consider what mechanisms are provided by the Chinese law, and how these compare to those provided by

中英仲裁法比较研究
A Comparative Study of the Chinese Arbitration
Law and the Arbitration Laws of the UK

the laws of the UK.

II. The Chinese Approach to Arbitral Jurisdiction

As mentioned in Chapter 4, to make the arbitration agreement valid, the arbitration agreement must satisfy a number of conditions. If the arbitration agreement is found to be invalid, the dispute cannot be resolved by arbitration, and the arbitral tribunal would have no jurisdiction over the dispute concerned. If a party has any doubt concerning the validity or existence of an arbitration clause or agreement, or the scope of such clause or agreement, it may make a jurisdictional challenge. The crucial question then is, which institution can entertain that challenge?

A. The Institutions Allowed to Entertain a Jurisdictional Challenge

In China, if a party wishes to make a jurisdictional challenge, three institutions could potentially be involved —the arbitration agency, the court and the arbitral tribunal.

1. The arbitration agency

As mentioned in Chapter 6, there are many arbitration agencies in China. The main two ones are CIETAC and CMAC. The main functions of arbitration agencies are accepting a case upon a written application and constituting arbitral tribunal. The principle that an arbitration agency has power to determine the arbitral tribunal's jurisdiction has recently been established by CIETAC and CMAC. The CIETAC Arbitration Rules provided for the first time that the Arbitration Commission shall have the right to rule on the validity of an arbitration agreement and on jurisdictional matters in a case.[1]

---

① Article 6 of the CIETAC Arbitration Rules(2015).

This provision enlarges the power of the arbitration agency. It not only has the right to make a decision on the validity of arbitration agreement and on the extent of the tribunal's jurisdiction, but also can even decide whether the arbitration agreement exists. The power of these arbitration agencies to decide upon the arbitral tribunal's jurisdiction has also been approved by legislation. Article 20 of the PRC Arbitration Law 2017 also provides that whereas parties concerned have doubt on the validity of an arbitration agreement, a request can be made to the arbitration commission for a decision or to the people's court for a ruling.

2. The arbitral tribunal

China adhered to the 1966 Washington Convention on the Settlement of Investment Disputes between States and Nationals of Other States in 1992. Article 41 of that Convention provides that, the Tribunal shall be the judge of its own competence; and any objection by a party to the dispute that that dispute is not within the jurisdiction of the Centre, or for other reasons is not within the competence of the Tribunal, shall be considered by the Tribunal which shall determine whether to deal with it as a preliminary question or to join it to the merits of the dispute. Thus according to the article, the arbitral tribunal should have right to decide its own jurisdiction. Nonetheless, the Convention applies in a very specialized set of circumstances — where the PRC is itself a party to an investment dispute with a foreign national — and seeks to create an entirely national arbitration system entirely free from supervision by the courts of any legal system. By contrast, under the PRC Arbitration Law and the arbitration rules of China, arbitrators have no power to decide upon their own jurisdiction in the first instance. The purpose of Chinese arbitration rules and regulations is to vest jurisdiction in the arbitration agency and the people's court, rather than in the arbitrators. While Article 19 of the Arbitration Law of the Republic of China provides that the arbitration tribunal has the power to confirm the validity of the contract, the tribunal may not consider the validity of the arbitration agree-

中英仲裁法比较研究
A Comparative Study of the Chinese Arbitration
Law and the Arbitration Laws of the UK

ment.

3. The court

The PRC Arbitration Law provides that, where the parties have doubt as to the validity of an arbitration agreement, a request can be made to the arbitration commission for a decision or to the people's court for a ruling.[①] As a result of this provision, the court is entitled to make a decision on such matters irrespective of the will of the parties.

Yet, if the parties have agreed in the arbitration clause to confer jurisdiction on the arbitration agency rather than the court, is the court still entitled to accept the claim? Due to the autonomy of arbitration, the arbitration agency is thought to be uniquely appropriate to adjudicate upon the jurisdiction of dispute by virtue of the agreement of the parties.[②]

As to the appropriate court to approach for a ruling on jurisdiction, the SPC delivered (July 20th, 2000) to the Shandong Province High Court. The Reply said, "We have received the report 'which court shall the parties request when they have doubt on the validity of arbitration agreement and how the court shall make a ruling'. Our response to the report is as following: if the parties choose an arbitration institution in China to resolve disputes and one party requests the people's court to make a ruling on the validity of the arbitration agreement, the intermediate court of the area where the arbitration institution is located would have jurisdiction. If the parties have not chosen any arbitration institution, the intermediate court of the area where the defendant is domiciled would have jurisdiction." The Official and Written Reply continues that if the parties have made an agreement to refer future disputes to CIETAC and they request the people's court for a ruling, Beijing

---

① Article 20 of the PRC Arbitration Law 2017.

② Feng Kefei, Doctrine of Competence —Competence and Its Practice in China, 78 (1) Arbitration and Law, 2002, 95-105.

No.2 Intermediate Court would have jurisdiction upon the request.①

Should the court hold a hearing as regards the validity of the arbitration agreement? No clear guidance can be found in the PRC Arbitration Law 2017. Yet, in light of considerations of due process, the court shall hold a hearing.② Are the parties entitled to appeal once the court has made a ruling about the validity of the arbitration agreement? No related section can be found in the PRC Arbitration Law 2017. However, Article 154 of the PRC Civil Procedure Law provides that an appeal may be made against the following:

a. Rejection of a lawsuit;

b. Objection to the jurisdiction of a court;

c. Rejection of a complaint.

Questions regarding the validity of arbitration agreement do not appear covered by such headings. Consequently, it is submitted that, on the basis of Article 154, the parties are not entitled to appeal. The SPC has promulgated "Notice about Treatment of the Courts as Regards the Arbitration concerning Foreign Affairs and Foreign Arbitration". This establishes the "Report System" with regard to arbitration concerning foreign affairs, and the refusal of courts to enforce foreign awards or awards concerning foreign affairs. The Report System operates as follows with regard to arbitration concerning foreign affairs. If the people's court makes a ruling that an arbitration agreement or arbitration clause is invalid or impossible to perform, the court shall submit the ruling to the High Court of its area. If the high court agrees with the ruling, it shall submit it to the SPC. Until the SPC responds, the court of first instance may not assert jurisdiction over the case. These provisions are clearly designed to protect the arbitral process from undue court interfer-

---

① Wang Shenchang, Arbitration Agreement and Its Validity, (One volume edition of 2001) Arbitration and Law, 2001, 280.

② Wang Shenchang, Arbitration Agreement and Its Validity, (One volume edition of 2001) Arbitration and Law, 2001, 280.

中英仲裁法比较研究
A Comparative Study of the Chinese Arbitration
Law and the Arbitration Laws of the UK

ence, by ensuring that lower courts cannot intervene without the sanction of the very highest court.[1]

B. Conflicts of Jurisdiction

1. Conflict between the arbitration agency and the court

The PRC Arbitration law 2017 says that, whereas parties concerned have doubt on the validity of an arbitration agreement, a request can be made to the arbitration commission for a decision or to the people's court for a ruling. If one party requests that the arbitration commission makes a decision while the other party requests the people's court to make a ruling, the people's court shall make a ruling.[2]

Yet the "Official and Written Reply to Questions about Validity of Arbitration Agreement made by the SPC on October 21st 1998" states that, whereas parties have doubts as to the validity of an arbitration agreement, should one party request the arbitration agency for a decision, while the other party requests the people's court for a ruling, if the arbitration agency makes a decision before the people's court accepts the request, the people's court shall not accept the request. If the arbitration agency has not made a decision, the court shall accept the request and instruct the agency to stay the proceedings. If, after the arbitration agency makes its decision on jurisdiction, a party appeals to arbitration, while the other party requests the people's court for a ruling regarding the validity of the arbitration agreement, the court shall accept the case and instruct the arbitral institution to stay the proceedings. After making a ruling, the court shall serve that ruling in writing on the arbitral institution. The arbitral institution shall then resume or withdraw from the arbitration on the basis of the ruling. If the court makes a ruling that the arbitration agreement is invalid, then that precludes

---

[1] Deng Jie, Discussion about Competence —Competence Principle, 5 Chinese Yearbook of Private International Law and Comparative Law, 2002, 406.

[2] Article 20 of the PRC Arbitration Law 2017.

a dissenting party from seeking to proceed with the arbitration. If the arbitration institution, which has been served with the ruling that the agreement is not valid, refuses to withdraw, the court is entitled to adjudicate regardless of that refusal.①

In Hongkong Cotton Textiles Company v. Hongkong Company, after CIETAC accepted the case, the Hongkong Company challenged the arbitrators' jurisdiction, claiming that there was no arbitration agreement. It commenced an action against Hongkong Cotton Textiles Company in Beijing No.2 Intermediate Court, making a request to the people's court for a ruling that CIETAC had no jurisdiction over the case. Meanwhile, CIETAC had already made a decision on the jurisdiction. Beijing No.2 Intermediate Court held that in respect that Hongkong Company had already made a request to the arbitration commission for a decision, it was not entitled to make the same request to the court. Consequently, the court would not accept the application. According to the decision made by Beijing No.2 Intermediate Court in Hongkong Cotton Textiles Company v. Hongkong Company, if the party at first asks an agency to consider the issue of jurisdiction, and then makes a similar application to the court, the court should not accept the application. The parties must choose one institution to rule on this issue.②

2. Conflict between the arbitration agency and the arbitral tribunal

Obviously, should any party challenge the validity of the arbitration agreement or the jurisdiction of the arbitral tribunal before the tribunal is composed, the matter cannot be dealt with by the tribunal, and so must be referred to the arbitration agency. If any jurisdictional issue is raised after the tribunal is composed, even after the agency has made a decision on the issue, the tribunal will hold a jurisdictional hearing, and must report the re-

---

① Deng Jie, Discussion about Competence-Competence Principle, 5 Chinese Yearbook of Private International Law and Comparative Law,2002,403.

② Feng Kefei, Either the Court or the Arbitration Agency should be Chosen by the Parties for Arising an Objection to Jurisdiction, 82(5) Arbitration and Law,2002,117.

中英仲裁法比较研究
A Comparative Study of the Chinese Arbitration
Law and the Arbitration Laws of the UK

sult in writing to the arbitration agency. This will still be so even if the a-gency has ruled that the tribunal has no jurisdiction, as the tribunal is regar-ded as better able to supply a definitive answer on this issue. The arbitration agency will then make a final decision based on the report made by the tribu-nal. Up till now, neither CIETAC nor CMAC has made a decision runs con-trary to the report of the arbitral tribunal.[1]

In order to reconcile the roles of the arbitral tribunal and the arbitration agency in jurisdictional matters, scholarly opinion recommends —

a. The arbitration agency can make a preliminary decision on the basis of prima facie evidence. If after hearing the evidence, the arbitral tribunal comes to the opposite conclusion, the agency could change its preliminary decision.

b. If the tribunal has already been constituted, unless the agency con-siders the position straightforward, it shall discuss it with the tribunal, in order that the tribunal and the agency do not reach contrary decisions.

c. Any decision made by the agency shall be communicated to the tribu-nal without unnecessary delay.

d. If, after hearing the evidence, the tribunal considers the preliminary decision made by the agency to be erroneous, the tribunal shall report this to the agency in writing. The agency shall then reconsider its decision, and de-cide whether to affirm, alter or disaffirm it. — In theory, the agency has the final decision, but as noted above, it will not in practice disagree with the tribunal.

---

[1] Gao Fei, Discussion about Arbitration Agreement, Arbitration and Law Reports 1996,11-12; also see Selections of the Decisions on Jurisdiction by CIETAC, Beijing: Chi-na Commercial Press, 2004.

C. Restrictions on the Right to Make Jurisdictional Challenges

There is no doubt that jurisdictional challenges can be an abuse of the arbitral process, causing substantial delay and extra cost. Chinese law seeks to deal with this problem as follows:

1. Time limit for raising challenges

The PRC Arbitration Law provides that a doubt to the effectiveness of an arbitration agreement should be raised before the first hearing at the arbitral tribunal.[1] The Arbitration Law also provides that after the respondent has received the copy of the application for arbitration, he shall file a counter-claim with the arbitration commission. After the commission has received the counter-claim, it shall deliver it to the claimant within the time limit set in the relevant arbitration rules. If a respondent fails to submit a counter-claim, it does not affect the arbitration proceedings.[2] The CIETAC Arbitration Rules provides that a counterclaim questioning the validity of the arbitration agreement, contesting the tribunal's jurisdiction may be put forward before the opening of the first arbitral hearing. Equally, a counterclaim contesting jurisdiction in a case proceeding on the basis of documents only shall be put forward before the first substantive defence by the respondent.[3]

2. Abandonment of the right to dissent

The PRC Arbitration Law 1994 provides that if a party knows or should have known that relevant arbitration rules, or any clauses or details of the arbitration agreement, are not observed, but still participates in the arbitration proceedings, without taking timely and explicit written exception to the non-observance, it shall be regarded as having given up the right to take exception. This provision could extend to situations where the tribunal exceeds

---

[1]   Article 20(2) of the PRC Arbitration Law 2017.
[2]   Article 25(2) of the PRC Arbitration Law 2017.
[3]   Article 6 of the CIETAC Arbitration Rules (2015).

中英仲裁法比较研究
A Comparative Study of the Chinese Arbitration
Law and the Arbitration Laws of the UK

its jurisdiction.[①]

3. The effect of a challenge

Article 6 (4) of the CIETAC Arbitration Rules (2015) provides that challenges to the arbitration agreement or jurisdiction generally, need not lead to the suspension of arbitration proceedings.

III. Disadvantages of the Chinese System

It is suggested that the Chinese system features many disadvantages, in that its rules are incomplete and of doubtful functionality. The system must also be dauntingly alien in appearance for foreign users, used to some version of the principle of competence-competence. The following are the main disadvantages of the system.

1. The fact that the arbitrators appointed by the parties cannot decide upon the extent of their own jurisdiction infringes the autonomy of the arbitral process.[②]

2. In some cases, a jurisdictional decision can only be made after hearing evidence, rather than on a prima facie basis. In those cases, it is necessary for the arbitral tribunal to make the decision, as strictly speaking, the arbitration agency is not a judicial organization and cannot hold a hearing.[③] In practice, the secretariat of arbitration agency would appoint coordinated secretary who is not expert in the field of the dispute to investigate. The

---

① Article 10 of the Arbitration Rules of SICA (2019).

② Deng Jie, Discussion about Competence-Competence Principle, 5 Chinese Yearbook of Private International Law and Comparative Law, 2002, 408.

③ Han Jian, Discussion about the Challenge against Jurisdiction in International Commercial Arbitration, 3 Chinese Yearbook of Private International Law and Comparative Law, 2000, 476.

agency's decision will be based in this badly informed and imperfect process. ①

3. If the decision is made by the arbitration agency, the arbitral proceedings would be suspended, adversely affecting the flexibility of arbitration. Were the arbitral tribunal permitted to continue the proceedings pending the decision on jurisdiction, such delay may be avoided. ②

4. Jurisdictional challenges are often an abuse of the arbitral process, making it possible for a party to prolong that process. ③ A doubt to the effectiveness of an arbitration agreement, should be raised before the first hearing at the arbitral tribunal. In some cases, the parties raise the challenge just several minutes before the first hearing and the tribunal proceedings has to stay. This can be an abuse of the arbitral process, causing substantial delay and extra cost. ④

5. Should issues of substance and jurisdiction be decided by different institutions, it is very possible that the decisions will be incompatible, especially where those issues cannot be separated completely. For example, an arbitration agency may decide that the parties have capacity, where that issue is raised before it. However when the arbitral tribunal hears the case, it may be persuaded that a party in fact lacks capacity. ⑤

6. The fact that the agency must make the decision on the basis of the

---

① Han Depei (ed), Current Issues of Private International Law, Wuhan: Publishing House of Wuhan University,2004,358.

② Han Depei (ed), Current Issues of Private International Law, Wuhan: Publishing House of Wuhan University,2004,358.

③ Han Jian, Discussion about the Challenge against Jurisdiction in International Commercial Arbitration, 3 Chinese Yearbook of Private International Law and Comparative Law,2000,474.

④ ZhangYi. Discussion about the Prevention of Delaying and Disturbing the Arbitral Process (new volume edition of 2001), Arbitration and Law,2001,206.

⑤ Kan Ming. Arbitration and Its Development in China, Arbitration and Law, March,2000,14.

中英仲裁法比较研究
A Comparative Study of the Chinese Arbitration
Law and the Arbitration Laws of the UK

adjudication of arbitral tribunal makes the process more complex.[①]

7. There is no guidance in the PRC Arbitration Law regarding how to deal with challenges which do not impugn the validity of arbitration agreement but raises other jurisdictional issues, such as the scope of the agreement, or questions of arbitrability. However, the CIETAC Arbitration Rules does explicitly confer jurisdiction to deal with such issues. Chinese arbitration law system is thus confusing and opaque in this area. One solution is to adopt the competence-competence principle which is enshrined in most developed legal systems and thus would be recognized and valued by foreign users of the Chinese system. But what version of that principle is most convenient to adopt. That is the question which the next section will attempt to answer.

Ⅳ. Competence-Competence in the UK

It is submitted that it is useful to look to the United Kingdom for a paradigm which may be followed, as it offers two models for consideration — the Arbitration Act 1996 in England, and the UNCITRAL Model Law on International Commercial Arbitration (the Model Law), which has been adopted in Scotland.

A. The Institutions with Jurisdiction to Determine the Tribunal's Jurisdiction

The principle of competence-competence whereby the arbitral tribunal may rule on its own competence, has long been recognized by all of the

---

① Han Jian. Discussion about the Challenge against Jurisdiction in International Commercial Arbitration, 3 Chinese Yearbook of Private International Law and Comparative Law, 2000, 478.

world's major arbitral jurisdictions①. The central idea is that any objection that a tribunal does not have jurisdiction should be dealt with, at least initially, by the tribunal itself. A statutory statement of the principle helps avoid the logical conundrum of how a tribunal, which rules that it has no jurisdiction, can be said to have jurisdiction to make such a ruling in the first place.

In England, Section 30(1) of the 1996 Act provides that, unless otherwise agreed by the parties, the arbitral tribunal may rule on its own substantive jurisdiction, that is, as to —

(a) whether there is a valid arbitration agreement;

(b) whether the tribunal is properly constituted; and

(c) what matters have been submitted to arbitration in accordance with the arbitration agreement.

It is noteworthy that the parties may choose to deprive the tribunal of this power. In other words, the principle of competence-competence is not regarded as so fundamental that it must apply whatever the wishes of the parties.② It may also be noted that Section 7 of the 1996 Act enshrines the principle of separability — the idea that the arbitration agreement is quite separate from the contract of which it forms part, and that the invalidity of the latter does not deprive the arbitration agreement of force. The practical idea which underpins it is that the tribunal acting under the arbitration clause in an invalid agreement should not be deprived by that invalidity of competence to rule on its jurisdiction. The issue of the separability of the arbitration agreement is rather more controversial and less universally accepted than that of competence-competence.③ What is thus particularly noteworthy is that, although the principle of separability has obvious links to the princi-

---

① e. g. Article 1052(1) of Netherlands Arbitration Act 1986, Article 178(3) of Swiss Private International Law Act 1987, Article 1466 of French Code of Civil Procedure.

② See the DAC's February 1996 Report para.139.

③ Davidson, Fraser P. Arbitration, Edinburgh: W. Green, 2000,pp.11-16.

中英仲裁法比较研究
A Comparative Study of the Chinese Arbitration
Law and the Arbitration Laws of the UK

ple of competence-competence, and is vital in order to allow the tribunal fully to exercise its competence.① the framers of the English Act were careful to emphasise the independence of the two principles②. Moreover, Section 7 equally only applies unless otherwise agreed by the parties. Once again therefore, the principle of separability is not regarded as so fundamental that it must apply whatever the wishes of the parties. It is therefore possible for the parties to choose to have separability without competence-competence or vice versa, or indeed to choose to have neither.

By contrast, Article 16(1) of the Model Law provides, "The arbitral tribunal may rule on its own jurisdiction, including any objections with respect to the existence or validity of the arbitration agreement. For that purpose, an arbitration clause which forms part of contract shall be treated as an agreement independent of the other terms of the contract. A decision by the arbitral tribunal that the contract is null and void shall not entail ipso jure the invalidity of the arbitration clause."

It will be seen than that the Model Law in this provision runs together two quite distinct ideas — the competence of the tribunal to rule on its own jurisdiction and the principle of separability — and treats one as the inevitable consequence of the other. Moreover, Article 16 is a mandatory provision, from which the parties cannot derogate. In other words, under the Model Law, the parties have to accept both separability and competence-competence, whether they like it or not.③ It would further appear that the Model Law features an extreme form of the doctrine of separability. Thus the Ana-

---

① As was indeed acknowledged by the English Court of Appeal in recognizing in Harbour Assurance Co (UK) (1993) Q. B. 705. that the two principles operated in tandem at common law.

② See the DAC Report para.43.

③ Brocha, Aron, Commentary on the Model Law on International Commercial Arbitration, Boston: Kluwer Law and Taxation Publishers,1990,78.

lytical Commentary on Article 16 states[1] that the principle of separability...
applies whatever the nature of the defect. This seems to have encouraged the
courts in states which have adopted the Model Law to take the idea of competence-competence to its logical extreme. So Henry J. states in the Ontario
case of Rio Algom Ltd v. Sammi Steel Co.:[2]

"The Courts in matters of contract interpretation do not appear to have
a role in determining matters of law or construction; jurisdiction and scope
of authority are for the arbitrator to determine in the first instance, subject
to later recourse to set aside the ruling or award."

So the Canadian courts have allowed the arbitrator to rule on even such
fundamental jurisdictional objections as sovereign immunity.[3] Courts elsewhere have regarded the tribunal's jurisdictional competence under the Model Law as extending beyond simple questions of whether the dispute falls
within the scope of the arbitration clause to entirely more fundamental issues
such as the validity or even the existence of the arbitration agreement it-

---

[1] U. N. AJCN. 9, 264, Analytical Commentary on Article 16, para.3.
[2] (1991) 47 C. P. C. 231 at 256.
[3] See International Civil Aviation Organisation v. Tripal Systems Pty Ltd (1998) 23
Yearbook of Commercial Arbitration 226.

中英仲裁法比较研究
A Comparative Study of the Chinese Arbitration
Law and the Arbitration Laws of the UK

self.①

The English Act and the Model Law take very different approaches here. Which is the more appropriate? At first sight the answer might appear obvious. One of the key principles which has driven the modernization of the world's arbitration systems has been that of party autonomy, the right of the parties to shape the arbitral process as they choose, a principle which is indeed espoused by both the Model Law and the English Act.② As the Act concedes autonomy to the parties in this regard, while the Model Law does not, it seems simple to conclude that the Act is to be preferred. Yet it might be asked whether it is sensible to insist that the centrality of the principle of competence-competence should be undermined, so that the principle of party autonomy might be carried to its logical extreme. One might also ask whether, given the inevitable relationship between the principles of competence-competence and separability, it makes sense to distinguish between the two concepts merely because it is logically possible to do so. In terms of Article 16 of the Model Law, an argument by a party that a fundamental flaw in the agreement between the parties deprived the arbitral tribu-

---

① See Tung Sang Trading Ltd v. Kai Sun Sea Products & Food Co Ltd [1992] A. D. R. U. 93, Canada Packers v. Terra Nova Tankers (1992) 11 O. R. 382. — It is worth pointing out, however, that courts under the English Arbitration Act have thus far adopted a fairly liberal view of competence-competence, holding that it is up to the tribunal to rule not only on matters which might be thought to be straightforwardly within the scope of the principle's Such as whether the tribunal is properly constituted — Minermet SpA Milan v. Luckfield Shipping Corporation SA [2004] EWHC 729 (Comm), the scope of the arbitration agreement — Al Naimi v Islamic Press Agency [2000] 1 Lloyd's Rep.122, whether the arbitration agreement has been repudiated — ABB LUMMUS Global Ltd v. Keppel Fels Ltd [1999]2 Lloyd's Rep.24, and whether the arbitration clause is valid —XL Insurance Ltd v. Owens Coming [2000] 2 Lloyd's Rep.500, but also more fundamental matters, such as whether the necessary preconditions for arbitration have been met — Mackley & Co v. Gosport Marina Ltd [2002] EWIIC 1313... and even whether particular matters are arbitrable at all — Azov Shipping Co v. Baltic Shipping Co [1999] 1 All E. R. (Comm) 716.

② Explicitly so in the case of Section 1(b) of the 1996 Act.

nal of jurisdiction would be considered in the first instance by the tribunal it-self. Even if it agreed that there was such a flaw, this would not rob it of ju-risdiction under the arbitration clause which formed part of this agreement, and it would be entitled to make a final disposal of the matter between the parties by dismissing the case of the party seeking to arbitrate an issue ari-sing under the agreement. (Equally, if it disagreed that such a flaw existed, it could proceed to try the substantive issue between the parties.) Prima fa-cie, the position would be the same under the Act. Yet if the parties were al-lowed to exclude the principles of competence-competence and separability, and did so, then the court rather than the tribunal would have to consider any jurisdictional issue which was raised, and would be bound to conclude that any serious flaw in the main agreement undermined the arbitration a-greement. This would tend to make a mockery of the parties' decision to ar-bitrate rather than litigate, and permit endless jurisdictional challenges.[1] The results might be even more absurd if the parties excluded only the prin-ciple of separability, since although the tribunal would retain the power to consider any jurisdictional objection, any conclusion that the main agreement was a nullity would rob it of the power to proceed further. The exclusion of only the principle of competence-competence would of course mean that such flaws in the main agreement would not undermine the arbitration clause, but that only the court, not the tribunal, would be empowered to make that rul-ing. There also remains the problem of whether certain commonly worded ar-bitration clauses serve to exclude (or worse still, partly exclude) either prin-ciple.[2]

Both the Act and the Model Law then, offer workable models. Adop-ting either one would represent a major step forward for the Chinese legal-

---

① A fact which is indeed recognized by the drafters of the Act — see the DAC Re-port, para.38.

② See Robert, Mertin, Arbitration law, Informa Legal Publishing UK, paras.7,5.4. 6 (1st edition 2004).

中英仲裁法比较研究
A Comparative Study of the Chinese Arbitration
Law and the Arbitration Laws of the UK

system. While the approach taken by the Act is superficially more attractive,
in light of the implications outlined above, it is suggested that China may
wish to consider carefully whether that taken by the Model Law is not in
practice more straightforward and best designed to serve the needs of a modem arbitration system. It is what foreign users might tend to expect, and
has the value of certainty. No real difficulties have been created by Article 16
in any of the many states which have adopted the Model Law.

B. Dealing with Jurisdictional Objections

In what circumstances should the arbitral tribunal take notice of jurisdictional questions? Under the Arbitration Act 1996, the arbitrator should
only do so if they are raised by agreement of the parties, or are the subject of
an objection or challenge by a party. In the latter event, the party making
the challenge has the burden of proof regarding any matter in relation to
which he challenges the tribunal's jurisdiction. By contrast, UNCITRAL
was of the view that the tribunal need not wait until a party raises a jurisdictional issue, but could raise such an issue of its own motion.[1] For example,
a tribunal operating under the Model Law in Scotland could raise the issue
under Article 16(1), if it believed that the subject of the dispute was not arbitrable under Scots law.

Turning to specifics, Article 16(2) demands that a plea that the tribunal lacks jurisdiction must be raised no later than the submission of a statement of defence to a claim or counterclaim, specifically conceding that a party is not barred from raising such a plea merely by appointing or participating in the appointment of an arbitrator —just in case such a step might otherwise be regarded as an admission of jurisdiction. Should a party take the
view that a tribunal has jurisdiction at the outset, but then proceeds to exceed its authority, Article 16(2) requires that the objecting party must raise

---

① U. N. A140/17. para.154.

the plea as soon as the matter alleged to be beyond its authority is raised① in the arbitral proceedings. UNCITRAL concedes however, "In some cases the governing law and therefore limitations on arbitrability of certain disputes might not be determined until the time of the award, making an earlier plea impossible".②

In other words, lack of initial jurisdiction or the fact that the tribunal has exceeded its jurisdiction may only become clear when the award is made. In such cases the award can still be challenged on a jurisdictional basis.

Moreover, in all cases, Article 16(2) permits the tribunal to entertain a later plea if it considers the plea to be justified, thus allowing the tribunal to save the merely hapless from the consequences of their inadvertence. UNCITRAL comments③:

"The concern was expressed that parties who were not sophisticated in international commercial arbitration might not realise that a matter exceeding the tribunal's jurisdiction had been raised and that they were compelled to object promptly."

What are the consequences of failing to raise a jurisdictional plea at the proper time? Disappointingly, Article 16 does not make this clear. However, Article 4, stating a principle of general application, provides, "A party who knows that any provision of this law from which the parties may derogate or any requirement under the arbitration agreement has not been complied with and yet proceeds with the arbitration without stating his objection to such non-compliance without undue delay, or if a time limit is provided therefore, within such period of time, shall be deemed to have waived his right to object."

It seems fairly certain then, that if a party does not raise a jurisdictional

① Whether by the tribunal itself or by the other party —U. N. A/40/17, para.155.
② ibid.
③ ibid.

中英仲裁法比较研究
A Comparative Study of the Chinese Arbitration
Law and the Arbitration Laws of the UK

plea timeously, he is barred from doing so at a later stage, e. g. in the form of a challenge to an award, and this is certainly how courts have interpreted the Model Law.[1] Nonetheless, during the drafting process there seemed to be a broad agreement that while, this should normally be the result of such a failure by a party, certain jurisdictional defects were so fundamental, e. g. violation of public policy or non-arbitrability, that they would provide grounds for attacking an arbitral award at any stage, even though they had not been raised at the proper time[2]. It was even mooted that this be made clear by an explicit provision to this effect[3]. Ultimately however, UNCITRAL[4], "decided not to embark on an in depth discussion with a view to elaborating a comprehensive provision covering all eventualities and details. It was agreed not to modify the text and, this to leave the question to the interpretation and possibly regulation by the States adopting the Model Law".

It is possible to sympathise with UNCITRAL on this point. The idea that, while failure to raise pleas which only involve the interests of the parties should preclude their consideration later in the arbitral process, jurisdictional issues involving the public interest cannot be a matter capable of being waived by a party, is easy to understand, but much harder to cast in the form of a rule. Yet the failure to make explicit what is implicit in the Model Law is here something of a weakness, and a state which was considering its adoption might indeed wish to consider a specific provision on this point.

Article 16(3) of the Model Law provides that the arbitral tribunal may rule on a jurisdictional plea either as a preliminary question or in an award on the merits, subject to the right of the parties to agree on the appropriate

---

[1] So in Case 214/1993, the Moscow City Court refused to entertain an action to have an award set aside on the basis that the applicant was not a party to the arbitration agreement, as the plea had not been raised before the tribunal.

[2] A/CN 9/246, para.51.

[3] U. N. A/40/17, para.288.

[4] U. N. A/40/17, para.289.

procedure. Where the tribunal rules on the plea as a preliminary question, if it rules that it has jurisdiction, it should continue the arbitral proceedings; if it rules that it has no jurisdiction, it should refuse to continue with the arbitration, or at least decline to consider the particular issue to which its jurisdiction does not extend. Where the tribunal decides to rule on the plea in an award on the merits, it may state that it is continuing with the arbitration on the assumption that it has jurisdiction, rather than ruling on the question of jurisdiction. Where a tribunal considers that a jurisdictional plea is plainly without merit, it will probably not issue a ruling at the preliminary stage, since there is little danger that the proceedings will be rendered pointless by the setting aside of the award. As UNCITRAL comments[1]: "such flexibility is desirable since it would enable the arbitral tribunal to assess in each particular case whether the risk of dilatory tactics was greater than the opposite danger of waste of money and time."

Yet, while the power of an arbitral tribunal to rule on its own jurisdiction may effectively prevent specious jurisdictional objections from being resorted to as a means of obstructing the proceedings, if the tribunal's determination of this issue were unreviewable, the potential for abuse would be immense. No serious legal system could permit an arbitral tribunal be the final determinator of its own jurisdiction. Thus any jurisdictional ruling, whether a separate ruling or as part of an award on the merits of the dispute, may be appealed to the courts. If the tribunal has dealt with jurisdiction as part of an award on the merits, then the appropriate form of challenge is an action to have the award set aside under Article 34(2)(a)(III), which is considered in more detail in chapter 12 below. Where the tribunal issues a separate ruling on its jurisdiction, Article 16(3) provide that a party may within 30 days of having received notice of that ruling ask the court to issue a final ruling on the matter —the decision of the court not being subject to further

---

① U. N. A/40/17, para.159.

中英仲裁法比较研究
A Comparative Study of the Chinese Arbitration
Law and the Arbitration Laws of the UK

appeal. Article 16(3) continues that while such a request is pending, the tribunal may continue with the proceedings, and may even make an award. Once again, this aspect of Article 16(3) is designed to ensure that unscrupulous parties do not use plainly unmeritorious appeals to delay the arbitral process. It would be a bold tribunal which would continue the proceedings, far less make an award, if it felt that a pending appeal stood a reasonable chance of success, given that in such an event its efforts would prove a waste of everyone's time and money.

It may be noted that the version of the Model Law promulgated by UNCITRAL permits an appeal to the court where the tribunal rules that it has jurisdiction, but not where it rules that it has no jurisdiction. The view of UNCITRAL was[1], "It was recognized that a ruling by the arbitral tribunal that it lacked jurisdiction was final as regards its proceedings since it was inappropriate to compel arbitrators who had made such a ruling to continue the proceedings."

Yet the Scottish Advisory Committee on Arbitration Law (the SAC), which recommended the adoption of the Model Law in Scotland, noted that if the parties, having been informed by the tribunal that it lacked jurisdiction, resorted to litigation, either could suggest to the court that there was a valid and binding arbitration clause. If the court agreed, it would in terms of Article 8, be bound to refer the matter to arbitration. The SAC opined[2], "This appears to be a very roundabout way to achieve a ruling by the court on whether or not the arbitral tribunal had jurisdiction." Accordingly, in the version of the Model Law adopted in Scotland, a ruling by the tribunal that it has no jurisdiction is also open to appeal. It may be suggested that the logic of the Scottish position is impeccable, and that if China were thinking of adopting a provision on the lines of Article 16(3), the Scottish version is

---

[1] U. N. A/40/17, para.163.

[2] In its Joint Consultation Document with the DAC, The UNCITRAL Model Law on International Commercial Arbitration (1987), p.57.

commended.

Once more the Model Law provides no answer to the question of whether a party who does not appeal against a jurisdictional ruling within the specified time limit is thereafter barred from raising the matter in an action to set aside the final award. It is by no means clear what the answer is in this instance. Nor is it clear whether the court's rejection of an appeal against a ruling by the tribunal that it has jurisdiction will preclude that issue being raised in an action to set aside the award, although any other conclusion would appear absurd. These are gaps which any Chinese legislation on the subject might address.

In comparing the position under the Arbitration Act 1996, it must first be observed that its provisions on this matter are directly inspired by Article 16, and thus very similar. Thus Section 31(1) insists that an objection that the tribunal lacks substantive jurisdiction must be raised by a party as soon as he takes any step to contest the merits[1]. He is not precluded from raising such an objection merely by appointing or participating in the appointment of an arbitrator. Again, should a party take the view that a tribunal has jurisdiction at the outset, but then proceeds to exceed that jurisdiction, Section 31(2) requires that the objecting party must raise the plea as soon as the matter alleged to be beyond its jurisdiction is raised in the arbitral proceedings[2]. And just like Article 16(2), Section 31(3) permits the tribunal to entertain a later plea if it considers the plea to be justified[3]. Section 31(4) then provides that where an objection is duly taken to the tribunal's substantive jurisdiction, if the parties agree on the course of action the tribunal should

---

[1]   See Athletic Union of Constantinople v. National Basketball Association (2001) unreported.

[2]   See JSC Zestafoni G Nikoladze Ferralloy Plant v. Ronly Holdings Ltd. [2004] EWHC 245 (Comm).

[3]   See Hussmann (Europe) Ltd. v. Al Ameen Development & Trade Co. [2000] 2 Lloyd's Rep.83.

中英仲裁法比较研究
A Comparative Study of the Chinese Arbitration
Law and the Arbitration Laws of the UK

take, the tribunal shall proceed accordingly. If there is no such agreement, the tribunal has the discretion as to whether it rules on the matter in an award as to jurisdiction, or deal with the objection in its award on the merits[1].

Yet despite the obvious similarities with the Model Law, the provisions of the Act contain subtle but important differences. In the first place, Section 30(1) of the Act speaks of a tribunal's "substantive jurisdiction" and goes on to define that term as referring to whether there is a valid arbitration agreement, or whether the tribunal is properly constituted, or what matters have been submitted to arbitration.

It can be appreciated that more fundamental objections to the arbitral proceedings such as arbitrability are not regarded as properly jurisdictional[2]. Moreover, Section 73 of the Act explicitly provides[3] that only in relation to certain specified matters — including lack of substantive jurisdiction — does a party lose his right to appeal against an award by failing to object at the appropriate time. Therefore the issue of whether fundamental questions such as arbitrability can still be raised to challenge an award, despite not being raised earlier in the proceedings, which issue is so obscure under the Model Law, is dealt with very clearly under the Act.[4] Moreover, the Act indicates that any ruling by the tribunal on jurisdiction shall itself take the form of an award. This means that any appeal will mean that the matter is res judicata and cannot be raised again in challenging the final award.[5] Once more then, the Act is clear where the Model Law is obscure. It is also clear that appeals

---

[1] And the tribunal's exercise of that discretion cannot be challenged — see AOOT Kalmneft v. Glencore International AG [2002] 2 All E. R. (Comm) 577.

[2] See DAC Report para.139, but see Mackley & Co Ltd v. Gosport Marina [2002] EWHC 1315.

[3] See also Section 67(1) of the 1996 Act.

[4] See DAC Report para.297.

[5] See DAC Report para.142.

can be made against negative as well as positive jurisdictional rulings, while the court as well as being able to confirm or set aside the award, has in terms of Section 67(3) the power to set the award aside only in part, or to vary it.①

At the same time, however, there are certain aspects of the regime introduced by the Act which are more questionable. First of all, although this is not clear from the terminology employed by the Act, it was always intended that in reviewing a tribunal's decision on jurisdiction, it would be open for a court to reconsider the tribunal's view of the facts as well as the law.② This has certainly been the approach taken by the English courts, who have reserved the right in jurisdictional appeals to rehear all the evidence on the question — an approach which may obviously add significantly to the cost and duration of the process.③ More importantly, while the determination of the court under the Model Law is final, the court's decision under the Act is, by virtue of Section 67(4), subject to appeal just like any other decision of the court, albeit that the court must give permission for that appeal. Given that one of the attractions of arbitration is its relative finality, anything which carries the potential of further extending the process is to be deplored. Mention should also be made of Section 72 which provides in effect that a party who disputes a tribunal's substantive jurisdiction may simply decline to take part in the arbitral proceedings and yet retain his right to question the tribunal's jurisdiction either by seeking an appropriate declaration or injunction, or by challenging the award. Describing this as a vital provision, the DAC comment④, A person who disputes that an arbitral tribunal has juris-

---

①   See Peterson Farms Inc v. C&.M Farming Ltd [204] EWHC 121 (Comm).
②   See DAC Report para.143.
③   Azov Shipping Co v. Baltic Shipping Co. [1999] 1 All E. R. (Comm) 716.
④   See DAC Report para.295. It has since been held that raising an objection to the arbitration does not amount to participation in arbitral proceedings — see Caparo Group Ltd v. Fagor Arrasate Sociedad Cooperative [2000] ADRLJ 254.

中英仲裁法比较研究
A Comparative Study of the Chinese Arbitration
Law and the Arbitration Laws of the UK

diction cannot be required to take part in the arbitration proceedings or to take positive steps to defend his position, for any such requirement would beg the question whether or not his objection has any substance and thus be likely to lead to gross injustice. Such a person must be entitled, if he wishes, to ignore the arbitral process. One can understand the logic of the DAC in this matter, and it is perhaps useful that they have made this position explicit. Yet the above approach surely represents a major inroad upon the principle of competence-competence①.

One further peculiarity of the English regime is that while both the Act and the Model Law envisage that in most circumstances the tribunal will, at least initially, rule on its own jurisdiction, the Act also contemplates that the court may sometimes have a role. Thus, Section 32(1) of Arbitration Act 1996 provides that the court may, on the application of a party to arbitral proceedings, (upon notice to the other parties), determine any question as to the substantive jurisdiction of the tribunal. This provision is mandatory, and thus will represent the only available means of challenge if the parties have deprived the tribunal of power to rule on its own jurisdiction②. Yet it is intended that only in rare would an application to the court under Section 32 would be justified in preference to seeking an award from the tribunal.③ To permit in most cases tribunals to rule on their own jurisdiction pursuant to Section 30 and 31, Section 32 procedure is narrowly drawn and limited. By virtue of Section 32(2) the application is required to be made either by agreement of all the parties or the permission of the tribunal. In the latter case, Section 32(2)(b) requires the court to be satisfied that, the application

---

① Although it does represent the view taken by the English courts prior to the passing of the Act — see the Gladys [1990] 1 All E. R. 397. See however Valedo Rio Duce Navegacos SA v. Shanghai Steel Ocean Shipping Co. Ltd. [2000] 2 All E. R. (Comm) 70.

② See Esso Exploration and Production UK Ltd. v. Electricity Supply Board [2004] EWHC 787 (Comm).

③ See DAC Report para.146.

was made promptly; it will save costs, and there is good reason why the matter should be decided by the court.

The DAC[1] expresses the hope 'that the Courts will take care to prevent this exceptional provision from becoming the normal route for challenging jurisdiction'. No appeal will lie against a decision as to whether these conditions have been complied with, unless the court gives leave[2]. And no appeal lies from the decision of the court on the question of jurisdiction without its leave, which leave shall not be given unless the court considers that the question involves a point of law which is one of general importance or is one which for some other special reason should be considered by the Court of Appeal.[3] This provides a clue to the possible circumstances in which Section 32 will apply. While the Act embraces the idea of competence-competence, it also recognises that there may be situations where it would be useful for the court, rather than the tribunal, to make the initial ruling on jurisdiction. This could be where both parties recognise that this is the case, such as where a difficult issue of jurisdiction is concerned, particularly a technical legal issue, and it is clear that one or both parties will not be satisfied with the tribunal's view of the issue. More importantly, where a point of law of general application may be at issue, —e. g. the meaning and scope of a standard form of arbitration clause[4] or the question of whether standard contract terms which incorporate standard terms from other standard form contracts are apt to incorporate an arbitration clause[5]—the framers of the Act regard it as valuable that such matters should be definitively determined by the

---

[1]   See DAC Report para.147.

[2]   Section 32(5) of the 1996 Act.

[3]   Section 32(6) of the 1996 Act.

[4]   See e. g. Asheville Investments Ltd. v. Elmer Construction Ltd. [1988] 2 All E. R. 577. C. A.

[5]   See e. g. Babcock Rosyth Defence Ltd. v. Grootcon (United Kingdom) Ltd. 1998 S. L. T. 1143.

中英仲裁法比较研究
A Comparative Study of the Chinese Arbitration
Law and the Arbitration Laws of the UK

courts, so that subsequent parties and arbitral tribunals may have guidance on such matters. Finally, it may be added that while an application is made to the court under Section 32, the tribunal, subject to the contrary agreement of the parties, has a discretion either to stay the arbitral proceedings, or to continue them and make an award.① The DAC comments② that by reason of this provision "a recalcitrant party will not be able to mount a spurious challenge as a means of delaying the arbitral process".

The question whether a provision such as Section 32 is useful depends on one's view of the role of the court in the arbitral process. Although the 1996 Act represents a dramatic move on the part of English law in the direction of party and tribunal autonomy, traditionally the courts have played a significant supervisory role in English arbitration law and it remains the case that they play much more of a role than in other developed arbitration systems. This can be seen not only in Section 32 but also in provisions such as Section 45③ which adopts a very similar model to Section 32, and which allows a party to apply to the court to determine a preliminary point of law arising in the course of the proceedings which the court is satisfied substantially affects the rights of one of the parties, and Section 69 which permits, albeit in very limited circumstances, an appeal against an arbitral award on a point of law④. To some degree, what drives English law here, is a conviction that part of its attraction as the governing law for many international commercial contracts, and part of the attraction of England as an arbitral forum is the view that English commercial law and English arbitration law in

---

① Section 32(4) of the 1996 Act.

② At para.148.

③ Which re-enacts in slightly different form 2 of the Arbitration Act 1979, which itself replaces the consultative case procedure (abolished by Section 1 of the Arbitration Act 1979) established by Section 21 of the Arbitration Act 1950. See the DAC Report, paras. 217-221.

④ See the DAC Report paras.284-292.

particular is extremely well developed due to the continued role of the courts in shaping its form①. This type of relationship between arbitration and the courts is therefore peculiar to England. Certainly, the courts in China do not share this tradition of assisting the development of arbitration law. Thus, while it might be argued that there may be merit, given that the decisions of tribunals on jurisdiction are reviewable by the courts in any case, in allowing the court rather than the tribunal in certain circumstances to rule on jurisdictional questions, any benefit gained thereby is probably lost by the damage such a possibility does to the principle of competence-competence. Suppose, however, the provision was modified so that the court could only play such a role, when invited to do so by both parties? Surely, it would be an extreme position to insist that the court could play no role here, even when this was the wish of the parties? Yet that is in effect the position taken by the Model Law, and such is the symbolic value of the principle of competence-competence that it must prevail over party autonomy in this context. It is difficult to believe that the attractiveness of China as an arbitral forum would be enhanced if there was any suggestion that its courts and not the tribunal could in any circumstances be the initial determinors of matters of jurisdiction. Accordingly, it is suggested that there is no merit, despite its superficial attractions, in commending the adoption of a provision like Section 32 (or any modification thereof) in China. It might be added that it is the case that Section 32 represents a qualification to the basic principles of competence-competence established by Section 30-31, rather than an indispensable element of the English regime, so that the provisions of Section 30-31 could be adopted without the addition of Section 32 to create a perfectly workable regime.

---

①   See the Commercial Court Committee Report on Arbitration,1978 (Cmnd 7284).

中英仲裁法比较研究
A Comparative Study of the Chinese Arbitration
Law and the Arbitration Laws of the UK

V. Conclusion

It has been seen that the provisions of existing Chinese law on the question of jurisdiction are obscure, fragmented and sometimes contradictory. In considering whether China could develop a new, modern, unified arbitration regime, reference has been had to the models of the Arbitration Act 1996 and the UNCITRAL Model Law on International Commercial Arbitration. It has been seen how both systems have adopted the principles of competence-competence and separability, now universally accepted by the world's leading arbitration systems. It was noted how, while the Model Law regarded those concepts as mandatory and interdependent, the Act saw them as non-mandatory and logically distinguishable. While at first sight the latter position appeared more attractive, it was concluded that the position adopted by the Model Law was practically more beneficial, as better supporting the arbitral process. Both regimes indicate how jurisdictional objections should be raised and the stage at which this should be done. However, the Model Law is less explicit than the Act as to what constitutes a jurisdictional plea, and thus correspondingly less clear as to the consequences of failing to raise a timely objection. If China were to consider adopting the provisions of the Model Law here, they might usefully adapted to offer similar clarification. It is not suggested that the provisions of the English Act are adopted wholesale, as they contemplate too extensive a role for the court. In particular, it is advised that China not adopt the procedure whereby a court on application by a party may render the initial decision on jurisdiction, as this represents too major an inroad upon the principle of competence-competence, and since China does not feature the peculiar relationship between arbitration and the courts which is unique to English law.

CHAPTER 10

CONDUCT OF PROCEEDINGS

I. Introduction

Where a party refers a dispute to arbitration, if the other party does not challenge the jurisdiction of the arbitral tribunal over the case, or if the arbitral tribunal is ruled to have jurisdiction in the face of such a challenge, the arbitral proceedings will be conducted. What role, if any, should the court have in the conduct of the arbitral proceedings? The main issues which will be dealt with in this chapter are, the discretion of the parties/arbitral tribunal, the need for each party to be treated equally and have an opportunity to present his case, the language of the proceedings, the role of statements of claim and defence, including supplementary claims and defences, rules of evidence, the power to order interim measures of protection, rules as to copies of evidential material, the location of arbitral proceedings, advance notice of hearings and meetings, the form and scope of hearings. As ever, the Chinese approach as to the above questions will be considered, and compared with the approach taken in English Law and the Model Law.

中英仲裁法比较研究
A Comparative Study of the Chinese Arbitration
Law and the Arbitration Laws of the UK

Ⅱ. The Chinese Approach to the Conduct of Proceedings

A. The Need to Be Treated Equally and Have an Opportunity of Presenting One's Case

By virtue of Article 4(2) of the CIETAC Rules (2015), the parties are free to agree on any issue, unless that agreement is inoperative or conflicts with the mandatory provisions of the law of the place of arbitration. Article 7 of the Arbitration Law, which is mandatory, provides that arbitration shall be made based on true facts and should be conducted according to the rules of law to reach a fair and reasonable settlement for parties concerned. Where the parties have no such agreement, Article 29 of the CIETAC Rules (2015) applies, and provides that the arbitral tribunal shall examine the case in any way that it deems appropriate, but must act impartially and fairly, and afford reasonable opportunities to all parties for presentations and debates.

B. The Language of the Proceedings

The Arbitration Law does not say anything about language, leaving the parties to make their own agreement.① However, while Article 67 of the CIETAC Rules 2015 allows the parties to agree on the language of the arbitral proceedings, it provides that, in the absence of such agreement, Chinese shall be the official language of the proceedings.

C. Statement of Claim and Defence

Statement of claim. By virtue of article 4(2) of the CIETAC Rules (2015), the parties are free to agree on the issues of statements of claim and defence, except where such agreement is inoperative or conflicts with a man-

---

① Article 4(3) of the CIETAC Arbitration Rules (2015).

datory provision. Article 22 of the Arbitration Law provides that in applying for arbitration, the parties shall submit copies of the arbitration agreement and application to arbitrate to the arbitration agency, while Article 23 states that the application shall specify the following matters:

—the name, gender, age, profession, work unit and residence of each party;

—the name and residence of any party who is a legal person or other organization;

—the name and position of the legal representatives or principal leading members. Where the applicant is a corporate body, the application shall specify the name and position of the legal representatives. Where the applicant is a partnership or an unincorporated association which does not have legal representatives, the applicant should specify the name and position of the most important leaders of the partnership or association;

—the nature of the claim and the facts and evidence on which it is based;

—sources of evidence, and the names and residences of witnesses.

By virtue of Article 24, an arbitration agency shall accept an application and notify the parties within five days of its receipt, if it deems the application to conform to the above requirements. If it deems otherwise, it shall notify the parties in writing and state its reasons. Article 25 continues that after the agency has accepted an application, it shall deliver a copy of the relevant arbitration rules and the list of the panel of arbitrators to both the claimant and respondent within the time limit prescribed in those rules, ensuring the latter also receives a copy of the application. If there is no agreement regarding how statements of claim and defence are to be handled, the default rules of the CIETAC Rules (2015) apply. Those Rules do not indicate clearly to whom the statement of claim should be submitted, but there are clues in the form of Articles 5(1) and 9 suggesting that it should be submitted to the arbitration agency. Article 5(1) provides that CIETAC shall,

中英仲裁法比较研究
A Comparative Study of the Chinese Arbitration
Law and the Arbitration Laws of the UK

upon receiving a written statement of claim from a party, accept a case in accordance with an arbitration agreement concluded between the parties. Article 9 states that the arbitral proceedings shall commence on the date on which CIETAC or one of its Sub-Agencies receives a statement of claim. As to the content of statement of claim, Article 10 states that a party applying for arbitration under these Rules shall submit a request for arbitration in writing signed by and/or affixed with the seal of the claimant and/or its authorized representative(s), which shall, inter alia, include:

a. the names and addresses of the claimant and the respondent, including the zip code, telephone, telex, fax and telegraph numbers, email addresses or any other means of electronic telecommunication;

b. a reference to the arbitration agreement that is invoked;

c. a statement of the facts of the case and the main issues in dispute;

d. details of the claim; and

e. the facts and grounds on which the claim is based.

I suggest that Article 10(b) and (c) should be deleted, since firstly, as the arbitration agreement must be submitted separately anyway, it is unnecessary to require the claimant to include a reference to it in the statement of claim; and secondly, the facts of the case and main issues in dispute are the facts and grounds on which the claim is based, so that (c) and (e) are virtually the same. Moreover, the CIETAC Rules also require the statement of claim to include details of evidence, its sources, and the names and residences of witnesses. Article 11 of the Rules provides that upon receipt of the request for Arbitration and its attachments, if CIETAC after examination finds the formalities required for an arbitration application to be incomplete, it may request the claimant to complete them. Where the formalities are found to be complete, CIETAC shall send a Notice of Arbitration to both parties together with a copy of its Arbitration Rules, panel of arbitrators and arbitration fee schedule. The request for arbitration and its attachments shall be sent to the respondent under the same cover. CIETAC or its Sub-Agency shall, after accepting a case, appoint a staff member of its secretariat to assist the arbitral tribunal in the procedural administration of the case. Article 68 of the Rules states that all documents, notices and written materials in relation to the arbitration may be sent to the parties and/or their representatives in person, or by registered mail or express mail, facsimile, telex, cable, or by any other means considered proper by the Secretariat of CIETAC or its Sub-Agency. Any written correspondence sent to a party and/or its representative(s) shall be deemed to have been properly served on the party if delivered to the addressee or delivered at his place of business, registration, domicile, habitual residence or mailing address, or where, after reasonable inquiries by the other party, none of the aforesaid addresses can be found, the written correspondence is sent by the Secretariat of CIETAC or its Sub-Agency to the addressee's last known place of business, registered address, domicile, habitual residence or mailing address by registered mail, or by any other means that provides a record of the attempt of delivery.

Statement of defence. The parties are free to agree on the issues of statement of defence, but their agreement cannot be inconsistent with the Arbitration Law.① Article 25 of the Arbitration Law provides that after the respondent has received the copy of the application for arbitration, he shall file a statement of defence with the arbitration agency. After the agency has received that statement of defence, it shall deliver it to the claimant within the time limit set in the arbitration rules. If a respondent fails to submit a statement of defence, it does not affect the arbitration proceedings, which will continue, and an award will be made. If there is no such agreement, the CIETAC Rules apply. Article 12(1) of those Rules provides that within 45 days of the date of receipt of the Notice of Arbitration, the respondent shall file a statement of defence in writing with the Secretariat of CIETAC or its Sub-Agency. The statement of defence shall be signed by and/or affixed with

---

① Article 4(3) of the CIETAC Arbitration Rules (2015).

中英仲裁法比较研究
A Comparative Study of the Chinese Arbitration
Law and the Arbitration Laws of the UK

the seal of the Respondent and/or its authorized representatives and shall, inter alia, include:

a. the names and addresses of the Respondent, including the zip code, telephone, telex, fax and telegraph numbers, email addresses or any other means of electronic telecommunications;

b. the defence to the Request for Arbitration setting forth the facts and grounds on which the defence is based;

c. the relevant evidence supporting the defence. Article 12(2) continues that the arbitral tribunal may accept a statement of defense submitted after expiration of the above time limit. It should be noted that unless otherwise agreed by the parties, a Summary Procedure shall apply to any case where the amount in dispute does not exceed RMB 5000000 yuan, or where the amount exceeds that sum, but one party applies to arbitrate under the Summary Procedure, and the other agrees in writing. Where no monetary claim is specified or the amount in dispute is not clear, CIETAC shall determine whether or not to apply the Summary Procedure after a full consideration of such factors as the complexity of the case and the interests involved, etc.[1] Where the amount in dispute under an amended claim or a counterclaim exceeds RMB 5000000 yuan, the procedure shall be changed from the Summary Procedure to the general procedure, unless the parties have agreed to the continuous application of the former.[2] Under the summary procedure, the respondent shall submit its Statement of Defense and relevant evidence to the Secretariat of CIETAC within twenty days from the date of receipt of the Notice of Arbitration, although the arbitral tribunal may extend this period if it considers it justified.[3] Article 12(3) states that failure of the respondent to file a statement of defence shall not affect the arbitral proceedings.

Statement of Counter-claim. There are no rules as regards counter claims

---

① Article 56(2) of the CIETAC Arbitration Rules (2015).
② Article 56(1) of the CIETAC Arbitration Rules (2015).
③ Article 59(1) of the CIETAC Arbitration Rules (2015).

in the Arbitration Law. Thus parties can make their own agreement on such issues as to whom a counter-claim should be submitted, what its content should be, time-limits for submission, and how a counter-claim should be served and accepted.[①] In the absence of such agreement, the CIETAC Rules apply. Article 13(1) provides that within 45 days of the date of receipt of the notice of arbitration, the respondent shall file with CIETAC any counter-claim in writing. The arbitral tribunal may extend time period if it believes that there is justification. Article 13(2) states that when filing a counter-claim, the respondent shall specify that counter-claim in a written statement of counter-claim, stating the facts and grounds upon which the counter-claim is based, with relevant evidence attached thereto. In summary procedure, counter-claims shall be filed with supporting evidence within 20 days, although again the tribunal may extend this period if it considers it justified.[②] Article 13 also provides that when filing a counter-claim, the respondent shall within a specified time period pay an arbitration fee in advance, according to the fee schedule of CIETAC.[③] Where the formalities required for filing a counter-claim are found to be complete, CIETAC shall send the statement of counter-claim and its attachments to the claimant.[④]

The Statement of Defence to a Counter-claim. As there are no rules in the Arbitration Law as to statements of defence to counter-claims, the parties are at liberty to agree on such issues.[⑤] If there is no such agreement, the CIETAC Rules apply. Article 13(4) provides that the claimant shall, within 30 days from the date of receipt of the statement of counter-claim and attachments, submit in writing its statement of defence to the counter-claim. The arbitral tribunal has the power to decide whether to accept a statement

---

① Article 4(3) of the CIETAC Arbitration Rules (2015).
② Article 59 of the CIETAC Arbitration Rules (2015).
③ Article 16(3) of the CIETAC Arbitration Rules (2015).
④ Article 16(4) of the CIETAC Arbitration Rules (2015).
⑤ Article 4(3) of the CIETAC Arbitration Rules (2015).

中英仲裁法比较研究
A Comparative Study of the Chinese Arbitration
Law and the Arbitration Laws of the UK

of defence submitted after expiration of the above time limit.[1] In summary procedure, the claimant shall file its statement of defence to the counter-claim within 20 days.[2] Article 13(6) states that failure of the claimant to file a statement of defence to a counter-claim shall not affect the arbitral proceedings.

D. Supplementary Claim and Defence

The Arbitration Law is silent on supplementary claims and defences, but under Article 4(3) of the CIETAC Rules (2015), the parties are free to agree on supplementary claims and defences. Where there is no such agreement Article 17 of the CIETAC Rules provides that a claimant may amend its claim and a respondent its counterclaim. However, the arbitral tribunal may not permit any such amendment if it considers that it is too late and may delay the arbitral proceedings.

E. Evidence

There are no detailed rules as to evidence in Chinese arbitration law. In practice, arbitrators conduct proceedings according to the system of evidence of the Civil Procedure Law. "Regulation of Evidence in Civil Procedure by the SPC" (hereinafter referred to as "Regulation of Evidence by the SPC")[3] lays down detailed rules as to burden of producing evidence, time-limits within which evidence should be produced, etc. Although arbitrators in China have been conducting arbitration according to the Regulation of Evidence by the SPC, I suggest it would be better if the arbitration law could adopt some of the rules of the Regulation of Evidence by the SPC, such as the burden of producing evidence, the power of tribunal to collect evidence, ap-

---

[1] Article 16(5) of the CIETAC Arbitration Rules (2015).

[2] Article 59(2) of the CIETAC Arbitration Rules (2015).

[3] Ayveral Rules on Evidence in Civil Procedure by the SPC, Law Interpretation, No.33 (2001), Dec. 21, 2001. The Regulations came into force on April 1, 2002.

praisal, and cross-examination, so that arbitration law could be made more developed.

1. The burden of producing evidence

The parties are free to agree on the burden of producing evidence, ① but their agreement should not conflict with the Arbitration Law, Article 43 of which provides that parties shall provide evidence to support their respective claims. If there is no agreement, the CIETAC Rules (2015) apply, and Article 10(2) provides that a party applying for arbitration shall attach to the request for Arbitration relevant evidence supporting the facts on which his claim is based. Article 13(2) deals similarly with counterclaims. Article 36 (1) states that each party shall have the burden of proving the facts relied on to support its claim, defence or counterclaim. The arbitral tribunal may specify a time period for the parties to produce evidence, and refuse to admit any evidence produced beyond the period. A party finding it difficult to produce evidence within the specified time period may apply for an extension before the expiration of the period, and the arbitral tribunal shall decide whether or not to extend the period.②If a party with the burden of proof of any issue fails to produce evidence within the specified period, or produces insufficient evidence to support its claim or counterclaim, it shall bear the consequences thereof.③

2. The power of tribunal to collect evidence

Again, the parties are free to agree on this matter, as long as that agreement is consistent with the Arbitration Law, and Article 43 provides that if an arbitration tribunal deems it necessary to collect evidence, it can do so on its own initiative, and the parties may not agree to deprive it of this power. Where there is no agreement on this issue, the CIETAC Rules apply, Article 37 providing that an arbitral tribunal may, on its own initiative,

---

① Article 4(3) of the CIETAC Arbitration Rules (2015).
② Article 41(2),59(3) and Article 68(3) of the CIETAC Arbitration Rules (2015).
③ Article 41(3) of the CIETAC Arbitration Rules (2015).

中英仲裁法比较研究
A Comparative Study of the Chinese Arbitration
Law and the Arbitration Laws of the UK

undertake investigations and collect evidence as it considers necessary. It can be seen that the CIETAC Rules envisage an inquisitorial role for the tribunal, which is in contrast with the adversarial approach favored by Anglo-American systems. From my point of view, to protect the autonomy of the parties, the arbitral tribunal should not be assigned an inquisitorial role, and the parties should be given the freedom to agree to preclude the tribunal from collecting evidence of its own motion. When thus investigating and collecting evidence, the tribunal shall inform each party of its right to be present at such investigation if it considers its presence necessary. In the event that one or both parties fail to be present, the investigation and collection shall proceed without being affected. The arbitral tribunal shall, through the Secretariat of CIETAC, transmit the evidence it collects to the parties and afford them an opportunity to comment.

I suggest that, to protect the autonomy of the parties, the parties shall be permitted to preclude the tribunal from collecting evidence on its own initiative. Where the parties have no such agreement, the tribunal may collect evidence if it considers it necessary. It is not possible to prescribe exhaustively the circumstances in which the tribunal may decide to collect evidence. The following are some examples of those circumstances.

a. Where the evidence produced by the parties is conflicting, so that after the hearing, the tribunal is still incapable of deciding upon the evidence, the tribunal might have the power to decide whether to collect evidence on its own initiative, or to make an award against the party with the burden of proof on that issue, as would happen in a common law system.

b. The parties or their attorneys are incapable of collecting evidence for objective reasons, and apply to the tribunal to collect the evidence. For example, where one party refuses to co-operate in supplying evidence, the other may want to ask the tribunal to collect the evidence.

c. The evidence is concerned with technical matters, and the tribunal needs to ask the expert agreed by the parties or appointed by it to assess the evidence.

It is not clear who should be liable if the tribunal cannot collect the evidence concerned. I suggest that it must be the party who is subject to the burden of producing evidence, as the arbitral tribunal does not have an obligation to collect evidence, but is simply helping the parties to do so. The arbitration law does not state whether the court should support the collection of evidence. I suggest that such support may be apt in certain cases. If a party wants to take evidence from a witness who refuses to co-operate, he should be able, with the permission of the tribunal, to apply to the court to collect that evidence. If the arbitral agency permits the application, it shall submit the application to the people's court at the place where the evidence was obtained. The tribunal should be able to refuse such an application if it considers that sufficient evidence has already been collected, or that the evidence the party wants to collect is not crucial.

F. Powers to Order Interim Measure of Protection

1. Attachment

As ever, the parties are free to agree on this, as long as their agreement does not conflict with the Arbitration Law,[①] Article 28 of which provides that if due to the acts of the other party or otherwise, the arbitration award cannot be executed or is difficult to execute, a party may apply to attach property. The people's court may, in the case of a party's actions or other reasons, make the judgment difficult to enforce or cause other damages to the party, according to the application of the other party, may decide to preserve its property, order it to perform certain acts or prohibit it from making certain acts. If the parties do not file an application, the people's court may also decide to take precautionary measures when necessary.[②] Where a claimant applies for attachment, the Civil Procedure Law directs that the arbitra-

---

① Article 4(3) of the CIETAC Arbitration Rules (2015).
② Article 100 of the PRC Civil Procedure Law 2017.

中英仲裁法比较研究
A Comparative Study of the Chinese Arbitration
Law and the Arbitration Laws of the UK

tion agency shall submit that application to the people's court. If there are errors in the application, the claimant shall compensate the respondent for any losses arising from the attachment. If the people's court adopts preservation measures, it may order the applicant to provide security. If the applicant does not provide security, the application shall be rejected.[1] Where any property may be extinguished or may be hard to obtain at a later time, if the circumstances are urgent, an interested party may, before instituting an action or applying for arbitration, apply for property attachment to a people's court at the place where the property is located or at the place of domicile of the respondent or a people's court having jurisdiction over the case.[2] If the applicant fails to file a lawsuit or apply for arbitration within 30 days after the people's court takes the preservation measures, the people's court shall cancel the preservation.[3] The applicant shall provide a guarantee. If no guarantee is provided, the application shall be rejected. The "Notice of the SPC about Several Problems in the Enforcement of the PRC Arbitration Law"[4] provides that if a party applies for attachment, the competent court is the basic-level People's Court in the region where the respondent is domiciled or where his property is located. If the dispute is foreign-related, Article 272 of the Civil Procedure Law makes the competent court the intermediate people's court in the place where the respondent is domiciled or where his property is located.[5] Article 102 of the Civil Procedure Law provides that

---

① Article 100 of the PRC Civil Procedure Law 2017.

② Article 101 of the PRC Civil Procedure Law 2017.

③ Article 101 of the PRC Civil Procedure Law 2017.

④ See "Notice of Several Problems on Application of the PRC Arbitration Law" by the SPC, Law Issue, No.4 (1997), Mar. 26,1997.

⑤ Article 272 of the PRC Civil Procedure Law 2017 provides that if any party has applied for the adoption of property preservation measures, the foreign affairs arbitration agency of the PRC shall submit for an order the party's application to the intermediate people's court in the place where the person against whom the application is filed has his domicile or where the said person's property is located.

property preservation shall be limited to the scope of the claim or to the property relevant to the case. Property preservation shall be carried out by sealing up, distraining, freezing or other methods as prescribed by law. Should the people's court freeze a property, it shall notify the person against whom the application is made. Property that has already been sealed up or frozen shall not be sealed up or frozen again. Article 100 of the "Opinion of the SPC about Several Problems as to the Enforcement of the PRC Civil Procedure Law" provides that the court may order a party to sell seasonal commodities, fresh and live goods, perishable articles, and other goods, which are not suitable for long-term preservation, the court retaining the money. The court may even itself sell goods and retain the money, if it considers it necessary. If there is no agreement, the CIETAC Rules apply, Article 23(1) stating that when any party applies for the preservation of property, CIETAC shall forward that application for a ruling by the competent court in the place where the respondent is domiciled or where his property is located.

There are several problems with the rules as to the power to order attachment. It is doubtful whether it is sensible that only the court has the power to order attachment, with the arbitral tribunal playing no role in the process. I submit that it is necessary for the court to order attachment if the application is made before the constitution of the arbitral tribunal, or if the attachment concerns a third party, or if a party refuses to cooperate with an order of attachment made by the tribunal. Where the application is made before the tribunal is constituted, clearly only the court could make such order.[①] Equally, where the attachment concerns a third party, an arbitration agency or tribunal should not have the power to order attachment, as the arbitration agreement is only between the parties concerned and cannot affect

---

①   Liu Yongming, Wang Xianrong, A Trend of the Development of the Interim Protection Measures in International Commercial Arbitration under Economic Globalization: Comment on Perfecting the Interim Protection Measures in China's International Commercial Arbitration, 21(2) Herbei Law Science, 2003,106.

中英仲裁法比较研究
A Comparative Study of the Chinese Arbitration
Law and the Arbitration Laws of the UK

third parties.① Finally, where a party refuses to honour an attachment, the court, unlike an arbitration agency or arbitral tribunal, has the power to force him to do so. Yet the approach of Chinese arbitration law to attachment has certain disadvantages:

(1) the tribunal is more aware of the case than the court;

(2) the fact that the parties are required to submit the application to the arbitration agency, which in turn submits it to the court, makes the process unnecessarily long;

(3) since the order of attachment issued by a court is subject to appeal, the process may be delayed and the interests of the applicant may not be well protected;

(4) one reason why the parties referred the dispute to arbitration may be because they do not wish to litigate. Thus, if they have to apply to the court for attachment, their preference is to some extent thwarted. Moreover, where the parties wish to ask the arbitral tribunal to order attachment, the requirement that they have to apply to the court for attachment infringes their autonomy. Therefore, I suggest that, the parties should have the right to elect whether the arbitral tribunal or the court has the right to order attachment. Where the parties have elected for the tribunal, the court may only play a role in the process of attachment when the arbitral tribunal has not been constituted, or where the attachment is concerned with a third party, or after the arbitral tribunal has ordered attachment and the party against whom the order is made refuses to enforce it.

2. Conservation of evidence

The parties are again free to make their own agreement, unless it conflicts with Mandatory Rules.② Article 81 of the Civil Procedure Law pro-

---

① Du Chengming, Discussion of Attachment in Arbitration, 10 Academic Research, 2002,87.
② Article 4(3) of the CIETAC Arbitration Rules (2015).

vides that where any evidence may be extinguished or may be hard to obtain at a later time, if the circumstances are urgent, an interested party may, before instituting an action or applying for arbitration, apply for evidence preservation to a people's court at the place where the evidence is located or at the place of domicile of the respondent or a people's court having jurisdiction over the case.[1] If the applicant fails to file a lawsuit or apply for arbitration within 30 days after the people's court takes the preservation measures, the people's court shall cancel the preservation.[2] If the people's court adopts preservation measures, it may order the applicant to provide guarantees. If the applicant does not provide guarantees, the application shall be rejected.[3] Article 46 of the Arbitration Law provides that if evidence is vulnerable to loss or destruction and would be hard to recover, a party may apply to put such evidence in custody. When a party so applies, the arbitration agency shall submit his application to the people's court at the place where the evidence was obtained. Article 68 of the Arbitration Law states that if a party involved in a foreign arbitration case applies for such custody, the arbitration agency shall submit the application to the intermediate people's court at the place where the evidence was obtained. In the absence of such agreement, the CIETAC Rules (2015) apply, Article 18 providing that when a party applies for the protection of evidence, CIETAC shall forward that application for a ruling to the competent court at the place where the evidence is located.

There are some problems in the rules as to the conservation of evidence. First of all, I suggest that the arbitral tribunal itself should have the power to order conservation of evidence, and the court may support the process if the application of attachment is made before the constitution of arbitral tribunal, or if the attachment concerns a third party, or if a party refuses to cooperate with the order of attachment which has been made. Secondly, the

---

[1]   Article 81 of the PRC Civil Procedure Law 2017.

[2]   Article 101 of the PRC Civil Procedure Law 2017.

[3]   Article 100 of the PRC Civil Procedure Law 2017.

中英仲裁法比较研究
A Comparative Study of the Chinese Arbitration
Law and the Arbitration Laws of the UK

arbitration law does not indicate the measures available to enforce orders regarding the conservation of evidence. It should provide that those measures are the same as those available to enforce attachment orders.

G. The Location of the Arbitral Proceedings

Since there are no rules as to the location of arbitral proceedings in the Arbitration Law, the parties are free to make their own decision.[1] In the absence of such agreement, the CIETAC Rules apply, Article 32(1) providing that where the parties have agreed on the place of oral hearings, the case shall be heard at that place, except as stipulated in Article 69(3). Article 69 (3) states that where the parties have agreed to hold an oralhearing at a place other than CIETAC's domicile, extra expenses including travel and accommodation expenses incurred thereby shall be paid in advance as a deposit by the parties. In the event that the parties fail to do so, the oral hearing shall be held at the domicile of CIETAC. Article 32 provides that if the parties have not agreed on the location of arbitral proceedings, a case accepted by CIETAC shall be heard in Beijing, or if the arbitral tribunal considers it necessary, at other places with the approval of the Secretary-General of CIETAC. A case accepted by a Sub-Agency of CIETAC shall be heard at the place where the Sub-Agency is located, or if the arbitral tribunal considers it necessary, at other places with the approval of the Secretary-General of the Sub-Agency.

H. Advance Notice of Hearings and Meetings

The parties are free to agree on the issues of advance notice of hearings and meetings, as long as their agreement is consistent with the mandatory rules[2], and Article 61 of the Arbitration Law provides that for a case exam-

---

①   Article 4(3) of the CIETAC Arbitration Rules (2015).
②   Article 4(3) of the CIETAC Arbitration Rules (2015).

ined by way of an oral hearing, after the arbitral tribunal has fixed a date for the first oral hearing, the parties shall be notified of the date at least fifteen days in advance of the oral hearing. A party having justified reasons may request a postponement of the oral hearing. However, the party shall communicate such request in writing to the arbitral tribunal within three days of its receipt of the notice of the oral hearing. The arbitral tribunal shall decide whether or not to postpone the oral hearing.

If a party has justified reasons for failure to submit a request for a postponement of the oral hearing in accordance with the preceding paragraph 1, the arbitral tribunal shall decide whether to accept such a request. A notice of a subsequent oral hearing, a notice of a postponed oral hearing, as well as a request for postponement of such oral hearing, shall not be subject to the time periods specified in the preceding paragraph.

I. Form and Scope of Hearings

The parties are free to agree on the form and scope of hearings, unless their agreement is inoperative or conflicts with mandatory rules. Article 39 of the Arbitration Law provides that an arbitration tribunal shall hold oral hearings unless the parties agree not to hold oral hearings, in which case the arbitral tribunal may render an award based on the application for arbitration, claims and counter-claims and other documents. Again while Article 40 provides that the arbitral tribunal may not hear a case in open session, if the parties so agree, hearings maybe held openly, except in cases that involve State secrets. Article 42 states that if a claimant is absent from a hearing without good reason, having been duly notified that it was being held, or withdraws during a hearing without the prior permission of the tribunal, he may be regarded as withdrawing his claim. The absence or withdrawal of a respondent in similar circumstances allows the tribunal to render an award by default. Article 47 states that the parties have the right to debate during the hearing. At the end of the debate, the chief or sole arbitrator shall ask

中英仲裁法比较研究
A Comparative Study of the Chinese Arbitration
Law and the Arbitration Laws of the UK

the parties for their final statement. Article 48 provides that the tribunal shall record the hearings in writing. If the parties or others involved in the arbitration find something in their statements left out of the record or misrecorded, they have the right to apply for correction. Even if corrections are not made, the application shall be recorded. The written records of the hearings shall be signed or affixed with seals by the arbitrators, minute keepers, the parties and others participating in the arbitration. Article 69 provides that if the dispute is foreign-related, the arbitral tribunal may write down its hearings on records or summary of records. The records shall be signed or affixed with the seals of the parties concerned and others participating in the arbitration. After an application for arbitration has been made the parties may settle the dispute of their own initiative. By virtue of Article 49, if a settlement agreement has been reached, a request may be made to the tribunal for an award based on that agreement, or the application for arbitration may be withdrawn. Should a party fail to honour the agreement, the other may again apply to arbitrate under the arbitration agreement.[①]

Where the parties have not reached agreement as to the form and scope of hearings, the CIETAC Rules apply, Article 35 providing that the arbitral tribunal may examine the case in the manner it considers appropriate. The arbitral tribunal may decide whether to examine the case solely on the basis of the written materials and evidence submitted by the parties or to hold an oral hearing after hearing from the parties of their opinions.[②] Moreover, under summary procedure the arbitral tribunal may examine the case in the manner it considers appropriate, and thus has discretion to conduct a case on the basis of the documents only or to hold oral hearings. Hearings shall be held in camera. Where both parties request an open hearing, the arbitral tribunal has discretion to grant or refuse that request.[③] If the Claimant fails to

---

① Article 50 of the PRC Arbitration Law 2017.
② Article 35 of the CIETAC Arbitration Rules (2015).
③ Article 60 of the CIETAC Arbitration Rules (2015).

appear at an oral hearing without showing sufficient cause for such failure, or withdraws from an on-going oral hearing without the permission of the tribunal, he may be deemed to have withdrawn his request for arbitration. In such a case, if the respondent has filed a counterclaim, the tribunal shall proceed with the hearing of the counterclaim and make a default award. If the respondent fails to appear at an oral hearing without showing sufficient cause for such failure, or withdraws from an on-going oral hearing without the permission of the tribunal, the tribunal may proceed with the arbitration and make a default award. In such a case, if the Respondent has filed a counterclaim, the respondent may be deemed to have withdrawn its counterclaim.① Unless otherwise agreed by the parties, the arbitral tribunal may adopt an inquisitorial or adversarial approach when examining the case, having regard to the circumstances of the case.② The arbitral tribunal may hold deliberation at any place or in any manner that it considers appropriate.③ The arbitral tribunal may, if it considers it necessary, issue procedural directions and lists of questions, hold pre-hearing meetings and preliminary hearings, and produce terms of reference, etc., unless otherwise agreed by the parties.④ Article 35 of the CIETAC Rules provides that during the oral hearing, the tribunal may arrange a stenographic and/or audio-visual record. The arbitral tribunal may, when it considers it necessary, take minutes stating the main points of the oral hearing and request the parties and/or their representatives, witnesses and/or other persons involved to sign and/or affix their seals to the minutes. The stenographic and/or audio-visual record of the oral hearing shall be available for the use and reference by the tribunal. Article 41 states that a party may file a request with CIETAC to withdraw its claim or counterclaim in its entirety. In the event that the respondent

---

① Article 39(2) of the CIETAC Arbitration Rules (2015).
② Article 35(3) of the CIETAC Arbitration Rules (2015).
③ Article 35(4) of the CIETAC Arbitration Rules (2015).
④ Article 35(5) of the CIETAC Arbitration Rules (2015).

中英仲裁法比较研究
A Comparative Study of the Chinese Arbitration
Law and the Arbitration Laws of the UK

withdraws its counterclaim in its entirety, the arbitral tribunal shall proceed with the examination of the claim and render an arbitral award thereon.①
Where a case is to be dismissed before the formation of the arbitral tribunal, the decision shall be made by the Secretary-General of CIETAC. Where the case is to be dismissed after the formation of the arbitral tribunal, the decision shall be made by the arbitral tribunal.②

Ⅲ. The Disadvantages of the Chinese Approach

1. Under Chinese arbitration law, the arbitral tribunal does not have the power to order interim measures of protection. I suggest that it should have such power, and that the court should only have a role where its support is required.

2. Article 33 of the Arbitration Law, which provides that where both parties request an open hearing, the arbitral tribunal has a discretion to refuse, breaches the autonomy of the parties. Moreover, it is unreasonable that, where both parties request an open hearing, the arbitral tribunal may have the power to refuse that request.

3. It is odd that the Arbitration Law does not contain any rule as to statements of counterclaim and the defence thereto, while it contains rules as to statements of claim and defence. I suggest that the Arbitration Law should lay down rules on statements of counterclaim and defence thereto, which rules could be in similar form to the rules on statements of claim and defence.

---

① Article 46(1) of the CIETAC Arbitration Rules (2015).
② Article 46(3) of the CIETAC Arbitration Rules (2015).

Ⅳ. The Approach of the Laws Operating in the UK

A. Introduction

As ever we refer to the United Kingdom for a paradigm which offers two models for consideration — the 1996 Arbitration Act and the Model Law. Chinese arbitration law, the Model Law, and the 1996 Act all require the parties to submit statement of claim and defence and to produce evidence. The court has the power to order interim measure of protection under the three laws. Since there are differences in culture and tradition, there are differences between the three laws as to the detail of the conduct of proceedings. One main difference is that in Chinese arbitration law, the court is never asked to support the collection of evidence, whereas under the 1996 Act and the Model Law, the court can play a role in evidence collection. There is also a difference between the role of court under the 1996 Act and under the Model Law. The 1996 Act gives the parties the right to exclude the court's power of collecting evidence, whereas under the Model Law, parties are not free to agree to prevent the court to collect evidence. Another main difference is that in the 1996 Act, the court may make an order requiring a party to comply with a peremptory order made by the tribunal and may make determination of preliminary point of law, whereas under the Chinese Law and the Model Law, the court does not have the power to do so.

B. The Right to Be Treated Equally and the Opportunity to Present One's Case

Model Law. Article 18 provides that the parties shall be treated with equality and each party shall be given a full opportunity of presenting his case.

1996 Act. Section 33 of the 1996 Act provides that the tribunal shall act

中英仲裁法比较研究
A Comparative Study of the Chinese Arbitration
Law and the Arbitration Laws of the UK

fairly and impartially as between the parties, giving each party a reasonable opportunity of putting his case and dealing with that of his opponent, and adopt procedures suitable to the circumstances of the particular case, avoiding unnecessary delay or expense, so as to provide a fair means for the resolution of the matters falling to be determined.① The tribunal shall comply with that general duty in conducting the arbitral proceedings, in its decisions on matters of procedure and evidence and in the exercise of all other powers conferred on it.② It is noteworthy that the 1996 Act has not adopted the term, a full opportunity of presenting its case, used in Article 18 of the Model Law. The term "a reasonable opportunity" conveys an objectively viewed balance of what is fair to the party, but is also compatible with expedition and economy.③

Chinese Law. The PRC Arbitration Law does not have a rule which provides clearly that the parties shall have the opportunity of being treated equally and presenting his case. Although the CIETAC Rules contains such rule, it is not a mandatory rule. The lack of a mandatory rule that the parties shall have the opportunity of being treated equally and presenting his case would not produce problem in practice. In very rare cases, the parties would make an agreement that they should be treated unequally. In the cases where they have no such agreement, if the arbitrator treats the parties differently, the parties could apply to the court to set aside the award, by virtue of Article 58(3) of the Arbitration Law, which provides that, if the composition of the arbitral tribunal or the arbitral proceedings is not conducted according to the law, the parties may apply to the intermediate court at the place where the arbitration agency is to set aside the award. Also the parties may apply to set aside the award under Article 58(6) of the Arbitration Law, which pro-

---

① Section 33(1) of the 1996 Act.
② Section 33(2) of the 1996 Act.
③ Harris, Bruce/Planterose, Rowan & Tecks, Jonathan, The Arbitration Act 1996: A Commentary, 3rd ed. Malden: Blackwell Publishing, Inc., 2003, 141.

vides that, if the arbitrator extorts bribes, receives a bribe, conducts irregularities for favoritism, or makes orders and judgments that misuse the law, the parties may apply to the intermediate court at the place where the arbitration agency is to set aside the award.

Where the parties have agreed to be treated differently, if a party is coerced into the arbitration agreement by the other party, the arbitration agreement is invalid, as Article 17(3) of the Arbitration Law provides that the arbitration agreement is invalid if one party is coerced by the other party to make the agreement. Article 58(1) of the Arbitration Law states that if there is no valid arbitration agreement, the party may apply to the intermediate court at the place where the arbitration agency is to set aside the award. If the parties have agreed to be treated differently and no party has been coerced into the agreement, the arbitration agreement should be deemed as valid. In this case, the party is not entitled to apply to set aside the award. Considering this situation is very rare, the lack of the rule as to parties being treated equally in the Arbitration Law does not cause any practical problem; but to make the Arbitration Law completed and sound, I suggest that the rule as to the party's opportunity of being treated equally and presenting his case should be added into the Chinese Arbitration Law.

C. Language

Model Law. Article 22 provides that the parties are free to agree on the language or languages to be used in the arbitral proceedings. Failing such agreement, the arbitral tribunal shall determine the language or languages to be used in the proceedings. This agreement or determination, unless otherwise specified therein, shall apply to any written statement by a party, any hearing and any award, decision or other communication by the arbitral tribunal. The Article also provides that the arbitral tribunal may order that any documentary evidence shall be accompanied by a translation into the language or languages agreed upon by the parties or determined by the arbitral

中英仲裁法比较研究
A Comparative Study of the Chinese Arbitration
Law and the Arbitration Laws of the UK

tribunal.

1996 Act. Similarly, Section 34(1) and (2)(b) of the 1996 Act states that it shall be for the tribunal to decide the language or languages to be used in the proceedings and whether translations of any relevant documents are to be supplied, subject to the right of the parties to agree any matter.

Chinese Law. In Chinese Arbitration law, if the parties have not agreed on the language, the language to be used in the proceedings would be Chinese. I suggest that, since in some circumstances, Chinese may not be the most suitable language for the proceedings, it would be more sensible for the arbitral tribunal to decide the language or languages, considering the particular case.

D. Statement of Claim and Defence

Model Law. Article 23(1) provides that within the period of time agreed by the parties or determined by the arbitral tribunal, the claimant shall state the facts supporting his claim, the points at issue and the relief or remedy sought, and the respondent shall state his defence in respect of these particulars, unless the parties have otherwise agreed as to the required elements of such statements. The parties may submit with their statements all documents they consider to be relevant or may add a reference to the documents or other evidence they will submit. Article 25 states that unless otherwise agreed by the parties, if, without showing sufficient cause, the claimant fails to communicate his statement of claim in accordance with article 23(1), the arbitral tribunal shall terminate the proceedings; if the respondent fails to communicate his statement of defence in accordance with article 23(1), the arbitral tribunal shall continue the proceedings without treating such failure in itself as an admission of the claimant's allegations.[1] The Analytical Commentary states that this rule "seems useful in view of the fact that under

---

① Article 25(a) and (b) of the Model Law.

many national laws on civil procedure, default of the defendant in court proceedings is treated as an admission of the claimant's allegations".① It adds
that that rule "does not mean that the arbitral tribunal would have no discretion as to how to assess the failure and would be bound to treat it as a full
denial of the claim".②

1996 Act. Under the 1996 Act, it shall be for the tribunal to decide,
subject to the right of the parties to agree any matter, whether any and if so
what form of written statements of claim and defence are to be used, and
when these should be supplied.③

Chinese Law. It can be seen that, in the Model Law and the 1996 Act,
statements of claim and defence may be supplied separately from the request
for arbitration, whereas under Chinese arbitration law the statements of
claim and defence shall be supplied together with the request for arbitration.
In my view, the approach of the Model Law and the 1996 Act gives the parties more time to make statements of claim and defence and therefore is
more attractive for the parties. Chinese arbitration law should adopt such an
approach, which might make more parties willing to arbitrate in China. Under Chinese arbitration law, the parties do not have the right to agree on the
content of statements of claim, and therefore the autonomy of the parties is
damaged. It would be beneficial for the Chinese law to adopt the approach of
the Model Law, which gives the parties the freedom to make their own a-
greement on this issue, and also provides default rules in the lack of such a-
greement.

E. Supplementary Claim and Defence

Model Law. Article 23(2) of the Model Law provides that unless otherwise agreed by the parties, either party may amend or supplement his claim

---

① Doc. A/CN. 9/264, p.56, Article 25, para.4.
② Doc. A/CN. 9/264, p.56, Article 25, para.4.
③ Section 34(1) and (2)(c) of the 1996 Act.

中英仲裁法比较研究
A Comparative Study of the Chinese Arbitration
Law and the Arbitration Laws of the UK

or defence during the course of the arbitral proceedings, unless the arbitral tribunal considers it inappropriate to allow such amendment having regard to the delay in making it.

1996 Act. The 1996 Act contains a similar rule, which provides that it shall be for the tribunal to decide the extent to which such statements can be supplied later, subject to the right of the parties to agree on any matter.

Chinese Law. The situation under the Chinese arbitration law is similar to the situation under the Model Law and the 1996 Act.

F. Evidence

1. Producing evidence

Model Law. Article 24(1) of the Model Law provides that, unless otherwise agreed by the parties, the claimant shall, within the period of time agreed by the parties or determined by the arbitral tribunal, state the facts supporting his claim, and the respondent shall state his defence in respect of the particulars.

1996 Act. Under the 1996 Act, the parties have the freedom to agree on producing evidence, and in the absence of such agreement, it is for the arbitral tribunal to decide the following issues: [1]

a. whether any and if so which documents or classes of documents should be disclosed between and produced by the parties and at what stage;

b. whether to apply strict rules of evidence (or any other rules) as to the admissibility, relevance or weight of any material (oral, written or other) sought to be tendered on any matters of fact or opinion, and the time, manner and form in which such material should be exchanged and presented;

c. whether and to what extent there should be oral or written evidence or submissions;

d. whether any and if so what questions should be put to and answered

---

[1] Section 34(1) and (2)(d), (f), (h) of the 1996 Act.

by the respective parties and when and in what form this should be done.

The tribunal may fix the time within which the directions given by it are to be complied with, and may if it thinks fit extend the time so fixed (whether or not it has expired).[①]

Chinese Law. In the Chinese arbitration law, the parties have no right to agree on whether they shall produce evidence. In my view, if the parties have agreed not to produce evidence, there is no reason why they shall be forced to do so. In order to protect the autonomy of the parties, the approach of either the Model Law or the 1996 Act shall be adopted by the Chinese arbitration law.

2. Investigation by the arbitral tribunal

Model Law. The Model Law does not contain any rule as to investigation by the arbitral tribunal.

1996 Act. Section 34(1) and (2)(g) states that it shall be for the tribunal to decide whether and to what extent the tribunal should itself take the initiative in ascertaining the facts and the law, subject to the right of the parties to agree any matter. Section 38(5) also provides that the tribunal may direct that a party or witness shall be examined on oath or affirmation, and may for that purpose administer any necessary oath or take any necessary affirmation.

Chinese Law. Under the Chinese arbitration law, the parties are not free to agree that the tribunal has no power to investigate. Again, to protect the autonomy of the parties, the Chinese law may adopt the instance of the 1996 Act and give the parties such freedom.

3. Court assistance in taking evidence

Model Law. Article 27 provides that the arbitral tribunal or a party with the approval of the arbitral tribunal may request from a competent court of this State assistance in taking evidence. The court may execute the request

---

　① 　Section 34(3) of the 1996 Act.

中英仲裁法比较研究
A Comparative Study of the Chinese Arbitration
Law and the Arbitration Laws of the UK

within its competence and according to its rules on taking evidence.

1996 Act. Section 43 provides that, with the permission of the tribunal or the agreement of the other parties, a party to arbitral proceedings may use the same court procedures as are available in relation to legal proceedings to secure the attendance before the tribunal of a witness in order to give oral testimony or to produce documents or other material evidence. A person shall not be compelled by virtue of this section to produce any document or other material evidence which he could not be compelled to produce in legal proceedings. Section 44(1) and (2)(a) indicates that, unless otherwise agreed by the parties, the court has for the purposes of and in relation to arbitral proceedings the same power of making orders about the taking of the evidence of witnesses as it has for the purposes of and in relation to legal proceedings. It should be noted that in any case the court shall act only if or to the extent that the arbitral tribunal, and any arbitral or other institution or person vested by the parties with power in that regard, has no power or is unable for the time being to act effectively.[1] If the court so orders, an order made by it under this section shall cease to have effect in whole or in part on the order of the tribunal or of any such arbitral or other institution or person having power to act in relation to the subject-matter of the order.[2]

Under the Model Law, the parties are not free to agree to preclude the court's power of taking evidence, whereas they are at liberty to do so under the 1996 Act. To protect the autonomy of the parties, they shall have the right to agree to preclude the court from taking evidence. Under the 1996 Act, the court may not only take evidence, but also secure the attendance of witness. The parties cannot preclude the power of the court to secure the attendance of witness by agreement. It is more beneficial that the court can also secure the attendance of witness, but it is odd that the parties are not free

---

① Section 44(5) of the 1996 Act.
② Section 44(6) of the 1996 Act.

to agree to preclude such power of the court, while they are free to agree to preclude the court's power of taking evidence. Under the 1996 Act, the courts' power of taking evidence is more strictly limited. To avoid too much intervention by the court to the arbitration, it is admirable to strictly limit the court's power in this regard.

Chinese Law. In China, the court can play no role in taking evidence. In my view, it is essentially important for the court to take evidence or secure the attendance of witness where the parties or the arbitral tribunal are unable to do so. The Chinese arbitration law may adopt the approach of the 1996 Act with a small change, which is to give the parties the freedom to agree to preclude the court from securing the attendance of witness.

G. Power to Order Interim Measures of Protection

Model Law. Chapter IV A on interim measures and preliminary orders was adopted by the Commission in 2006. It replaces Article 17 of the original 1985 version of the Model Law. Section 1 provides a generic definition of interim measures and sets out the conditions for granting such measures. An interim measure is any temporary measure, whether in the form of an award or in another form, by which, at any time prior to the issuance of the award by which the dispute is finally decided, the arbitral tribunal orders a party to: (a) maintain or restore the status quo pending determination of the dispute; (b) take action that would prevent, or refrain from taking action that is likely to cause, current or imminent harm or prejudice to the arbitral process itself; (c) provide a means of preserving assets out of which a subsequent award may be satisfied; or (d) preserve evidence that may be relevant and material to the resolution of the dispute. Unless otherwise agreed by the parties, the arbitral tribunal may, at the request of a party, grant interim

中英仲裁法比较研究
A Comparative Study of the Chinese Arbitration
Law and the Arbitration Laws of the UK

measures.①

The party requesting an interim measure under article 17(2)(a), (b) and (c) shall satisfy the arbitral tribunal that: (a) harm not adequately reparable by an award of damages is likely to result if the measure is not ordered, and such harm substantially outweighs the harm that is likely to result to the party against whom the measure is directed if the measure is granted;and (b) there is a reasonable possibility that the requesting party will succeed on the merits of the claim. The determination on this possibility shall not affect the discretion of the arbitral tribunal in making any subsequent determination. With regard to a request for an interim measure under Article 17(2)(d), the requirements in paragraphs (1)(a) and (b) of this article shall apply only to the extent the arbitral tribunal considers appropriate.②

The arbitral tribunal may modify, suspend or terminate an interim measure it has granted, upon application of any party or, in exceptional circumstances and upon prior notice to the parties, on the arbitral tribunal's own initiative.③ The arbitral tribunal may require the party requesting an interim measure to provide appropriate security in connection with the measure.④ The party requesting an interim measure or applying for a preliminary order shall be liable for any costs and damages caused by the measure or the order to any party if the arbitral tribunal later determines that, in the circumstances, the measure or the order should not have been granted. The arbitral tribunal may award such costs and damages at any point during the

---

① Article 17 of the UNCITRAL Model Law on International Commercial Arbitration (1985), with amendments as adopted in 2006.

② Article 17A of the UNCITRAL Model Law on International Commercial Arbitration (1985), with amendments as adopted in 2006.

③ Article 17D of the UNCITRAL Model Law on International Commercial Arbitration (1985), with amendments as adopted in 2006.

④ Article 17E of the UNCITRAL Model Law on International Commercial Arbitration (1985), with amendments as adopted in 2006.

proceedings.①

An interim measure issued by an arbitral tribunal shall be recognized as binding and, unless otherwise provided by the arbitral tribunal, enforced upon application to the competent court, irrespective of the country in which it was issued, subject to the provisions of Article 17I. The party who is seeking or has obtained recognition or enforcement of an interim measure shall promptly inform the court of any termination, suspension or modification of that interim measure. The court of the State where recognition or enforcement is sought may, if it considers it proper, order the requesting party to provide appropriate security if the arbitral tribunal has not already made a determination with respect to security or where such a decision is necessary to protect the rights of third parties.②

Recognition or enforcement of an interim measure may be refused only: (a) at the request of the party against whom it is invoked if the court is satisfied that: (i) such refusal is warranted on the grounds set forth in article 36(1)(a)(i), (ii), (Ⅲ) or (iv); or (ii) the arbitral tribunal's decision with respect to the provision of security in connection with the interim measure issued by the arbitral tribunal has not been complied with; or (Ⅲ) the interim measure has been terminated or suspended by the arbitral tribunal or, where so empowered, by the court of the State in which the arbitration takes place or under the law of which that interim measure was granted; or (b) if the court finds that: (i) the interim measure is incompatible with the powers conferred upon the court unless the court decides to reformulate the interim measure to the extent necessary to adapt it to its own powers and procedures for the purposes of enforcing that interim measure and without modifying its substance; or (ii) any of the grounds set forth in article 36(1)(b)(i) or (ii),

---

① Article 17G of the UNCITRAL Model Law on International Commercial Arbitration (1985), with amendments as adopted in 2006.

② Article 17H of the UNCITRAL Model Law on International Commercial Arbitration (1985), with amendments as adopted in 2006.

中英仲裁法比较研究
A Comparative Study of the Chinese Arbitration
Law and the Arbitration Laws of the UK

apply to the recognition and enforcement of the interim measure.

Moreover, any determination made by the court on any ground in paragraph (1) of this article shall be effective only for the purposes of the application to recognize and enforce the interim measure. The court where recognition or enforcement is sought shall not, in making that determination, undertake a review of the substance of the interim measure.①

1996 Act. Section 38 provides that the parties are free to agree on the powers exercisable by the arbitral tribunal for the purposes of and in relation to the proceedings. Unless otherwise agreed by the parties the tribunal has the following powers:

a. The tribunal may order a claimant to provide security for the costs of the arbitration.②

b. The tribunal may give directions in relation to any property which is the subject of the proceedings or as to which any question arises in the proceedings, and which is owned by or is in the possession of a party to the proceedings for the inspection, photographing, preservation, custody or detention of the property by the tribunal, an expert or a party, or ordering that samples be taken from, or any observation be made of or experiment conducted upon, the property.③

c. The tribunal may give directions to a party for the preservation for the purposes of the proceedings of any evidence in his custody or control.④

It appears that the tribunal may exercise these powers of its own motion, as well as upon the application of a party.

Section 44(1) and (2) indicate that the parties are free to preclude the power of the court to order interim measures of protection; in the lack of

---

① Article 17I of the UNCITRAL Model Law on International Commercial Arbitration (1985), with amendments as adopted in 2006.

② Section 38(3) of the 1996 Act.

③ Section 38(4) of the 1996 Act.

④ Section 38(6) of the 1996 Act.

such agreement, the court has for the purposes of and in relation to arbitral proceedings the same power of making orders about the matters listed below as it has for the purposes of and in relation to legal proceedings:

a. the preservation of evidence;

b. making orders relating to property which is the subject of the proceedings or as to which any question arises in the proceedings for the inspection, photographing, preservation, custody or detention of the property, or ordering that samples be taken from, or any observation be made of or experiment conducted upon, the property; and for that purpose authorizing any person to enter any premises in the possession or control of a party to the arbitration;

c. the sale of any goods which is the subject of the proceedings;

d. the granting of an interim injunction or the appointment of a receiver.

Section 44(3) provides that if the case is one of urgency, the court may, on the application of a party or proposed party to the arbitral proceedings, make such orders as it thinks necessary for the purpose of preserving evidence or assets.[1] If the case is not one of urgency, the court shall act only on the application of a party to the arbitral proceedings (upon notice to the other parties and to the tribunal) made with the permission of the tribunal or the agreement in writing of the other parties.[2] In any case the court shall act only if or to the extent that the arbitral tribunal, and any arbitral or other institution or person vested by the parties with power in that regard, has no power or is unable for the time being to act effectively.[3] If the court so orders, an order made by it under this section shall cease to have effect in whole or in part on the order of the tribunal or of any such arbitral or other institution or person having power to act in relation to the subject-matter of

---

[1]　Section 44(3) of the 1996 Act.
[2]　Section 44(4) of the 1996 Act.
[3]　Section 44(5) of the 1996 Act.

中英仲裁法比较研究
A Comparative Study of the Chinese Arbitration
Law and the Arbitration Laws of the UK

the order.① The leave of the court is required for any appeal from a decision of the court under this section.②

To some extent, the powers of the tribunal in Section 38 run in parallel with the corresponding powers of the court in Section 44, the scheme of the Act being, so far as possible, to enable the tribunal to act rather than require the parties to submit to the inconvenience and expense of an application to the court.③ It should also be noted that unlike those powers which may exercised by both the tribunal and by the court, the tribunal alone has power to order security for costs, the court having no such power.④ Moreover, the court may support the enforcement of peremptory orders of tribunal by making an order requiring a party to comply with a peremptory order made by the tribunal. Section 41 provides that the parties are free to agree on the powers of the tribunal in case of a party's failure to do something necessary for the proper and expeditious conduct of the arbitration.⑤ In the absence of such agreement, if without showing sufficient cause a party fails to comply with any order or directions of the tribunal, the tribunal may make a peremptory order to the same effect, prescribing such time for compliance as it considers appropriate.⑥ If a claimant fails to comply with a peremptory order of the tribunal to provide security for costs, the tribunal may make an award dismissing his claim.⑦ If a party fails to comply with any other kind of peremptory order, then, without prejudice to Section 42 (enforcement of the tribunal's peremptory orders by the court), the tribunal may do any of the

---

① Section 44(6) of the 1996 Act.

② Section 44(7) of the 1996 Act.

③ Harris, Bruce/Planterose, Rowan & Tecks, Jonathan, The Arbitration Act 1996: A Commentary, 3rd ed. Malden: Blackwell Publishing, Inc., 2003,158.

④ Harris, Bruce/Planterose, Rowan & Tecks, Jonathan, The Arbitration Act 1996: A Commentary, 3rd ed. Malden: Blackwell Publishing, Inc., 2003,158.

⑤ Section 41(1) of the 1996 Act.

⑥ Section 41(5) of the 1996 Act.

⑦ Section 41(6) of the 1996 Act.

following:

a. direct that the party in default shall not be entitled to rely upon any allegation or material which was the subject matter of the order;

b. draw such adverse inferences from the act of non-compliance as the circumstances justify;

c. proceed to an award on the basis of such materials as have been properly provided to it;

d. make such order as it thinks fit as to the payment of costs of the arbitration incurred in consequence of the non-compliance.[1]

Section 42 states that unless otherwise agreed by the parties, the court may make an order requiring a party to comply with a peremptory order made by the tribunal.[2] An application for an order under this section may be made by the tribunal (upon notice to the parties), or by a party to the arbitral proceedings with the permission of the tribunal (and upon notice to the other parties), or where the parties have agreed that the powers of the court under this section shall be available.[3] The leave of the court is required for any appeal from a decision of the court under this section.[4] This section permits the court to supplement the sanctions available to the tribunal by applying those sanctions that are available to the court for breach of a court order. For example, the court would be able to fine a party, or send him to prison for contempt.[5] To prevent much intervention of the court to arbitration, the power of the court to support the enforcement of peremptory orders of tribunal is restricted. The court shall not act unless it is satisfied that the applicant has exhausted any available arbitral process in respect of failure to com-

---

① Section 41(7) of the 1996 Act.

② Section 42(1) of the 1996 Act.

③ Section 42(2) of the 1996 Act.

④ Section 42(5) of the 1996 Act.

⑤ Harris, Bruce/Planterose, Rowan & Tecks, Jonathan, The Arbitration Act 1996: A Commentary, 3rd ed. Malden: Blackwell Publishing, Inc.,2003,174.

中英仲裁法比较研究
A Comparative Study of the Chinese Arbitration
Law and the Arbitration Laws of the UK

ply with the tribunal's order.① Moreover, no order shall be made under this section unless the court is satisfied that the person to whom the tribunal's order was directed has failed to comply with it within the time prescribed in the order or, if no time was prescribed, within a reasonable time.② At para. 212 of their Report, the DAC said: "In our view there may well be circumstances where in the interests of justice, the fact that the court has sanctions which in the nature of things cannot be given to arbitrators (e. g. committal to prison for contempt) will assist the proper functioning of the arbitral process." There is difficulty in envisaging circumstances where it will be necessary for tribunal or party to look beyond the powers available to the tribunal in Section 41. A possible example might be where a party refused to comply with a peremptory order for discovery and was prepared to suffer such sanctions as the tribunal could impose; however, the continuing non-availability of the documents affected another party's right to recover. Only the threat of imprisonment might actually produce the documents.③

Chinese Law. In Chinese arbitration law, the tribunal has no power to order interim measure of protection and the parties are not free to agree to preclude the power of the court to order attachment or conservation of evidence. I suggest that, unless other wise agreed by the parties, the tribunal should have such power, and the court should only have a role where its support is required. In other words, the approach of either the Model Law or the 1996 Act shall be adopted. As far as the role of the court is concerned, the Chinese law may adopt the instance of the Model Law and the 1996 Act, and give the court the power which run in parallel with the power of the tribunal and also the power to support the enforcement of peremptory order of the tribunal. The Model Law permits the arbitral tribunal to require any par-

---

① Section 42(3) of the 1996 Act.
② Section 42(4) of the 1996 Act.
③ Harris, Bruce/Planterose, Rowan & Tecks, Jonathan, The Arbitration Act 1996: A Commentary, 3rd ed. Malden: Blackwell Publishing, Inc., 2003, 174.

ty to provide appropriate security in connection with such measure. It is admirable for the Chinese arbitration law to adopt this instance.

H. Location of Arbitral Proceedings

Model Law. Article 20(2) provides that the arbitral tribunal may, unless otherwise agreed by the parties, meet at any place it considers appropriate for consultation among its members, for hearing witnesses, experts or the parties, or for inspection of goods, other property or documents.

The 1996 Act. Section 34(1) and (2)(a) states that it shall be for the tribunal to decide when and where any part of the proceedings is to be held, subject to the right of the parties to agree any matter.

Chinese Law. Under the Chinese arbitration law, where the parties have no agreement as to the location of proceedings, the proceedings shall be conducted in the places indicated by the CIETAC Rules and the tribunal has no power to decide the location of arbitral proceedings; and if the tribunal intends to hold proceedings in the places rather than those indicated by the CIETAC Rules, the permission of the Secretary-General is needed. In my view, the Secretary-General may not be aware of the details of the case as much as the tribunal does, therefore, it is more sensible for the tribunal to decide where to hold the proceedings if the parties have no agreement on this issue. Thus, either the instance of the Model Law or that of the 1996 Act shall be adopted by the Chinese arbitration law.

I. Advance Notice of Hearings and Meetings

Model Law. Article 24(2) provides that the parties shall be given sufficient advance notice of any hearing and of any meeting of the arbitral tribunal for the purposes of inspection of goods, other property or documents.

1996 Act. There is no rule as to advance notice of hearings and meetings in the Act.

Chinese Law. In Chinese arbitration law, the arbitral tribunal shall give

中英仲裁法比较研究
A Comparative Study of the Chinese Arbitration
Law and the Arbitration Laws of the UK

the parties sufficient advance notice of hearings and meetings, similar as the situation under the Model Law.

J. Forms and Scope of Hearings

Model Law. Article 24 provides that, subject to any contrary agreement by the parties, the arbitral tribunal shall decide whether to hold oral hearings for the presentation of evidence or for oral argument, or whether the proceedings shall be conducted on the basis of documents and other materials. However, unless the parties have agreed that no hearings shall be held, the arbitral tribunal shall hold such hearings at an appropriate stage of the proceedings, if so requested by a party.[1] The Article incorporates the following ideas:

a. that the parties should be free to decide whether an oral hearing should take place;

b. that if not expressly prohibited by the parties, either party had a right to an oral hearing upon request;

c. that if the parties took no decision on the matter and neither applied for an oral hearing, the arbitral tribunal could decide how the proceedings were to be conducted.[2]

It must also be noted, however, and was so noted by the Commission, that Article. 18 of the Law may in exceptional circumstances provide a compelling reason for holding an oral hearing. The Report then goes on to say:

"It was understood that parties who had earlier agreed that no hearings should be held were not precluded from later modifying their agreement,

---

[1] Article 24(1) of the 1996 Act.
[2] Doc. A/CN. 9/SR. 324, para.1.

thus to allow a party to request oral hearings."①

Article 25(c) states that unless otherwise agreed by the parties, if, without showing sufficient cause, any party fails to appear at a hearing or to produce documentary evidence, the arbitral tribunal may continue the proceedings and make the award on the evidence before it. This sub-paragraph does not state time limits either directly or by reference to another provision. The Analytical Commentary states that "failure to appear at hearing" presupposes that the party was given sufficient advance notice as required by Article 24(3) and that "failure to produce documentary evidence" presupposes that the party was requested to do so within a specified period of time which was reasonable in accordance with the fundamental principles of Article 18 of the Law.②

1996 Act. Section 34 provides that, subject to the right of the parties to agree any matter, it shall be for the tribunal to decide when and where any part of the proceedings is to be held③; whether and to what extent there should be oral or written evidence or submissions④; and whether any and if so what questions should be put to and answered by the respective parties and when and in what form this should be done.⑤ Section 41 provides that the parties are free to agree on the powers of the tribunal in case of a party's failure to do something necessary for the proper and expeditious conduct of the arbitration. Unless otherwise agreed by the parties, the following provisions apply. If the tribunal is satisfied that there has been inordinate and in-

---

① Ibid., para. 205. The Tanzanian delegate, supported by a few other delegations, had expressed the view that a party which had originally agreed that no hearing should be held might subsequently decide that one was necessary after all (Doc. A/CN. 9/233, paras. 55 and 57).

② Doc. A/CN. 9/SR. 264, para.5.

③ Section 34(1) and (2)(a) of the 1996 Act.

④ Section 34(1) and (2)(e) of the 1996 Act.

⑤ Section 34(1) and (2)(h) of the 1996 Act.

中英仲裁法比较研究
A Comparative Study of the Chinese Arbitration
Law and the Arbitration Laws of the UK

excusable delay on the part of the claimant in pursuing his claim and that the delay gives rise, or is likely to give rise, to a substantial risk that it is not possible to have a fair resolution of the issues in that claim, or has caused, or is likely to cause, serious prejudice to the respondent, the tribunal may make an award dismissing the claim. If without showing sufficient cause, a party fails to attend or be represented at an oral hearing of which due notice was given, or where matters are to be dealt with in writing, fails after due notice to submit written evidence or make written submissions, the tribunal may continue the proceedings in the absence of that party or, as the case may be, without any written evidence or submissions on his behalf, and may make an award on the basis of the evidence before it. Section 35 provides that the parties are free to agree that the arbitral proceedings shall be consolidated with other arbitral proceedings, or that concurrent hearings shall be held, on such terms as may be agreed.[1]

Unless the parties agree to confer such power on the tribunal, the tribunal has no power to order consolidation of proceedings or concurrent hearings.[2] The structure of the section reflects the fact that the parties may themselves agree to consolidate arbitrations or have concurrent hearings either at a stage prior to the appointment of the tribunal or thereafter. Alternatively they may agree to confer the relevant powers on the tribunals.[3] The rationale behind this approach is that the parties should not have to find their agreed procedure for the private resolution of their own disputes being used to deal with other parties and their disputes, or to find themselves part of someone else's arbitration, unless they specifically so agree. Consolidation in the absence of agreement could operate as a disincentive to arbitrate. On an international level it might equally result in the award being unenforcable,

---

[1] Article 35(1) of the 1996 Act.
[2] Article 35(2) of the 1996 Act.
[3] Harris, Bruce/Planterose, Rowan & Tecks, Jonathan, The Arbitration Act 1996: A Commentary, 3rd ed. Malden: Blackwell Publishing, Inc.,2003,151.

where the tribunal, for instance, had been imposed on an unwilling party. The DAC Report (para.180) also noted that difficulties over discovery might arise. [1]

　　Chinese Law. Chinese arbitration law does not contain rules dealing with consolidation of proceedings and concurrent hearings. To fill the gap it would be beneficial for China to adopt a provision on the lines of Section 35 of the 1996 Act. It is noteworthy that the 1996 Act gives the court the power to determine preliminary points of law. Section 45 provides that, unless otherwise agreed by the parties, the court may on the application of a party to arbitral proceedings (upon notice to the other parties) determine any question of law arising in the course of the proceedings which the court is satisfied substantially affects the rights of one or more of the parties. An agreement to dispense with reasons for the tribunal's award shall be considered an agreement to exclude the court's jurisdiction under this section. Section 45 also limits the court's power to determine preliminary point of law by providing that an application under this section shall not be considered unless it is made with the agreement of all parties to the proceedings, or it is made with the permission of the tribunal and the court is satisfied that the determination of the question is likely to produce substantial savings in costs, and that the application was made without delay. [2] The application shall identify the question of law to be determined and, unless made with the agreement of all parties to the proceedings, it shall state the grounds on which it is said that the question should be decided by the court. [3] Unless otherwise agreed by the parties, the arbitral tribunal may continue the arbitral proceedings and make an award while an application to the court under this section is pending. [4]

　　Unless the court gives leave, no appeal lies from a decision of the court

---

　　[1]　Harris, Bruce/Planterose, Rowan & Tecks, Jonathan, The Arbitration Act 1996: A Commentary, 3rd ed. Malden: Blackwell Publishing, Inc.,2003,152.

　　[2]　Section 45(2) of the 1996 Act.

　　[3]　Section 45(3) of the 1996 Act.

　　[4]　Section 45(4) of the 1996 Act.

中英仲裁法比较研究
A Comparative Study of the Chinese Arbitration
Law and the Arbitration Laws of the UK

as to whether the conditions specified in subsection (2) are met.① The decision of the court on the question of law shall be treated as a judgment of the court for the purposes of an appeal. But no appeal lies without the leave of the court which shall not be given unless the court considers that the question is one of general importance, or is one which for some other special reason should be considered by the Court of Appeal.② The usefulness of the section would arise, for example, where a particular point of law is central to the arbitration, and an authoritative decision one way or the other will effectively determine the whole or a large part of the dispute between the parties. It may also be invoked where a particular question is central to a large number of arbitrations, and early and definitive consideration thereof by the court would assist a large number of parties to different proceedings, subject of course to the proviso that there must be a substantial effect on the rights of one or more parties to the arbitration in question.③ However, in my view, it is unnecessary to give the court the power to determine preliminary point of law, as in all of the above situations the tribunal can deal with the issue itself. Moreover, it is notable that Section 40(2)(b) refers to this section as a specific example of the general duty of the parties to proceed with expedition. Delay is likely to be measured from the time when the question of law might first be identified, such as the close of any pleading stage. If substantial progress has been made in the arbitration, and particularly if there have been steps towards the determination of the question of law in the course of the arbitration itself, it is likely that the court would refuse the request to hear the application.④ It can be seen that since the power of enforce-

---

① Section 45(5) of the 1996 Act.

② Section 45(6) of the 1996 Act.

③ Harris, Bruce/Planterose, Rowan & Tecks, Jonathan, The Arbitration Act 1996: A Commentary, 3rd ed., Malden: Blackwell Publishing, Inc.,2003,183.

④ Harris, Bruce/Planterose, Rowan & Tecks, Jonathan, The Arbitration Act 1996: A Commentary, 3rd ed., Malden: Blackwell Publishing, Inc.,2003,183-184.

ment of the court is not needed in those situations, even if the court does not intervene, the tribunal can resolve the problems by itself. Intervention of the court will not save time and energy, as the process in the court might be more complex than that in the arbitration and the determination would have to be transferred from the court to the tribunal.

V. Conclusion

To resolve the problems existing in Chinese arbitration law, it might be useful to look to the UNCITRAL Model Law and the 1996 Act. In Chinese arbitration law, the parties cannot agree to exclude the arbitral tribunal's power to collect evidence. To protect the autonomy of the parties, Chinese arbitration law might adopt the position of the 1996 Act permitting the parties to prevent the arbitral tribunal from collecting evidence on its own initiative. Chinese arbitration law does not give the court the power to collect evidence. Since under some circumstances, the support of the court in this regard is needed, Chinese law might usefully adopt the approach of the 1996 Act and give the court such power, subject to the agreement of the parties. In Chinese arbitration law, the arbitral tribunal cannot order interim measure of protection. Considering the utility of giving the tribunal such power, it would be beneficial for Chinese law to adopt the approach of either the Model Law or the 1996 Act and give the tribunal this power. Under the 1996 Act, where a party fails to obey a peremptory order of the tribunal, the court may intervene and make an order requiring the party to comply with the tribunal's order. Chinese arbitration law may follow this lead.

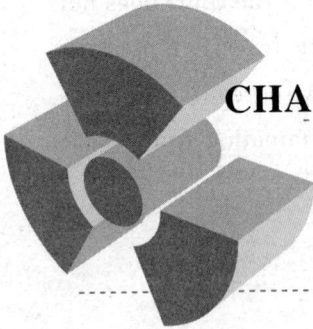

中英仲裁法比较研究
A Comparative Study of the Chinese Arbitration
Law and the Arbitration Laws of the UK

CHAPTER 11

THE ARBITRAL AWARD

Ⅰ. Introduction

The ultimate goal of arbitration is the making of an arbitral award. This chapter aims to discuss different types of awards, and the substance of awards, including the power to award damages, interest, and expenses, and to make other orders, plus the delivery, correction and effect of the award. As ever, the Chinese approach as to the above questions will be considered, and compared with the approach taken in English Law and the Model Law.

Ⅱ. The Chinese Approach to Arbitral Award

A. Types of Awards

1. Partial award

Article 55 of the Arbitration Law provides that, in arbitrating disputes, the arbitration tribunal may rule on those facts that are already clear, while

Article 44 of the CIETAC Rules (2015) provides that a partial award may be made on any issue before the final award is made, if considered necessary by the arbitral tribunal, or if the arbitral tribunal accedes to the request of the parties to do so. A partial award is a part of the final award and has the same effect. Neither the Arbitration Law nor the CIETAC Rules indicates the sort of problems a partial award can deal with. However, since a partial award is a part of the final award, it must deal with matters related to the substance of the dispute, such as whether one party owes the other a sum of money.[1]

2. Interlocutory award

Article 44 of the CIETAC Rules states that an interlocutory award may be made by the arbitral tribunal on any issue in the case at any time before the final award is made either if considered necessary by the arbitral tribunal, or if the tribunal accedes to the request of the parties to do so. A party's failure to comply with an interlocutory award will not affect the continuation of the arbitration proceedings, nor prevent the arbitral tribunal from making a final award. Again, the CIETAC Rules do not indicate the sort of problems an interlocutory award can deal with.

In practice, where a procedural problem needs to be resolved before the making of the final award, and if the decision regarding the procedural problem needs to be explained, the tribunal will make an interlocutory award informing the parties of the decision, incorporating the explanation in that interlocutory award. If an explanation is not needed, as in the case of audits and valuations, the tribunal will request the appropriate secretariat to send the parties a letter, procedural order or instruction. Yet in a very small number of cases the tribunal will make an interlocutory award to inform the parties of audit and appraisal. It can be seen that it is within the discretion of

---

[1]   Song Hang, Recognition and Enforcement of International Commercial Arbitration Awards, Beijing: Law Press, 2000, 55; Han Jian, Theory and Practice on Modern International Commercial Law, Beijing: Law Press, 2000, 331.

中英仲裁法比较研究
A Comparative Study of the Chinese Arbitration
Law and the Arbitration Laws of the UK

the tribunal to deal with this matter either via an interlocutory award, or via a letter, procedural order or instruction.[①] In my opinion, since the CIETAC Rules provide that the arbitral tribunal can make an interlocutory award, to make the Rules complete and executable, the Rules should define "interlocutory award" and specify clearly an interlocutory award shall deal with procedural problem. However, as to a particular procedural problem, the arbitral tribunal shall remain to have the discretion to decide whether to make an interlocutory award or simply send a letter, procedural order or instruction.

Article 4(2) of the CIETAC Rules states that the parties may agree to preclude the arbitral tribunal from making interlocutory awards. This is also the effective position under the Arbitration Law, as it does not contain a mandatory rule giving the arbitral tribunal the power to make an interlocutory award.

3. Final award

A final award resolves the dispute between the parties. When a final award is made, the arbitrators have accomplished their duty and no longer have competence over the case. The particular relationship of the parties and the arbitrators is terminated.[②]

4. Amicable award

In international commercial arbitration, the tribunal can only make an effective award if the parties agree to confer competence on the tribunal. The source of the tribunal's power is the agreement of the parties. Thus, during the process of arbitration and before the award is made, the parties are free to reach a conciliation agreement, which of course cancels the arbitration agreement. To ensure that the conciliation agreement is effectively enforced, the parties may ask the tribunal to make an award to confirm that agree-

---

① Song Hang, Recognition and Enforcement of International Commercial Arbitration Awards, Beijing: Law Press, 2000, 55.

② Han Jian, Theory and Practice on Modern International Commercial Law, Beijing: Law Press, 2000, 325.

ment. The arbitral tribunal may refuse to make an award to confirm the conciliation agreement if it considers that the agreement breaches mandatory legal rules or harms the rights of a third party. Where parties have referred a dispute to arbitration, and make a conciliation agreement part of which breaches mandatory rules or harms a third party's interests, the arbitral tribunal shall inform the parties of this fact and suggest that they amend that part. If the parties refuse to make such amendment and do not withdraw the case, the tribunal shall make an award confirming the non-offending part of the agreement, while continuing the arbitration and making an award to deal with the offending part. Where parties to an arbitration agreement make a conciliation agreement and request the arbitral tribunal to make an award to confirm the conciliation agreement without referring the dispute to the arbitration, if part of the conciliation agreement breaches mandatory rules or harms a third party's interest, the tribunal shall inform the parties of the fact and suggest they amend the offending part. If the parties refuse to make such amendment and do not withdraw their request, the tribunal may only make an agreed award confirming the non-offending part of the conciliation agreement, and will not commence arbitral proceedings to deal with the rest of the agreement. Such an award has the same status as any other arbitration award and is called an amicable award. The advantage of an amicable award is that it has more sanction than a mere conciliation agreement. A conciliation agreement is not legally binding, and any party is permitted to change his mind and refuse to abide by the agreement, but an amicable award becomes legally binding immediately upon issue. Where a party refuses to enforce an amicable award, the other party can apply to the court for enforcement.[1]

5. Default award

Article 42(2) of the Arbitration Law provides that whereas a respond-

---

[1]   Han Jian, Theory and Practice on Modern International Commercial Law, Beijing: Law Press, 2000, 333.

中英仲裁法比较研究
A Comparative Study of the Chinese Arbitration
Law and the Arbitration Laws of the UK

ent is absent from the hearing without justifiable reasons after receiving the written notice, or withdraws from hearing without the prior permission by of the tribunal, the tribunal may make an award by default. Article 34 of the CIETAC Rules (2015) provides that if the respondent fails to appear at an oral hearing without showing sufficient cause for such failure, or withdraws from an on-going oral hearing without the permission of the tribunal, the tribunal may proceed with the arbitration and make a default award.[1] Article 34 also states if the claimant fails to appear at an oral hearing without showing sufficient cause for such failure, or withdraws from an on-going oral hearing without the permission of the tribunal, the claimant may be deemed to have withdrawn its request for arbitration. In such a case, if the respondent has filed a counterclaim, the tribunal shall proceed with the hearing of the counter-claim and make a default award.[2]

B. Substance of Awards

1. The Process of making awards

Article 7 of the Arbitration Law states that an award shall be made on the basis of true facts and relevant laws to achieve a fair and reasonable settlement for the parties. Article 43 of the CIETAC Rules (2015) provides that the tribunal shall independently and impartially make its award on the basis of the facts, in accordance with the law and the terms of the contract, with reference to international practices and in compliance with principles of fairness and reasonableness.

As to how to make an award where the arbitrators have different views, Article 53 of the Arbitration Law provides that an arbitral award shall be decided by the majority of the arbitrators and the views of the minority can be written down in the record. Where a majority vote cannot be reached, the a-

---

[1] Article 34(2) of the CIETAC Arbitration Rules (2015).

[2] Article 34(1) of the CIETAC Arbitration Rules (2015).

ward shall be decided on the basis of the opinion of the chief arbitrator. Article 43 of the CIETAC Rules provides that where the tribunal is composed of three arbitrators, the award shall be rendered by all three or by a majority. Where the arbitral tribunal cannot reach a majority opinion, the award shall be rendered in accordance with the presiding arbitrator's opinion. In either case, dissenting opinions shall be docketed into the file and may be attached to the award, but shall not form part of the award.① The Arbitration Law does not say whether, where the award is decided based on the opinion of the chief arbitrator, the other arbitrators' opinion should be written into the record. This is an apparent omission, and such a requirement should be added to the Arbitration Law. The Arbitration Law does not provide whether the written dissenting opinion or the written opinion of other arbitrators shall be docketed into the file or may be attached to the award, or shall form a part of the award. The Arbitration Law leaves this problem to be dealt with by the Arbitration Rules of Arbitral Agency.

Article 54 of the Arbitration Law provides that the arbitral award shall be signed by arbitrators and affixed with the seals of the arbitration commission. An arbitrator holding different views may or may not sign the award. Article 43 of the CIETAC Rules (2015) states that CIETAC's stamp shall be affixed to the award.②Unless the award is made in accordance with the opinion of the presiding arbitrator or the sole arbitrator, the arbitral award shall be signed by a majority of arbitrators. An arbitrator who has a dissenting opinion may or may not sign his/her name on the award.③ Article 43 of the CIETAC Rules (2015) does not say where the award is made in accordance with the opinion of the presiding arbitrator or the sole arbitrator, whether the presiding arbitrator or the sole arbitrator shall sign the award. Yet it can be inferred from the fact that the majority of arbitrators must sign

---

① Article 43(5) of the CIETAC Arbitration Rules (2015).
② Article 43(3) of the CIETAC Arbitration Rules (2015).
③ Article 43(6) of the CIETAC Arbitration Rules (2015).

中英仲裁法比较研究
A Comparative Study of the Chinese Arbitration
Law and the Arbitration Laws of the UK

where a majority award is made, that the presiding or sole arbitrator must sign the award in the above circumstances. This omission should be rectified. Similarly, where the award is made on the basis of the opinion of the presiding arbitrator, the other arbitrators may or may not sign the award.

The Arbitration Law is silent regarding time limits for making awards, but the CIETAC Rules state that the tribunal shall render an award within six months of the date on which the arbitral tribunal is formed.① In summary procedure the tribunal shall render an award within three months of the above date.② In both cases, upon the request of the arbitral tribunal, the Chairman of CIETAC may extend the time period if he/she considers it truly necessary and the reasons for the extension truly justified.③

2. Content of awards

Article 54 of the Arbitration Law provides that the arbitral award shall specify the claims, the facts in disputes, the reasons for the award, the result of the award, the arbitration expenses and the date of the award. Where parties object to the specification of the facts in dispute and reasons for the ruling, such specification and reasons may be omitted. Article 43 of the CIETAC Rules 2015 states that the arbitral tribunal shall state in the award the claims, the facts of the dispute, the reasons on which the award is based, the result of the award, the allocation of the arbitration costs and the date on which and the place at which the award is made. The facts of the dispute and the reasons on which the award is based may not be stated in the award if the parties have so agreed, or if the award is made in accordance with the terms of a settlement agreement between the parties. The arbitral tribunal is also given the power to determine in the arbitral award the specific time period for the parties to execute the award and the liabilities to be borne

---

① Article 42(1) of the CIETAC Arbitration Rules (2015).
② Articles 42(2) and 56(1) of the CIETAC Arbitration Rules (2015).
③ Article 56(2) of the CIETAC Arbitration Rules (2015).

by a party failing to execute the award within the specified time.[1] Yet, since there is no mandatory rule in the Arbitration Law giving the tribunal such a power, the parties may exclude that power by agreement. There is an argument that the award should not include reasons, as this may encourage the losing party to challenge the award. However, the opinion that the parties are entitled to be aware of the reasons for the award prevails.[2]

3. Delivery of awards

Article 68 of the CIETAC Rules (2015) provides that all documents, notices and written materials in relation to the arbitration may be sent to the parties and/or their representatives in person, or by registered mail or express mail, facsimile, telex, cable, or by any other means considered proper by the secretariat of CIETAC or its sub-commission.[3] Any written correspondence to a party and/or its representative(s)s hall be deemed to have been properly served on the party if delivered to the addressee or delivered at his place of business, registration, domicile, habitual residence or mailing address, or where, after reasonable inquiries by the other party, none of the aforesaid addresses can be found, the written correspondence is sent by the secretariat of CIETAC or its sub-commission to the addressee's last known place of business, registered address, domicile, habitual residence or mailing address by registered mail or by any other means that provides a record of the attempt of delivery.[4] The Arbitration Law does not deal with the delivery of awards, thus the parties are free to make their own agreement as to delivery.[5] It may be noted that an award becomes effective on the date on which the award is made, whether the award has been delivered or not.

---

[1]   Article 43(2) of the CIETAC Arbitration Rules (2015).

[2]   Han Jian, Theory and Practice on Modern International Commercial Law, Beijing: Law Press, 2000, 336.

[3]   Article 68(1) of the CIETAC Arbitration Rules (2015).

[4]   Article 68(2) of the CIETAC Arbitration Rules (2015).

[5]   Article 4(2) of the CIETAC Arbitration Rules (2015).

中英仲裁法比较研究
A Comparative Study of the Chinese Arbitration
Law and the Arbitration Laws of the UK

4. Correction of awards

Article 56 of the Arbitration Law provides that a tribunal may correct errors of expression or computation, and add things omitted from the award. The parties may apply to the tribunal for such correction within 30 days of receipt of the award. Article 47 of the CIETAC Rules (2015) states that within thirty days of receipt of the award, either party may request in writing a correction of any error of a clerical, typographical, calculation or similar nature in the award. The tribunal shall correct any such error within thirty days of the date of receipt of such a request. The arbitral tribunal may likewise correct any such errors of its own initiative within a reasonable time after the award is issued. Such a correction shall form a part of the arbitral award. Article 48 of the CIETAC Rules (2015) indicates that within thirty days from the date on which the ward is received, either party may request the tribunal in writing for an additional award on any claim or counterclaim which was advanced in the arbitration proceedings but omitted from the award. If such omission does exist, the tribunal shall make an additional award within thirty days from the date of receipt of the written request. The arbitral tribunal may also make an additional award on its own initiative within a reasonable period of time after the arbitral award is issued. Such additional award shall form a part of the arbitral award previously rendered.

The Arbitration Law does not provide a time limit for making corrections. Thus, in light of Article 4(2) of the CIETAC Rules, the parties are free to agree on another time limit rather than the 30 days specified in the Rules. In my view, the parties may not be sufficiently aware of how much time the proceedings may take. If they agree to require the arbitral tribunal to correct the error in a too short period of time, the arbitrators may be under too much pressure and the making of any correction may be adversely affected. Therefore, I suggest the Arbitration Law should contain a rule which provides that the arbitral tribunal shall make a correction in writing within thirty days from the date of receipt of the written request for the correction,

so that the parties have no right to agree on the time limit for making corrections. The Arbitration Law does not provide that the arbitral tribunal may
correct the error or make an additional award on its own initiative. Thus, the
parties can by virtue of Article 4(2) of the CIETAC Rules agree to prevent
the tribunal correcting the error or making an additional award on its own initiative. However, such agreement would be rare, as the parties would not
benefit. The Arbitration Law does not state that a correction in writing or an
additional award shall form a part of the arbitral award previously rendered,
so that the parties are at liberty to agree otherwise. Again such agreement
would be rare. Neither the Arbitration Law nor the CIETAC Rules contains
any provision regarding the explanation of ambiguities in the arbitral award.
In practice, CIETAC allows the tribunal to explain ambiguities, if either
party applies and the tribunal considers it necessary.[①] This is a necessary
and sensible power, which should be provided for explicitly in both the Arbitration Law and the CIETAC Rules 2015.

Neither the Arbitration Law nor the CIETAC Rules deal with correction
of errors other than clerical and similar errors. In practice, such other errors
are not and should not be corrected, so that the finality of the arbitral award
is not adversely affected.

5. Effect of awards

Article 9 of the Arbitration Law provides that the arbitration award is
final. After the award is given, neither the arbitration commission nor the
courts may entertain any action concerning that dispute. Article 57 of the
Arbitration Law provides that the award takes legal effect upon its issuing.
Article 62 provides that the parties shall execute the award. If one of the parties refuses, the other may apply to the people's court for enforcement. Article 43 of the CIETAC Rules states that the date on which the award is made

---

① Han Jian, Theory and Practice on Modern International Commercial Law, Beijing: Law Press, 2000, 337.

中英仲裁法比较研究
A Comparative Study of the Chinese Arbitration
Law and the Arbitration Laws of the UK

shall be the date on which the award comes into legal effect.① The award is final and binding upon both parties. Neither party may bring a suit before a court or request any other organization to revise the award.② Article 49 of the CIETAC Rules (2005) provides that the parties must automatically execute the award within the time period specified in the award. If no time limit is specified in the award, the parties shall execute it immediately.③ Where one party fails to execute the award, the other may apply to a competent Chinese court for its enforcement pursuant to Chinese law, or apply to a competent court for enforcement of the award according to the 1958 United Nations Convention on Recognition and Enforcement of Foreign Arbitral Awards or other international treaties that China has concluded or acceded to.④ Since the Arbitration Law does not provide that the parties must automatically execute the arbitral award within the time period specified in the award, the parties are free to agree to execute the arbitral award immediately regardless of the time period specified in the award.

C. Special Substance of Amicable Awards

1. Reconciliation on parties own initiative

Article 49 of the Arbitration Law provides that after the parties have applied for arbitration, they may reach conciliation on their own initiative. Where a conciliation agreement has been reached, a request may be made to the tribunal for an award based on that agreement, or the application for arbitration may be withdrawn. Article 50 continues that where a conciliation agreement is not observed, either party may apply for arbitration according to the arbitration agreement.

Article 40(5) of the CIETAC Rules (2015) states that a settlement a-

---

① Article 43(7) of the CIETAC Arbitration Rules (2015).
② Article 43(8) of the CIETAC Arbitration Rules (2015).
③ Article 49(1) of the CIETAC Arbitration Rules (2015).
④ Article 49(2) of the CIETAC Arbitration Rules (2015).

greement reached between the parties during the course of conciliation by the arbitral tribunal, but without the involvement of the arbitral tribunal, shall be deemed as one reached through conciliation by the arbitral tribunal. Thus, under the Rules, there is no difference between conciliation on the parties' own initiative and conciliation by the arbitral tribunal. The rules as to conciliation by the arbitral tribunal under the CIETAC Rules will be discussed in the following paragraphs.

2. Situations under which the arbitral tribunal may conciliate

Article 51 of the Arbitration Law provides that, where the parties so desire, the tribunal may conciliate a case before making the award. Article 40 of the CIETAC Rules states that where both parties desire conciliation, or one party so desires and the other party agrees when approached by the tribunal, the tribunal may conciliate the case during the course of the proceedings.[1] It can be seen that the parties may not agree that the tribunal may conciliate only if a certain condition is satisfied, since the mandatory rules of the Arbitration Law give the tribunal the power to conciliate. Thus party autonomy is been damaged. Accordingly, I suggest that the Arbitration Law should not give the tribunal the power to conciliate of its own motion.

Article 40(3) of the CIETAC Rules states that the tribunal may conciliate the case in the manner it considers appropriate, but the parties are at liberty to restrict the discretion given by Article 40(3).

3. Failure of conciliation

The Arbitration Law states that if conciliation fails, the tribunal shall continue the arbitration and make an arbitral award. The CIETAC Rules provide that the tribunal shall terminate the conciliation and continue the proceedings if one of the parties requests a termination, or if the tribunal be-

---

① Article 40(2) of the CIETAC Arbitration Rules (2015).

中英仲裁法比较研究
A Comparative Study of the Chinese Arbitration
Law and the Arbitration Laws of the UK

lieves that further efforts to conciliate will be futile.[①] Where conciliation fails, the tribunal shall proceed with the arbitration and render an award.[②] Moreover, any opinion, view or statement, and any proposal or expression of acceptance or opposition by either party or the tribunal in the process of conciliation, shall not be invoked as grounds for any claim, defence or counterclaim in subsequent proceedings, arbitral, judicial or otherwise.[③] Since the Arbitration Law does not prevent such matters from being invoked as grounds in any subsequent proceedings, the parties are permitted to agree that they may be so invoked.[④]

4. Success of conciliation

The Arbitration Law provides that where an agreement is reached through conciliation, the tribunal shall produce a reconciliation document or make an award based on the results of the agreement. The document and the award are equally binding legally.[⑤] As for the application for refusing enforcement of a conciliation document or an award based on the results of the agreement, it shall be dismissed by the people's court.[⑥]

Article 52 of the Arbitration Law provides that the reconciliation document shall specify the arbitration claims and the result of the agreement between the parties. It must be signed by the arbitrator and affixed with the seal of the arbitration commission before being delivered to the parties. It becomes legally binding immediately upon receipt by the parties. If any party fails to honour the reconciliation document before receiving it, the tribunal shall continue the arbitration and make an arbitral award. The Arbitration

---

① Article 40(4) of the Arbitration Law 2017.
② Article 40(7) of the Arbitration Law 2017.
③ Article 40(8) of the Arbitration Law 2017.
④ Article 4(2) of the CIETAC Arbitration Rules (2015).
⑤ Article 51 of the Arbitration Law 2017.
⑥ Section of the Interpretation of the SPC on Application of the PRC Arbitration Law, Law Interpretation No.7. Sept. 8, 2006.

Law leaves the issue of an amicable award to be dealt with by the Arbitration Rules of the Arbitral Agency. The CIETAC Rules state that where settlement is reached through conciliation by the tribunal, the parties shall sign a written settlement agreement. Unless otherwise agreed by the parties, the arbitral tribunal will close the case and render an arbitral award in accordance with the terms of the settlement agreement.① The CIETAC Rules contain no provision as to the making of a conciliation agreement. Thus, if the parties decide that a conciliation agreement rather than a conciliation award shall be made, the tribunal shall make that agreement according to Articles 51 and 52 of the Arbitration Law.②The CIETAC Rules require the agreement to be in writing, unlike the Arbitration Law. Therefore, under the Law an oral conciliation agreement is valid.

Ⅲ. Suggested Improvements to the Chinese Law

1. The CIETAC Rules should define interlocutory award and specify clearly the sorts of problems which can be dealt with by such an award.

2. The tribunal should not have the power to conciliate on its own initiative, but should conciliate only if both parties desire for conciliation or one party so desires and the other party agrees.

3. The CIETAC Rules should state clearly that the award is made by the presiding or sole arbitrator, he/she shall sign the award.

4. The Arbitration Law and the CIETAC Rules should provide that if a party applies to the arbitral tribunal to explain an ambiguity of the award, the arbitral tribunal must do so.

---

① Article 40(6) of the CIETAC Arbitration Rules (2015).
② Article 4(2) of the CIETAC Arbitration Rules (2015).

中英仲裁法比较研究
A Comparative Study of the Chinese Arbitration
Law and the Arbitration Laws of the UK

Ⅳ. The Approach of the Laws Operating in the UK

A. Introduction

As ever it is useful to refer to the United Kingdom for paradigm which offers two models for consideration —the 1996 Arbitration Act and the Model Law. There are similarities among the three laws as to the contents, delivery and effect of awards. Yet, as a result of differences in culture and tradition, there are points where the three laws differ in their treatment of arbitral awards. One main difference is that in Chinese arbitration law and the Model Law, unlike the 1996 Act, the court has no role to play as the extension of time-limits. Another major difference is that in Chinese arbitration law and the Model Law, an arbitral tribunal is not allowed to withhold an award in case of non-payment of the fees and expenses of the arbitrators, whereas under the 1996 Act, the tribunal is allowed to do so. The last main difference is regarding the method of enforcement the awards.

B. Types of Awards

1. Partial and interim awards

Model Law. Its drafters at one time considered giving the tribunal the power to make interim interlocutory and partial awards, but did not reach a clear conclusion, due to the fact that Article 3 suggests that the Model Law contemplates that other types of award may be made. That is then a matter for the domestic law of the state adopting the Model Law.

1996 Act. Section 47 provides that, unless otherwise agreed by the parties, a tribunal may make more than one award at different times on differ-

CHAPTER 11   THE ARBITRAL AWARD

ent aspects of the matters to be determined.① In Particular, it may make an award relating to an issue affecting the whole claim, or to a part only of the claims or cross-claims submitted to it for decision. If the arbitral tribunal makes the latter type of award, it must specify in its award the issue, or the claim or part of a claim, which is the subject matter of the award.② It is important to appreciate that the awards to which Section 47 refers are final as to the matters which they determine.③ So they are essentially partial awards. This facility to male awards on different issue is an important tool whereby an arbitrator can implement his duty under s. 33(1)(b) to adopt procedures suitable to the circumstance of the particular case, avoiding unnecessary delay or expense, so as to provide a fair means for the resolution of the matters falling to be determined. It is also very flexible. The procedure may secure the early determination of an issue fundamental to the whole award, thus enabling the parties to settle their remaining difference.

Chinese Law. Under Chinese arbitration law, unless otherwise agreed by the parties, the arbitral tribunal has the power to make partial④ and interlocutory awards.⑤ However, it is not clear which sorts of issues shall be dealt with which types of award. I have two suggestions. First, Chinese arbitration law could stipulate the sort of issues which may be dealt with by each type of awards. Alternatively, it could approach of the 1996 Act and simply give the arbitral tribunal power to make more than one award at different times on different aspects of the matters to be determined and give the tribunal power to make orders in relation to the proceedings.

---

① Section 47(1) of the 1996 Act.
② Section 47(3) of the 1996 Act.
③ Harris, Bruce/Planterose, Rowan & Tecks, Jonathan, The Arbitration Act 1996: A Commentary, 3rd ed. Malden: Blackwell Publishing, Inc., 2003. Sutton, David St. John & Gill, Judith, Russell on Arbitration, 22 ed. London: Sweet & Maxwell, 2003.
④ Article 55 of the Arbitration Law 1994; Article 44 of the Arbitration Rules of CIETAC (2015).
⑤ Article 44 of the CIETAC Arbitration Rules (2005).

中英仲裁法比较研究
A Comparative Study of the Chinese Arbitration
Law and the Arbitration Laws of the UK

2. Final awards

Model Law. Article 32(1) provides that the arbitral proceedings are terminated by the final award.

1996 Act. Unless otherwise agreed by the parties, the tribunal may make an award relating to an issue affecting the whole claim,[①] i.e. a final award.

Chinese Law. Under Chinese arbitration law, the arbitral tribunal can make a final award. There being no difference between the Model Law, the 1996 Act, and Chinese arbitration law on this issue, there is no need for Chinese arbitration law to be amended in this respect.

3. Amicable awards

Model Law. Article 30(1) provides that if, during arbitral proceedings, the parties settle the dispute, the arbitral tribunal shall terminate the proceedings and, if requested by the parties and not objected to by the arbitral tribunal, record the settlement in the form of an arbitral award on agreed terms. It is apparent that the arbitral tribunal has the right to decide whether to record the settlement in the form of an award. It was thought that the arbitral tribunal should not be compelled to issue an award in such circumstances since in the words of the Commission Report, "the words of such settlement, in exceptional case, be in conflict with binding laws or public, including fundamental notions of fairness and justice".[②] The Commission Report states after deliberation it was agreed "that there must be the dual will of the two parties that the settlement by recorded as an award, but that the formal request needed to be made by only one of them.[③] It seems that since the arbitral tribunal must be satisfied as to the "dual will": a joint request is likely to save time.

1996 Act. Section 51(1) and (2) of the 1996 Act, if during arbitral pro-

---

① Section 47(1) of the 1996 Act.
② Doc. A/CN. 9/SR.328, para.249.
③ Doc. A/CN. 9/SR. 328, para.250.

ceedings the parties settle the dispute, unless otherwise agreed by the parties, the tribunal shall terminate the substantive proceedings, and, if so requested by the parties not objected to by the tribunal, shall record the settlement in the form of an agreed award. It is notable that, unlike Article 30 of the Model Law, Section 51 of the 1996 Act is non-mandatory, thus the parties are entitle to exclude the section by agreement. As under the Model Law both parties must agree that settlement be recorded as an award, but to save time, the formal request needs to be made by only one of them. Like the Model Law, the tribunal may refuse to make an award if settlement contains objectionable features that might comprise the tribunal. In the wording of the section used strongly indicates, that the object is very much a matter of last resort rather than a question of general discretion. It is unclear exactly when arbitrators might be justified in objecting, although the DAC suggested in its February 1996 Report, para. 242, that one situation might be where they believe the agreed award to be part of an elaborate tax fraud by the parties,① or to conflict with public policy. If arbitrators do refuse to make an agreed award, it would seem that the appropriate remedy is an application for their removal under Section 24 of the 1996 Act, although in practice the real sanction may be a refusal by the parties to pay the arbitrators' fees insofar as payment has not been made.

Chinese Law. Chinese arbitration law does not formally give the arbitral tribunal the right to refuse to make an award on agreed terms, but arbitrators have such a right in practice. To properly develop the law, it is suggested that Chinese arbitration law adopt the stance of either the Model Law or the 1996 Act, and explicitly give the tribunal such a right. Under Chinese arbitration law, if the dispute is settled through mediation by the tribunal, it will make an agreed award unless otherwise agreed by the parties, whether

---

① Although the DAC also recognized that, if this was the case, the award would scarcely be binding on the revenue or customs authorities, as third parties.

中英仲裁法比较研究
A Comparative Study of the Chinese Arbitration
Law and the Arbitration Laws of the UK

the parties request this or not.① If the dispute is settled by the parties themselves, the tribunal may make an agreed award only at their request.② It can
be appreciated that, where the dispute is settled through mediation by the
tribunal, an agreed award will be issued even if one of the parties requests
otherwise. In this situation, the autonomy of the parties is damaged. Therefore, I suggest that Chinese law could adopt the approach of either the Model Law or the 1996 Act and provide that an agreed award should be made only if both parties have so agreed, and one or both of them have requested the
tribunal to do so.

4. Default Awards

Model Law. Article 25 of the Model Law provides that unless otherwise
agreed by the parties, if without showing sufficient cause, the respondent
fails to communicate his statement of defence in accordance with Article
23(1), the arbitral tribunal shall continue the proceedings without treating
such failure in itself as an admission of the claimant's allegation.③ If any party fails to appear at a hearing or to produce documentary evidence, the arbitral tribunal may continue the proceedings and make the award on the evidence before it.④

1996 Act. Section 41 of the 1996 Act states that the parties are free to a-
gree on the powers of the tribunal in case of a party's failure to do something
necessary for the proper and expeditious conduct of the arbitration.⑤If there
is no such agreement,⑥ if without showing sufficient cause, a party fails to

---

① Article 51 of the PRC Arbitration Law 2017; Article 40(6) of the CIETAC Arbitration Rules (2015).
② Article 49 of the PRC Arbitration Law 2017.
③ Article 25(b) of the Model Law.
④ Article 25(c) of the Model Law.
⑤ Section 41(1) of the 1996 Act.
⑥ Section 41(2) of the 1996 Act.

attend or be represented at an oral hearing of which due notice was given, ①
or where matters are to be dealt with in writing, fails after due notice to
submit written evidence or make written submissions, the tribunal may continue the proceedings in the absence of that party or, as the case may be,
without any written evidence or submissions on his behalf, and may make an
award on the basis of the evidence before it. ②

   Chinese Law. Under Chinese arbitration law, the tribunal may also
make default awards. Unlike the Model Law and the 1996 Act, the parties
have no freedom to agree on the powers of the tribunal in case of a party's
failure to do something necessary for the proper and expeditious conduct of
the arbitration. To protect the autonomy of the parties, I suggest that the
Chinese arbitration law should allow the parties to make their own agreement as to the powers of the tribunal in such cases.

C. The Substance of Awards

1. Process of making awards

[The principle of majority rule]

Model Law. Article 29 provides that in arbitral proceedings with more
than one arbitrator, any decision of the arbitral tribunal shall be made, unless otherwise agreed by the parties, by a majority of all its members. However, questions of procedure may be decided by a presiding arbitrator, if so
authorized by the parties or all members of the arbitral tribunal. The Analytical Commentary states that this does not mean that obviate the need for all
arbitrators to take part in the deliberations, or at least be afforded the op-

---

① Section 41(4)(b) of the 1996 Act.
② Section 41(4)(b) of the 1996 Act.

中英仲裁法比较研究
A Comparative Study of the Chinese Arbitration
Law and the Arbitration Laws of the UK

portunity to do so.① It is noteworthy that the Model Law does not indicate how an award is to be made if there is no majority. It has been suggested that one disadvantage of this is that in the event of three different opinions being held, the presiding arbitrator may be tempted to agree to a judicially dubious solution in order to attain the necessary majority. More problematically, situations may arise where no award is made, leading to a total waste of time and expense.② Yet on the other hand, it is more likely that all issues will be fully considered as a result of the arbitrators' need to reach agreement. This will make the parties more ready to accept the decision, thus reducing the likelihood of subsequent litigation or appeals.③ Moreover, the non-mandatory character of Article 29 would permit the parties, where the arbitral tribunal was unable to reach a decision, to authorize a presiding arbitrator to decide alone.④ It should be noted that the principle of majority rule also applies to an agreed award.

1996 Act. Section 20 of the 1996 Act provides that where the parties have agreed that there is to be a chairman, they are free to agree what the functions of the chairman are to be in relation to the making of decisions, or-

---

① Doc. A/CN. 9/264, p.64, para.2. A majority view at the second session of the Working Group favoured an express statement that all arbitrators must have had an opportunity to participate in the deliberations, although under another view this condition was self-evident. (Doc. A/CN. 9/232, para.138). Language in accordance with the majority view was included in a draft provision considered by the Working Group at its fourth session, which adopted a simplified version omtting that language (Doc. A/CN. 9/245, paras. 101-102).

② Doc. A/CN. 9/263, para.43, Article 29, para. 1. Korea suggested that in cases where no majority can be obtained, the arbitration agreement shall come to an end.

③ Doc. A/CN. 9/SR. 327, para.48.

④ Doc. A/CN. 9/SR. 327, para.50. The Analytical Commentary had mentioned as examples of this flexibility that parties might authorize a presiding arbitrator, if no majority can be reached, to case the decisive vote, or to decide as if he were the sole arbitrator. They might also, for quantum decisions, agree on a formula for the calculation of the decisive amount (Doc. A/CN. 9/ 264, p.64, para.3).

ders and awards. If or to the extent that there is no such agreement, decisions, orders and awards shall be made by all or a majority of the arbitrators (including the chairman). The view of the chairman shall prevail in relation to a decision, order or award in respect of which there is neither unanimity nor a majority of the arbitrators. Section 22 states that where the parties agree that there shall be two or more arbitrators with no chairman or umpire, the parties are free to agree how the tribunal is to make decisions, orders and awards. If there is no such agreement, decisions, orders and awards shall be made by all or a majority of the arbitrators. There would be a deadlock where a tribunal comprising an even number of arbitrators is evenly divided in respect of a matter. However, the parties have nothing to gain from agreeing a panel with an equal number of arbitrators or from not providing for a chairman or umpire, thus deadlock is unlikely to happen in practice.

Chinese Law. Under Chinese arbitration law, an arbitral award is made according to the opinion of the majority, and where there is no majority the Chief arbitrator decides. This is a mandatory rule and the parties cannot agree otherwise. On the surface, the autonomy of the parties seems to be compromised here. However, in cases of deadlock the only practical solution is to entrust the decision to one arbitrator. Since there is no "presiding arbitrator" in Chinese law, the Chief arbitrator appointed by both parties or the arbitration agency would most likely be chosen to make the decision. In other words, where a majority vote cannot be reached, the parties are very unlikely to make any other agreement than asking the Chief arbitrator to decide. Their choice will mirror the law, so that in reality the law does not infringe their autonomy.

[Dissenting opinions]

Model Law. The question of how to deal with dissenting opinions was not addressed in the Model Law. The opinion is therefore that this is a matter to be determined pursuant to Article 19 by the parties or, failing deter-

中英仲裁法比较研究
A Comparative Study of the Chinese Arbitration
Law and the Arbitration Laws of the UK

mination by them, by the arbitral tribunal.① Thus, the Model Law left the problem to be concretely resolved by the parties and national law.

1996 Act. The 1996 Act does not contain any rule as to how to deal with the dissenting opinions.

Chinese Law. Chinese arbitration law provides that an arbitral award shall be decided by the majority of the arbitrators and the views of the minority can be written down in the record. Where a majority vote cannot be reached, the award shall be decided on the basis of the opinion of the chief arbitrator. The CIETAC Rules provide that in either case, dissenting opinions shall be docketed into the file and may be attached to the award, but shall not form part of the award. The Arbitration Law itself does not indicate whether the written dissenting opinion or the written opinion of other arbitrators shall be docketed into the file or may be attached to the award, or shall form a part of the award, leaving this problem to be dealt with by the Arbitration Rules of Arbitral Agencies. It does not say whether, where the award is decided based on the opinion of the chief arbitrator, the other arbitrators' opinion should be written into the record. This is an apparent omission, and such a requirement should be added to the Arbitration Law.

[Signature]

Model Law. Article 31 (1) provides that the award shall be made in writing and signed by the arbitrator(s). In proceedings with more than one arbitrator, the signatures of the majority of the members of the arbitral tribunal shall suffice, provided that the reason for any omitted signature is stated. It was said that the requirement that the reason for any omitted sig-

---

① Article 19 of the Model Law provides that subject to the provisions of this Law, the parties are free to agree on the procedure to be followed by the arbitral tribunal in conducting the proceedings. Failing such agreement, the arbitral tribunal may, subject to the provisions of this Law, conduct the arbitration in such manner as it considers appropriate. The power conferred upon the arbitral tribunal includes the power to determine the admissibility, relevance, materiality and weight of any evidence.

nature be stated is a compromise between two extreme positions: on the one hand, that the majority of the arbitrators could take any decision they wished; on the other, that all the arbitrators must sign an award.[1] The Analytical Commentary noted that there were two different possible causes for a missing signature. The first was that after the award was finalized an arbitrator died, became physically unable to sign or could not be reached. The second possible reason was that an arbitrator dissented from the award and refused to sign.[2] Where the award is made by a majority, while it is possible for only the majority to sign, all the arbitrators may wish to sign. In that case it will be impossible for the parties to discover who was in the majority and who dissented, or indeed that the award was not unanimous, unless (as often happens) the award otherwise identifies the dissentient. Article 30(2) provides that an award on agreed terms shall be made in accordance with the provisions of Article 31 and shall state that it is an award. Such an award has the same status and effect as any other award on the merits. Article 33(5) provides that the provisions of Article 31 shall also apply to a correction or interpretation of the award or to an additional award.

1996 Act. Section 52(3) provides that the award shall be in writing and signed by all the arbitrators or all those assenting to the award. It can be seen that both the Model Law and the 1996 Act require the arbitrators assenting to the award to sign the award. The difference between the Model Law and the 1996 Act is that the former requires the reason for an omitted signature to be stated, whereas the latter has no such requirement.

Chinese Law. Under Chinese arbitration Law, minority arbitrators need not sign the award, and no reason for any omitted signature is needed. However as Chinese arbitration law requires dissenting opinions to be recorded, the reason for an omitted signature is obvious in such a case. Yet Chinese ar-

---

① Doc. A/CN. 9/ SR. 328, paras.25-26.

② Broches, Aron, Commentary on the Model Law on International Commercial Arbitration, Boston: Kluwer Law and Taxation Publishers,1990,162.

中英仲裁法比较研究
A Comparative Study of the Chinese Arbitration
Law and the Arbitration Laws of the UK

bitration law might follow the Model Law in requiring that the award should state the reason for an omitted signature if that reason is that the arbitrator concerned died, became physically unable to sign or could not be reached. Such a provision is needed where there is no dissenting opinion contained in the award, but only two of the arbitrators have signed it. In this case parties would probably want to know why the third signature is missing, and I submit that they are entitled to know the reason.

[Provisions regarding time limits for making awards]

Model Law. There is no such provision in the Model Law.

1996 Act. While the 1996 Act does not provide a time limit for making an award, Section 50(1) provides that, unless otherwise agreed by the parties, the court may extend any agreed time limit. Section 50(2) provides that an application for an order under this section may be made by the tribunal (upon notice to the parties), or by any party to the proceedings (upon notice to the tribunal and the other parties), but only after exhausting any available arbitral process for obtaining an extension of time. Under certain institutional rules awards must be made within certain time limits, and provision is made for extensions to be granted by the institution. It will be rare, therefore, for such a matter to come before the court since it will normally have been considered by the institution first.[1] The court may only grant an extension if it satisfied that a substantial injustice would result if it did not do so.[2] It may extend the limit for such period and on such terms as it thinks fit, and may do so whether or not the time previously fixed (by or under the agreement or by a previous order) has expired.[3] The leave of the court is required for any appeal from a decision of the court under this section.[4] It is

---

[1] Harris, Bruce/Planterose, Rowan & Tecks, Jonathan, The Arbitration Act 1996: A Commentary, 3rd ed. Malden: Blackwell Publishing, Inc.,2003,196.

[2] Section 50(3) of the 1996 Act.

[3] Section 50(4) of the 1996 Act.

[4] Section 50(5) of the 1996 Act.

difficult to see how the effect of Section 50 differs from that of Section 79, which generally empowers the court to extend any time limit in relation to any matter relating to the arbitral proceedings.

Chinese Law. Under Chinese arbitration law, the court has no power to extend the time limit for making an award. Since giving the court such power subject to strict qualifications provides the parties with another means of recourse, with no possibility of adverse effects, I suggest that Chinese law should follow the lead of the 1996 Act in this instance. Since the parties may agree to exclude this power, their autonomy is not infringed.

[Form of agreed awards]

Model Law. Article 30(2) states that an award on agreed terms shall be made in accordance with the provisions of Article 31, i. e. just like any other award.

1996 Act. The effect of Section 51(1) and(4)[1] is that, unless otherwise agreed by the parties, the provisions of Section 52(directing the form an award is to take) apply to an agreed award.

Chinese Law. Chinese arbitration law makes no provision for this matter, although in practice, agreed awards are made in the same way as other awards. It is suggested that Chinese arbitration law should adopt the approach of the Model Law and the 1996 Act, by making it clear that the provisions which apply to the form of awards also apply to the form of an agreed award.

2. Content of awards

Model Law. Article 31(2) provides that an award shall state the reasons upon which it is based, unless the parties have agreed that no reasons are to be given or the award is an award on agreed terms under Article 30. In the

---

[1]　Section 51(1) of the 1996 Act provides that if during arbitral proceedings the parties settle the dispute, the following provisions apply unless otherwise agreed by the parties. Section 51(4) provides that the following provisions of this Part relating to awards (Section 52 to 58) apply to an agreed award.

中英仲裁法比较研究
A Comparative Study of the Chinese Arbitration
Law and the Arbitration Laws of the UK

Analytical Commentary, the Secretariat suggests that an agreement that no reasons are to be given may be implied, for example, by submitting a dispute to an established arbitration institution which is known not to contemplate the giving of reasons, and or which operates a practice of stating the reasons in a separate and confidential document.[①] Article 31(3) states that the award shall state its date and the place of arbitration as determined in accordance with Article 20(1). The award shall be deemed to have been made at that place. Article 20(1) provides that the parties are free to agree on the place of arbitration. Failing such agreement, the place of arbitration shall be determined by the arbitral tribunal having regard to the circumstances of the case, including the convenience of the parties. At the Commission session, it was proposed to extend the second sentence of Article 31(3) to the date of the award, and to have it read, "the award shall be deemed to have been made at that place and on that date".[②] It was stated in support that the date of the award might have legal implications with regard, for example, to the payment of interest "from the date of the award",[③] and that since the award might be circulated among the arbitrators by mail for their signature, it would be difficult to determine its date. However, the prevailing view was that the date fixed in the award by the arbitral tribunal should be open to re-

---

① Doc. A/CN. 9/264, p.67, Article 31, para.3. The Analytical Commentary and the report of the first session of the Working Group (n. 31.6 supra) speak in terms of a "waiver" of the requirement that reasons are to be given. In my submission that is too limited a characterization: if an agreement states that no reasons are to be given it precludes the giving of reasons.

② Doc. A/CN. 9/SR. 328, paras.29 and 33.

③ The date of the award has, on the other hand, no significance for the application of the Law. Time limits, including the limit for an application under Article 34 for setting an award aside, run, not from the date of award; but from the date on which the party received it. See Broches, Aron, Commentary on the Model Law on International Commercial Arbitration, Boston: Kluwer Law and Taxation Publishers, 1990, 164.

buttal.①

1996 Act. Section 52(1) gives the parties the freedom to agree on the form of an award. In the absence of such agreement, the award shall contain reasons, unless it is an agreed award.② It is increasingly recognized that those making such significant decisions are expected to explain the reasons for them. It should be noted that an agreement not to have reasons would exclude the jurisdiction of the court to determine a preliminary point of law,③ or to entertain an appeal on a question of law arising out of the a-ward.④ Section 52(5) states that the award shall state the seat of the arbitration and the date when the award is made. Section 53 provides that unless otherwise agreed by the parties, where the seat of the arbitration is in England, any award in the proceedings shall be treated as made there, regardless of where it was signed, despatched or delivered to any of the parties. The seat of arbitration means the juridical seat of the arbitration designated by the parties to the arbitration agreement, or by an arbitral or other institution or person vested by the parties with powers in that regard, or by the arbitral tribunal if so authorized by the parties, or determined, in absence of any such designation, having regard to the parties' agreement and all the

---

① Commission Report, para.255.

② Section 52(4) of the 1996 Act.

③ Section 45(1) of the 1996 Act provides that unless otherwise agreed by the parties, the court may on the application of a party to arbitral proceedings (upon notice to the other parties) determine any question of law arising in the course of the proceedings which the court is satisfied substantially affects the rights of one or more of the parties. An agreement to dispense with reasons for the tribunal's award shall be considered an agreement to exclude the court's jurisdiction under this section.

④ Section 69(1) of the 1996 Act provides that unless otherwise agreed by the parties, a party to arbitral proceedings may (upon notice to the other parties and to the tribunal) appeal to the court on a question of law arising out of an award made in the proceedings. An agreement to dispense with reasons for the tribunal's award shall be considered an agreement to exclude the court's jurisdiction under this section.

中英仲裁法比较研究
A Comparative Study of the Chinese Arbitration
Law and the Arbitration Laws of the UK

relevant circumstances.① Section 54(1) indicates that unless otherwise a-
greed by the parties, the tribunal may decide what is to be taken to be the
date on which the award was made. The "decision" may not be straightforward in all cases. Where there is more than one arbitrator, the award is likely to circulate, and may even go overseas. Signatures may be days or weeks
apart. It will usually be most practical for the arbitrators either to ask the
last signatory to date the award (as has in fact been common practice hither-
to), or to return it to the chairman, who will do so.② Thus Section 54(2)
continues to provide that in the absence of any such decision, the date of the
award shall be taken to be the date on which it is signed by the arbitrator or,
where more than one arbitrator signs the award, by the last of them.

Section 51 provides that, unless otherwise agreed by the parties, an a-
greed award shall state that it is an award of the tribunal,③ and that Section
52 to Section 54 apply to an agreed award.④ The requirement for stating it is
an award of the tribunal will be satisfied by reciting the appointment of the
arbitrator(s) and terms of the award, and by the signature(s) of the arbitra-
tor(s).⑤

Chinese Law. Under Chinese arbitration law, the date of award is required to be contained in an award, but it is silent regarding how to determine the date of award.⑥ The CIETAC Rules (2015) requires an award to
contain "the place of award"⑦, but do indicate how to determine the place of

---

① Section 3 of the 1996 Act.

② Harris, Bruce/Planterose, Rowan & Tecks, Jonathan, The Arbitration Act
1996: A Commentary, 3rd ed. Malden: Blackwell Publishing, Inc., 2003,207.

③ Section 51(3) of the 1996 Act.

④ Section 51(4) of the 1996 Act.

⑤ Harris, Bruce/Planterose, Rowan & Tecks, Jonathan, The Arbitration Act
1996: A Commentary, 3rd ed. Malden: Blackwell Publishing, Inc.,2003,200.

⑥ Article 54 of the PRC Arbitration Law 2017; Article 43(2) of the CIETAC Arbitration Rules (2015).

⑦ Article 43(2) of the Arbitration Rules of CIETAC (2015).

arbitration. Although the Rules does not explicitly provide that the place of award is actually the place of arbitration, that is the case in practice. To make the Rules clearer, I suggest that they should use the term "place of arbitration" concurrently, instead of using "place of arbitration" in one provision and "place of award" in another. Also, Chinese arbitration law should follow the 1996 Act and provide how to determine the date of arbitration. Chinese arbitration law does not indicate whether the provisions regarding the content of awards apply to the making of an agreed award. It is, therefore, suggested that Chinese law should make it clear that the provisions which apply to the making of an award also apply to the making of an agreed award, as under the 1996 Act.

3. Remedies of awards

Model Law. The Model Law does not mention remedies. This problem has been left to be resolved by the rules of law chosen by the parties as applicable to the substance of the dispute.[①]

1996 Act. Section 48(1) provides that the parties are free to agree on the powers exercisable by the arbitral tribunal as regards remedies. These powers are not restricted to those that are available to the court in court proceedings. It is therefore possible for the parties to agree that the tribunal should have different, and even greater, powers than the court. They may, for example, agree that the tribunal should be able to use a remedy on different grounds from those on which it would be available to the court; or that the tribunal should be able to adopt remedies that are known only in other jurisdictions — for example, punitive damages; or that the tribunal should be able to adopt remedies suitable to the type of contract — such as the power to "open up, review and revise certificates" found in many build-

---

① Harris, Bruce/Planterose, Rowan & Tecks, Jonathan, The Arbitration Act 1996: A Commentary, 3rd ed. Malden: Blackwell Publishing, Inc.,2003,192.

中英仲裁法比较研究
A Comparative Study of the Chinese Arbitration
Law and the Arbitration Laws of the UK

ing contracts.[①] Where the parties have not agreed on the powers exercisable by the arbitral tribunal, the tribunal has the following powers.[②] It may make a declaration as to any matter to be determined in the proceedings,[③] or order the payment of a sum of money in any currency[④](the most commonly used remedy). It also has the same powers as the court to order a party to do or refrain from doing anything, and to order specific performance of a contract (other than a contract relating to land), and to order the rectification, setting aside or cancellation of a deed or other document.[⑤] Under English law the power to order a party to do or refrain from doing anything is discretionary. It is to be noted that there are limits on the remedies which can be awarded by arbitrators. Where there is no authorization under the parties' agreement under either Section 46(1)[⑥] or Section 48(1) of the 1996 Act, the arbitrators cannot rewrite the contract between the parties, e.g., by depriving a buyer of goods of the contractual right to reject them.

Again, a remedy may not contravene public policy in a manner which may affect a third party or society as a whole, e.g., by authorizing a criminal act[⑦] or requiring the invasion of the rights of a third party.[⑧] If the tribunal does decide to make the order, it must be careful to set out clearly what the respondent party must do.[⑨] Specific performance is a discretionary remedy

---

① Harris, Bruce/Planterose, Rowan & Tecks, Jonathan, The Arbitration Act 1996: A Commentary, 3rd ed. Malden: Blackwell Publishing, Inc.,2003,190.

② Section 48(2) of the 1996 Act.

③ Section 48(3) of the 1996 Act.

④ Section 48(4) of the 1996 Act.

⑤ Section 48(5) of the 1996 Act.

⑥ Section 46(1) of the 1996 Act provides that the arbitral tribunal shall decide the dispute — (a) in accordance with the law chosen by the parties as applicable to the substance of the dispute, or(b) if the parties so agree, in accordance with such other considerations as are agreed by them or determined by the tribunal.

⑦ Wood v. Griffith (1818) 1 Swanst 55.

⑧ Alder v. Savill (1814) 5 Taunt 454. Turner v. Swainson (1836) 1M & W 572.

⑨ Redland Bricks v. Morris [1970] AC 652.

by which a party in breach of contract is ordered to complete its perform-ance. Its usefulness arises when the subject matter of the contract is unique or not readily available elsewhere, such as a rare book or a commodity that is in short supply.[1] The tribunal has the same powers as the court to order rectification.[2] Rectification is a remedy by which a written contract that does not set out the true agreement between the parties in some important respect may be amended to reflect that agreement. It therefore operates to correct a mistake on the part of the relevant parties that is common to them all. The remedies of setting aside or cancellation of contracts may be appropriate where other kinds of mistake are alleged. Such remedies may also apply where agreements are challenged by allegations of misrepresentation, du-ress, illegality and so on.[3] One problem not expressly dealt with by the 1996 Act is how a court would, on an appeal on a point of law under the Ar-bitration Act 1996, Section 69, treat the exercise of a consensual power to a-ward a remedy not open to the court itself, as there are no established judi-cial criteria against which the exercise of such a power can be tested. It must be assumed that, provided that the arbitrators have been correct in law in holding that a right has been infringed, the remedy for the infringement is a matter for them alone. A further potential problem is posed by Section 66 of the Arbitration Act 1996, which allows the court to enforce an award as if it were an order of the court. It is difficult on the surface for a court to enforce an award where the remedy is not one which could have been awarded by the court itself. However, the problem can be overcome by the court granting a

---

[1]   Harris, Bruce/Planterose, Rowan &. Tecks, Jonathan, The Arbitration Act 1996: A Commentary, 3rd ed. Malden: Blackwell Publishing, Inc.,2003,192.

[2]   Section 48(5)(c) of the 1996 Act.

[3]   Harris, Bruce/Planterose, Rowan &. Tecks, Jonathan, The Arbitration Act 1996: A Commentary, 3rd ed. Malden: Blackwell Publishing, Inc.,2003,192.

中英仲裁法比较研究
A Comparative Study of the Chinese Arbitration
Law and the Arbitration Laws of the UK

mandatory injunction enforceable by contempt proceedings.①

Chinese Law. There are no comparable provisions under Chinese arbitration law, although in practice, arbitrators use the similar remedies to those provided by the 1996 Act. To aid the development of Chinese arbitration law, it is suggested to follow the example of the 1996 Act and expressly indicate that the parties are, free to agree on the remedies available to the tribunal, and where the parties have no such agreement, the tribunal may make a declaration as to any matter to be determined in the proceedings, ② or order the payment of a sum of money in any currency, or order a party to do or refrain from doing anything, and to order specific performance of a contract, or order the rectification, setting aside or cancellation of a deed or other document.

4. Delivery of awards

Model Law. Article 31 (4) provides that after the award is made, a signed copy shall be delivered to each party.

1996 Act. Section 55 provides that the parties are at liberty to agree what requirements there should be for the tribunal to notify them of the award, but if there is no such agreement, the award shall be notified to the parties by service on them of copies of the award without delay after the award is made. This is without prejudice to the power conferred by Section 56 to withhold the award except upon full payment of the fees and expenses of the arbitrators. Section 56 is mandatory, and may not be excluded by the parties. Section 56(2) provides that if the tribunal refuses on that ground to deliver an award, on an application by a party, the court may order the award to be released against the applicant paying into court the full amount claimed, or such lesser amount as the court may specify. This deals with the

---

① The solution suggested by the SPC of Tasmania in Ridler v. Waters [2001] TASSC 98.

② Section 48(3) of the 1996 Act.

possibility of a grossly excessive claim by the tribunal making it impossible for a party to obtain the award.① In that case the amount of the fees and expenses properly payable shall be determined by such means and upon such terms as the court may direct.② Out of the money paid into court there shall be paid out such fees and expenses as may be found to be properly payable, with any surplus being refunded to the applicant.③ The amount of fees and expenses properly payable is the amount the applicant is liable to pay under Section 28④ or any agreement relating to the payment of the arbitrators⑤. It should be noted that no such application to the court may be made where there is a possibility of appeal or review of the arbitrators' fees and expenses by some other arbitral process, for instance by applying to a relevant institution or appellate arbitral tribunal.⑥ In Section 56, "arbitrators" includes an

---

①　Section 56(2)(a) of the 1996 Act.

②　Section 56(2)(b) of the 1996 Act.

③　Section 56(2)(c) of the 1996 Act.

④　Section 28(Joint and several liability of parties to arbitrators for fees and expenses) provides that(1) The parties are jointly and severally liable to pay to the arbitrators such reasonable fees and expenses (if any) as are appropriate in the circumstances. (2) Any party may apply to the court (upon notice to the other parties and to the arbitrators) which may order that the amount of the arbitrators' fees and expenses shall be considered and adjusted by such means and upon such as it may direct. (3) If the application is made after any amount has been paid to the arbitrators by way of fees or expenses, the court may order the repayment of such amount (if any) as is shown to be excessive, but shall not do so unless it is shown that it is reasonable in the circumstances to order repayment. (4) The above provisions have effect subject to any order of the court under Section 24(4) or 25(3) (b) (order as to entitlement to fees or expenses in case of removal or resignation of arbitrator). (5) Nothing in this section affects any liability of a party to any other party to pay all or any of the costs of the arbitration(see Sections 59 to 65) or any contractual right of an arbitrator to payment of his fees and expenses. (6) In this section references to arbitrators include an arbitrator who has ceased to act and an umpire who has not replaced the other arbitrators.

⑤　Section 56 (3) of the 1996 Act.

⑥　Section 56(4) of the 1996 Act.

中英仲裁法比较研究
A Comparative Study of the Chinese Arbitration
Law and the Arbitration Laws of the UK

umpire who has not replaced the other arbitrators, and arbitrators who have ceased to act.① Section 56 also applies to any arbitral or other institution or person vested by the parties with powers in relation to the delivery of the tribunal's award. In such a case, "fees and expenses of the arbitrators" shall be construed as including the fees and expenses of that institution or person.② The leave of the court is required for any appeal from a decision of the court under Section 56.③ Nothing in this section shall be construed as excluding an application under section 28 where payment has been made to the arbitrators in order to obtain the award. Parties thus have a choice between an application to the court under Section 56(2), or the payment of the full amount to the arbitrators and subsequent challenge under Section 28.

Chinese Law. Chinese arbitration law requires that awards shall be delivered to the parties, without explicitly requiring the delivery shall be made without delay. To improve Chinese arbitration law, it would be beneficial for it to demand explicitly that the award be delivered "without delay". In the Chinese arbitration law, the tribunal does not have the power to withhold an award in case of non-payment and there is no other method to force the parties to make payment. Since withholding an award can force the parties to make payment, the Chinese arbitration law might usefully adopt the stance of the 1996 Act, and provide that the tribunal has the power to withhold an arbitral award upon non-payment, and that in the case, the court may order to release the award requiring the applicant to pay into the court the full amount or such lesser amount as the court specifies, surplus of which shall be refunded to the applicant.

5. Correction of awards

[Computational, clerical or typographical errors]

Model Law. Article 33(1)(a) provides that within thirty days of receipt

---

① Section 56(5) of the 1996 Act.
② Section 56(6) of the 1996 Act.
③ Section 56(7) of the 1996 Act.

of the award, unless another period of time has been agreed upon by the parties, a party, with notice to the other party, may request the arbitral tribunal to correct in the award any error in computation, any clerical or typographical error or any errors of similar nature. If the arbitral tribunal considers the request to be justified, it shall make the correction or give the interpretation within thirty days of receipt of the request. The correction shall form part of the award. The arbitral tribunal may extend, if necessary, the period of time within which it shall make a correction, interpretation or an additional award[1] and may correct any error of the type referred to above on its own initiative within thirty days of the day of the award.[2] As to content and form, the provisions of Article 31 apply to a correction.[3] The provision of Article 18 that the parties shall be treated with equality and each party shall be given a full opportunity of presenting his case presumably implies that before the tribunal makes a correction, it shall give the other parties a full opportunity of making representation. However, it is not completely clear that that is how Article 18 is to be interpreted.

1996 Act. Unlike the Model Law, Section 57 of the 1996 Act gives the parties the freedom to agree on the powers of the tribunal to correct an award.[4] Where there is no such agreement, under Section 57(3), acting either on its own initiative or on the application of a party, the tribunal may correct an award so as to remove any clerical mistake or error arising from an accidental slip or omission.[5] The tribunal must give the other parties a reasonable opportunity to make representations before exercising any of these powers. Any correction of an award shall form part of the award.[6] The

---

[1]   Article 33(4) of the Model Law.
[2]   Article 33(2) of the Model Law.
[3]   Article 33(5) of the Model Law.
[4]   Section 57(1) of the 1996 Act.
[5]   Section 57(3)(a) of the 1996 Act.
[6]   Section 57(7) of the 1996 Act.

中英仲裁法比较研究
A Comparative Study of the Chinese Arbitration
Law and the Arbitration Laws of the UK

meaning of "the other parties" is plain where the application is made by one party. It presumably means "all parties" where the tribunal acts on its own initiative. This requirement accords with the tribunal's duty under Section 33 (1)(a) to act fairly and give each party a reasonable opportunity of putting his case. Section 57(4) provides that any application for the exercise of those powers must be made within 28 days of the date of the award or such longer period as the parties may agree. Section 57(5) indicates that any correction of an award shall be made within 28 days of the date the application was received by the tribunal or, where the correction is made by the tribunal on its own initiative, within 28 days of the date of the award or, in either case, such longer period as the parties may agree. The "date of award" may not always be the date of the (last) signature, but it will often be a date earlier than receipt of notification of the award, and will almost always be earlier than receipt of a copy of it. Thus, in practice, the applicant will have fewer than 28 days in which to apply.① However, the time may be extended by the court under Section 79.②

---

① Harris, Bruce/Planterose, Rowan & Tecks, Jonathan, The Arbitration Act 1996: A Commentary, 3rd ed. Malden: Blackwell Publishing, Inc., 2003,215.

② Section 79 of the 1996 Act provides: (1) Unless the parties otherwise agree, the court may by order extend any time limit agreed by them in relation to any matter relating to the arbitral proceedings or specified in any provision of this Part having effect in default of such agreement. This section does not apply to a time limit to which section 12 applies (power of court to extend time for beginning arbitral proceedings. (2) An application for an order may be made — (a) by any party to the arbitral proceedings (upon notice to the other parties and to the tribunal), or (b) by the arbitral tribunal (upon notice to the parties). (3) The court shall not exercise its power to extend a time limit unless it is satisfied — (a) that any available recourse to the tribunal, or to any arbitral or other institution or person vested by the parties with power in that regard, has first been exhausted, and (b) that a substantial injustice would otherwise be done. (4) The court's power under this section may be exercised whether or not the time has already expired. (5) An order under this section may be made on such terms as the court thinks fit. (6) The leave of the court is required for any appeal from a decision of the court under this section.

Chinese Law. Under Chinese arbitration law, the parties are not allowed to agree that any party may not apply to the tribunal to correct such errors, as this right is given by a mandatory rule. In practice it would be very rare for the parties to agree to exclude this right, as the parties would gain nothing from making such agreement. Additionally, the party autonomy would be taken to an extreme if it is elevated over the consideration that errors shall be corrected. The Chinese arbitration does not allow the parties to agree time limits for applications, and neither the tribunal nor the court has power to extend such time limits. I suggest that the approach taken by the 1996 Act is dictated by the fact that the time limit it sets starts from the date of award, rather than the date of receipt of the award, which means that a party has fewer than 28 days in which to apply. Therefore, it is unnecessary for Chinese arbitration law to give the tribunal and the court the power to extend the time for application, as its time limit starts from the date of receipt of award. Chinese arbitration law neither requires the applicant to notify the other parties nor gives the other parties a reasonable opportunity to make representations to the tribunal before a correction is made. The Model Law requires the party to notify the other parties when it makes an application, and the 1996 Act requires the parties to be given an opportunity to make representation before the tribunal. In my view, the approach of the 1996 Act in this respect is more better than that of the Model Law, as where the other parties are given a reasonable opportunity to make representations, they will certainly be notified first and they also have an opportunity to make representations, which is not allowed in the Model Law. Thus Chinese arbitration law would benefit from adopting the approach of the 1996 Act. In Chinese arbitration law, the parties are free to make their own agreement regarding the time limit for a tribunal making a correction. To avoid parties agreeing upon a period of time which is unreasonably short and adversely affects the conduct of the arbitrators, I suggest that Chinese law should give the parties the right only to agree upon a longer period of time, as the 1996

中英仲裁法比较研究
A Comparative Study of the Chinese Arbitration
Law and the Arbitration Laws of the UK

Act does. Moreover, Chinese arbitration law gives neither the arbitral tribunal nor the court the power to extend the time in which it shall make a correction. In my view, if the arbitral tribunal has the power to extend the time, the power would potentially be abused and unnecessary delay would be caused. Therefore, it is better for the Chinese arbitration law to require the arbitral tribunal to apply to the court to extend the time where it considers the time limit set by the law too short, as the 1996 Act does.

[Omissions]

Model Law. Article 33(3) provides that unless otherwise agreed by the parties, a party, with notice to the other, may request, within thirty days of receipt of the award, the arbitral tribunal to make an additional award as to claims presented in the arbitral proceedings but omitted from the award. If the arbitral tribunal considers the request to be justified, it shall make the additional award within sixty days. Article 33(4) gives the arbitral tribunal the power to extend the period of time within which it shall make an additional award. The provisions of Article 31 apply to the content and form of an additional award.① Again, it is not clear whether Article 18 implies that the arbitral tribunal shall give the other parties an opportunity to make representations.

1996 Act. Section 57(3) provides that the tribunal may, on its own initiative or on the application of a party, make an additional award in respect of any claim (including a claim for interest or costs) which was presented to the tribunal but was not dealt with in the award. Section 57(4) indicates that any such application must be made within 28 days of the date of the award or such longer period as the parties may agree. The period may be extended by the court under Section 79. According to Section 57(6), any additional award shall be made within 56 days of the date of the original award or such longer period as the parties may agree. Again, this time limit may be ex-

---

① Article 33(5) of the Model Law.

tended by the court under Section 79. Before making an additional award, the other parties shall be afforded a reasonable opportunity to make representations to the arbitral tribunal.①

Chinese Law. Under Chinese arbitration law, the parties may not exclude the right of a party to apply for an additional award. I suggest that Chinese arbitration law should adopt the stance of the Model Law and the 1996 Act in allowing such exclusion, so that the autonomy of the parties would be protected. Again, Chinese arbitration law does not require that a party making such an application should notify all other parties. Nor does it require the tribunal to give the other parties an opportunity to make representations as under the 1996 Act. In my view, Chinese law would benefit from adopting the approach of the 1996 Act in this regard. Chinese arbitration law allows the parties agree on the time in which the arbitral tribunal shall make an additional award.

I suggest that it should only allow the parties to agree on a period of time longer than that laid down by law, as under the 1996 Act. Again, neither the arbitral tribunal nor the court may extend time limits under Chinese arbitration law. I suggest that it should allow the arbitral tribunal to apply to the court to extend such limits, where it considers the time limit set by the law too short, as under the 1996 Act.

[Interpretation]

Model Law. Article 33(1)(b) provides that within thirty days of receipt of the award, unless another period of time has been agreed upon by the parties, if so agreed by the parties, a party, with notice to the other, may request the arbitral tribunal to give an interpretation of a specific point or part of the award. If the arbitral tribunal considers the request to be justified, it shall give the interpretation within thirty days of receipt of the request. The interpretation shall form part of the award. Article 33(4) indicates that the

---

① Section 57(3) of the 1996 Act.

中英仲裁法比较研究
A Comparative Study of the Chinese Arbitration
Law and the Arbitration Laws of the UK

arbitral tribunal may extend, if necessary, the period of time within which it shall make an interpretation. In the drafting process it was proposed that this provision be restricted to interpretation "of the reasons on which the award is based" rather than of the dispositive part of the award.① Other delegates suggested its deletion,② since it was felt to encourage attempts on the part of both the winner and the loser to change the award, the former to seek to protect the award against annulment, the latter to lay a basis for recourse against the award. A compromise was reached on the basis that the provision can only be invoked with the agreement of both parties.③ The Chairman indicated that the phrase "if so agreed by the parties" meant that the parties should either have agreed before the award was made to allow the arbitral tribunal to interpret it, or should agree to ask for an interpretation after the award was made.④ It is uncertain whether the parties, by virtue of Article 18, should be given an opportunity of making representations before the tribunal interprets the award.

1996 Act. Section 57(3)(a) provides that where the parties have not agreed on the powers of the tribunal in this regard (which agreement might of course be to the effect that it shall have no powers), the tribunal may, on its own initiative, or on the application of a party, clarify or remove any ambiguity in the award. This power shall not be exercised without first affording the other parties a reasonable opportunity to make representations to the tribunal. Any application for the exercise of those powers must be made within 28 days of the date of the award or such longer period as the parties may a-

---

① Doc.A /CN.9 /263, 645, Article 33,para.1.

② Doc. A/CN. 9/SR. 329, para.41(Tanzania), 44(German Democratic Republic), 45(Finland), 49(Sweden), 50(Federal Republic of Germany) and 51(India).

③ Doc. A/CN. 9/SR. 329, para.45.

④ Broches, Aron, Commentary on the Model Law on International Commercial Arbitration, Boston: Kluwer Law and Taxation Publishers, 1990,175.

gree.① However, this time may be extended by the court under Section 79. Interpretation shall be made within 28 days of the date the application was received by the tribunal or, where the correction is made by the tribunal on its own initiative, within 28 days of the date of the award or, in either case, such longer period as the parties may agree.②

Chinese Law. Chinese arbitration law is silent on the issue of interpretation. I consider that it should adopt the approach of the 1996 Act and give the parties the power to ask the tribunal to interpret the award, subject to their right to agree to exclude the power. As regards the time limit for such application, Chinese law might adopt the approach of either the Model Law or the 1996 Act. Chinese arbitration law should require the tribunal to give the other parties a reasonable opportunity to make representations before making interpretation, and permit the arbitral tribunal make interpretations on its own initiative, as under the 1996 Act. It should also adopt the stance of the 1996 Act in setting a period within which the interpretation must be made, while allowing the parties to agree on a longer period and the court to extend that period upon application.

6. Effect of awards

[Binding effect and termination of the arbitral proceedings]

Model Law. Article 32(1) provides that the arbitral proceedings are terminated by the final award. The point of time of the termination of the arbitral proceedings may be relevant, for example, for the determination of the running of periods of limitation which, if suspended by the institution of arbitral proceedings, would resume upon their termination, or in terms of the possibility of instituting legal proceedings on the same dispute. An award will not fix that time with certainty, as its date is open to rebuttal.③ A

---

① Section 57(4) of the 1996 Act.
② Section 57(5) of the 1996 Act.
③ See Article 31 of the Model Law.

中英仲裁法比较研究
A Comparative Study of the Chinese Arbitration
Law and the Arbitration Laws of the UK

lengthy discussion arose about the desirability of adding a definition of the time when an award becomes binding and the criteria to be employed in such a definition. A number of delegates saw no need for such a provision, although some of them saw no objection thereto if a suitable definition were found. However, the proponents of a definition could not agree on the criteria to be employed. The two principal, possible criteria are the date of the award and the date on which the award is delivered to the parties. As discussed above, the date of the award is a difficult criterion to rely on, while the date of delivery would require proof of that fact. Ultimately, no provision was added, as it appeared to be impossible to satisfy all points of view.

The question when an award became binding then is to be determined by the law of the arbitral seat.[①] Article 32(3) indicates that the mandate of the arbitral tribunal terminates with the termination of the arbitral proceedings, subject to the provisions of Articles 33 and 34(4).[②] If the interpretation of the term "final award" includes the decisions of the arbitral tribunal pursuant to Articles 33 and 34(4), the references to those articles in Article 32(3) would have been unnecessary. Since Article 33 deals with correction and interpretation of the award and the making of additional awards, while Article 34(4) deals with the suspension of setting aside proceedings to allow the tribunal to take such steps as will eliminate the grounds for setting the award aside, the decision or award under those provisions would apparently be made later than a final award. Therefore, according to Article 32(1), where the tribunal is correcting or interpreting an award or making an addi-

---

① Broches, Aron, Commentary on the Model Law on International Commercial Arbitration, Boston: Kluwer Law and Taxation Publishers, 1990, 205.

② Article 34(4) of the Model Law provides that, the court, when set asked to set aside an award, may, where appropriate and so requested by a party, suspend the setting aside proceedings for a period of time determined by it in order to give the arbitral tribunal an opportunity to resume the arbitral proceedings or to take such other action as in the tribunal's opinion will eliminate the grounds for setting aside.

tional award, or court proceedings for setting aside an award are suspended, the arbitral proceedings have been terminated already. On the other hand, according to Article 32(3), in those cases, the mandate of the arbitral tribunal has not yet terminated. A conflict thus seemingly arises, but I suggest that the apparent conflict is eliminated if in cases where Articles 33 or 34(4) apply the time of termination of the arbitral proceedings is not regarded as the date of the "final award", but the time of the decision or award under those articles. Consequently, Article 32(1) must be read as if it provides that the arbitral proceedings "are terminated by the final award, subject to the provisions of Articles 33 and 34(4)... etc". In fact, if paragraph(1) had been so drafted, paragraph (3) could simply have read: "the mandate of the arbitral tribunal terminates with termination of the arbitral proceedings."

1996 Act. Section 58(1) provides that, unless otherwise agreed by the parties, an award made by the tribunal pursuant to an arbitration agreement is final and binding both on the parties and on any person's claiming through or under them. Section 58(2) indicates that this does not affect the right of a person to challenge the award by any available arbitral process of appeal or review or in accordance with the provisions of the Act. While the Act does not explicitly state when an award becomes binding, since it requires an award to contain its date, it is presumably that date on which the award becomes binding.

Chinese Law. Under Chinese arbitration law, an award is binding and the parties are not at liberty to agree otherwise. Chinese arbitration law provides clearly that an award becomes binding on the date on which the award is made. I consider it is rational to deprive the parties of the right to agree that the award is not binding, since it is surely the essence of an award that it finally disposes of the issue. Moreover, it is preferable for the law rules to make explicit provision as to when an award becomes binding, so that the parties and the arbitrators can easily be aware of that fact.

[Enforceability]

中英仲裁法比较研究
A Comparative Study of the Chinese Arbitration
Law and the Arbitration Laws of the UK

Model Law. Article 35(1) provides that an arbitral award, irrespective of the country in which it was made, upon application in writing to the competent court, shall be enforced subject to the provisions of Articles 35 and 36.① Article 35(2) continues that the party relying on an award or applying for its enforcement shall supply the duly authenticated original award or a duly certified copy thereof, and the original arbitration agreement referred to in Article 7 or a duly certified copy thereof. If the award or agreement is not made in an official language of the enforcing State, the party shall supply a duly certified translation thereof into such language. The Model Law does not prescribe the procedure to be followed in order to enforce an award, leaving this to be determined by national procedural law.② The Working Group agreed that the award should be enforced by the court designated by such procedural law "since the function envisaged here was one of enforcement for which States have well established systems of competence".③

1996 Act. Section 66(1) provides that an award may, by leave of the court, be enforced in the same manner as a judgment or order of the court to the same effect. Section 66(2) indicates that where leave is so given, judgment may be entered in terms of the award. Apparently, two cumulative methods of enforcement of an award are available under these sections. The first is that the applicant may apply directly to enforce the award in the same manner as a judgment. If leave is given, the applicant may seek execution of the award as if it were a judgment, without actually obtaining a judgment. The second method, where leave has been given, is to apply for an actual judgment in terms of the award. There may be advantages in the latter process. For example, the applicant seek enforcement or recognition of the judgment in a foreign court, or may rely on the judgment as a judicial reso-

---

① Article 36 of the Model Law —Grounds for refusing recognition or enforcement.

② Cf. Article Ⅲ of the New York Convention which provides for enforcement "in accordance with the rules of procedure of the territory where the award is relied upon".

③ Report of fourth session of Working Group, Doc. A/CN. 9/264, p.76, para.4.

lution of the issues that prevents any further action being brought in a foreign court.[1] Section 66(3) provides that leave to enforce an award shall not be given where, or to the extent that, the person against whom it is sought to be enforced shows that the tribunal lacked substantive jurisdiction to make the award.[2] Where that defence is successfully raised, the award cannot be enforced. Otherwise, the use of the word "may" indicates that the court is not required to order enforcement in every case, but has a discretion whether to grant or refuse leave. While there are a number of other obvious situations in which the person against whom enforcement is sought may successfully oppose the grant of leave to enforce the award, it was considered that the provision of a non-exhaustive list of such grounds would be unsatisfactory, since parties might think that matters not mentioned were not covered. Therefore, instead of providing a non-exhaustive list, the section gives the court an unfettered discretion to grant or withhold leave to enforce in relation to objections made on a basis other than lack of substantive jurisdiction.[3]

Chinese Law. Under Chinese arbitration law, the Model Law, and the 1996 Act, an award is enforceable and the parties are not allowed to agree otherwise. In terms of procedure, under Chinese law, the only method of enforcement by a party is applying to the court for enforcement. It has been seen that the 1996 Act provides two methods of enforcement. In light of the advantages of obtaining a judgment in terms of the award, Chinese arbitration law might benefit from adopting the approach of the 1996 Act to this issue.

[1]   Harris, Bruce/Planterose, Rowan & Tecks, Jonathan, The Arbitration Act 1996: A Commentary, 3rd ed. Malden: Blackwell Publishing, Inc., 2003,243.

[2]   Section 66(3) of the 1996 Act.

[3]   Harris, Bruce/Planterose, Rowan & Tecks, Jonathan, The Arbitration Act 1996: A Commentary, 3rd ed. Malden: Blackwell Publishing, Inc., 2003,243-244.

中英仲裁法比较研究
A Comparative Study of the Chinese Arbitration
Law and the Arbitration Laws of the UK

D. Powers to Make Other Orders

1. Power to make orders to terminate the arbitral proceedings

Model Law. Article 32(1) provides that the arbitral proceedings are terminated by an order of the arbitral tribunal, while Article 32(2) indicates
the circumstances in which the tribunal shall issue such an order. The first is
where the claimant withdraws his claim, unless the respondent objects
thereto and the arbitral tribunal recognizes a legitimate interest on his part in
obtaining a final settlement of the dispute. The second is where the parties a-
gree on the termination of the proceedings. While at one time it was proposed to allow the parties to terminate the proceedings by agreement, it was
conceded that as a matter of legal principle and in order to be consistent with
Articles 30, only the arbitral tribunal should have power to terminate the
proceedings, so that the agreement by the parties to terminate is thus made
one of the bases for an order to that effect of the arbitral tribunal.[①] The
third is where the arbitral tribunal finds that the continuation of the proceedings has for any other reason become unnecessary or impossible. It was not
clear why the arbitral tribunal, having made that finding, should nevertheless have the right to permit a continuation of the proceedings which could
only be a waste of time and money.

1996 Act. The 1996 Act does not address the above issue.

Chinese Law. In Chinese arbitration law, if the claimant withdraws his
claim before the arbitral tribunal is constituted, the Secretary-General of the
Arbitration agency shall decide whether to terminate the arbitral proceedings. If the claimant withdraws his claim after the arbitral tribunal is constituted, the tribunal shall decide whether to terminate the arbitral proceedings. In my view, the tribunal's discretion is too wide, as where the claimant
wants to withdraw the claim, if the respondent does not object and the arbi-

---

① Doc. A/CN. 9/SR. 329, para.26. It became subparagraph (b) of paragraph (2).

tral tribunal does not recognize a legitimate interest on his part in obtaining a final settlement of the dispute, it is not clear why the arbitral proceedings should be continued. Moreover, I consider that where the parties agree on the termination or the tribunal finds that continuation of the arbitral proceedings has become unnecessary, or impossible, the arbitral tribunal should terminate the proceedings. Therefore, I suggest the Chinese arbitration law should adopt the stance of the Model Law and restrict the discretion of the arbitral tribunal accordingly.

2. Power to make provisional orders

Model Law. As the framers of the Model Law could not know the range of orders available within a state which chose to adopt the Model Law, it does not give the arbitral tribunal the power to make provisional orders.

1996 Act. Section 39(1) states that the parties are free to agree that the tribunal shall have power to order on a provisional basis any relief which it would have power to grant in a final award, Section 39(4) making it clear that, unless the parties agree to confer this power on the tribunal, it has no such power. The 1996 Act does not give any indication as to how the tribunal's discretion in this regard should be exercised, but it is clear that the arbitrators may exercise this power in a manner which may diverge from the approach a court would take as regards the making of provisional orders, as long as it fulfills its general duties under Section 33. Section 39(2) provides some examples of provisional orders: a provisional order for the payment of money or the disposition of property as between the parties, or an order to make an interim payment on account of the costs of the arbitration. It is clearly not exclusive. The tribunal should generally be cautious about using any such power, for if liability may not be clearly determined where a provisional order is sought, it is difficult to imagine the circumstances in which it would be fair to make one, and there is a possibility that long-term injustice could be caused. For example, if after a provisional order for the payment of money was made and complied with, it was found that in fact a

中英仲裁法比较研究
A Comparative Study of the Chinese Arbitration
Law and the Arbitration Laws of the UK

smaller sum was due, the respondent might not be able to obtain reimbursement because the claimant has become impecunious.[1] Section 39(4) also provides that the power to make provisional awards does not affect its powers under Section 47(awards on different issues). It can be seen that the Act specifically distinguishes between provisional orders and awards on different issues pursuant to Articles 47. The word "provisional" has no doubt been carefully chosen to avoid the use of "interim", as an interim award is nevertheless final as regards the matters which it determines. It follows that although the marginal note to the Act refers to "provisional awards", what the section in fact concerns should properly be termed "provisional orders". The terminology is important since the power under Section 39 is subject to later adjustment, whereas awards, unless otherwise agreed, are "final and binding". Since the power is to make an "order", Section 52 which deals with the form of awards does not apply here.

Chinese Law. Chinese arbitration law does not give the arbitral tribunal the power to make provisional awards and the parties may not confer that power by agreement. Since such a power is useful for the tribunal to arbitrate economic disputes impartially and promptly, I suggest that Chinese arbitration law should adopt the stance of the 1996 Act and give the tribunal such power.

V. Conclusion

It has been suggested that while in Chinese arbitration law, the tribunal has the power to conciliate on its own initiative, to protect the autonomy of the parties, it might require that the tribunal should conciliate only if both

---

[1] Hais, Bruce/Planterose, Rowan & Tecks, Jonathan, The Arbitration Act 1996: A Commentary, 3rd ed. Malden: Blackwell Publishing, Inc.,2003,163-164.

parties desire it, or one party so desires and the other party agrees. Neither the Model Law nor the Act says anything about conciliation. Yet as conciliation is a well established form of dispute resolution in China in a way that is not yet the case with arbitration, Chinese law cannot afford to ignore this subject. It goes without saying that in Chinese legal culture the assumption by the tribunal of the role of conciliator is not regarded as inimical to its role as impartial adjudicator. Chinese arbitration law is silent about any power to interpret ambiguities in an award, even though in practice the tribunal may make such interpretation. To improve the law, it is beneficial for Chinese law to adopt the stance of the 1996 Act allowing the tribunal to make such interpretation unless otherwise agreed by the parties. In Chinese arbitration law the court has no power to extend the time within which an arbitral award, or an application for correction or an actual correction, shall be made. Since sometimes, the time agreed by the parties or provided by law is too limited, the tribunal or the parties may need recourse to a longer time. Chinese arbitration law might thus usefully adopt the approach of the 1996 Act and allow the court to extend such periods. The 1996 Act allows the court not only to enforce an award in the same manner as a judgment, but also issue a judgment in terms of the award. Since the second method of enforcement has the advantages which the first lacks, Chinese law should adopt this approach. Under the 1996 Act, the arbitral tribunal is allowed to withhold an arbitral award in case of non-payment of fees, while the court may order the tribunal to deliver the award on the payment into court by the applicant. This seems an effective means of obliging payment, and since Chinese arbitration law lacks such means, it is suggested that it may once again follow the example of the Act.

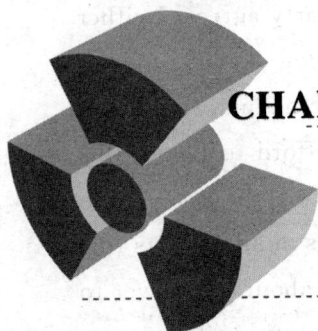

中英仲裁法比较研究
A Comparative Study of the Chinese Arbitration
Law and the Arbitration Laws of the UK

CHAPTER 12

CHALLENGING AWARDS

Ⅰ. Introduction

After an arbitral award is made, any dissenting party is entitled to challenge it. Whether the challenge is justified depends on the applicable procedural law. If the challenge is thus justified, the award may be set aside or be subject to any other remedy available under the applicable law. Moreover, while a losing party will usually comply with the award conscientiously, sometimes that party may refuse to comply. In this case, the winning party is entitled to apply to the court to enforce the award.

This chapter aims to discuss the grounds and procedures for challenging an award, adopting the viewpoint that resisting enforcement of an award is a type of challenge. It will also consider the possibility of remitting challengeable awards for reconsideration by the tribunal. As ever, the Chinese approach as to the above questions will be considered, and compared with the approach taken in English Law and the Model Law.

II. The Chinese Approach to Challenging Awards

According to the Arbitration Law and the Civil Procedure Law, there are three sorts of arbitration award — domestic awards, foreign-related awards, and foreign awards.

A. Cancellation of Awards

1. Grounds for cancellation

Domestic Awards. Neither the Arbitration Law or the Civil Procedure Law clearly defines domestic awards. However, in both of these laws there are special provisions dealing with Foreign-related awards. ① Accordingly, Chinese awards which are not foreign-related must be domestic awards. Moreover, the "Opinion as to Several Problems about Application of the Civil Procedure Law" of the SPC states that a domestic award is an award which fulfills the following requirements: it is made in Mainland China; the parties, whether natural persons, legal persons, or other organizations must be Chinese; the creation, modification, and termination of the juridical relation must happen within China; the object of arbitration shall be within China.② Article 58 of the Arbitration Law provides that the parties may apply to the court for cancellation of an award if they provide evidence proving that the award involves one of the following circumstances:

    a. there is no arbitration agreement between the parties;

    b. the matters of the award are beyond the extent of the arbitration a-

---

    ①   Part VII, Special provisions on Foreign-Related Arbitration, of the Chinese Arbitration Law 2017. Chapter XVIII, Arbitration, Part IV, Special Provisions on Foreign-related Civil Lawsuit, of the PRC Civil Procedure Law 2017.

    ②   "Section 304 of Opinion on Application of the PRC Civil Procedure Law by the SPC", Law Issue No.22(1992), July 14,1992.

中英仲裁法比较研究
A Comparative Study of the Chinese Arbitration
Law and the Arbitration Laws of the UK

greement or not within the jurisdiction of the arbitration commission;

c. the composition of the arbitration tribunal or the arbitration procedure is contrary to law;

d. the evidence on which the award is based is falsified;

e. the other party has concealed evidence which is sufficient to affect the impartiality of the award; and

f. the arbitrator(s) has (have) demanded or accepted bribes, committed graft or perverted the law in making the arbitral award.

The peoples' court shall cancel the award if the existence of one of the circumstances prescribed in the preceding clause is confirmed by its collegiate bench. The people's court shall also cancel the award if it holds that the award is contrary to the social and public interests.

Foreign-related Awards. According to the Arbitration Law, an award made by a foreign-related arbitration institution or foreign-related arbitration agency is a foreign-related arbitration award.[①] Thus under the Arbitration Law, the question whether an award is foreign-related depends on the arbitration institution or agency by which the award is made. Yet the SPC issued "Opinion as to Several Problems on Enforcement of Civil Procedure Law" on July 14th, 1992. This provides that an award is foreign-related only if one or more party is a foreigner, stateless person, foreign corporation or organization; or if the creation, modification, or termination of the legal relation happens in a foreign country; or if the object of arbitration is within a foreign country.[②] It can be seen that there is a conflict between the Arbitration law and the Opinion made by the SPC. Chinese law lacks any device for the resolution of such conflict. In practice arbitrators tend to be guided by the views of the SPC, but the theoretical position is unclear.

---

① Article 66-68,72 of the PRC Arbitration Law 1994 and Article 66-68,72 of the PRC Arbitration Law 2017.

② "Opinion on Application of the PRC Civil Procedure Law by the SPC", Law Issue, No.22 (1992), July 14,1992.

Article 70 of the Arbitration Law states that the court shall cancel an a-
ward if a party provides evidence proving that the arbitration award involves
one of the circumstances prescribed in Clause 1 of Article 274 of the Civil
Procedure Law (2017). These are: (1) there is no written arbitration agreement; (2) the party against whom the application for enforcement is made
was not given notice for the appointment of an arbitrator or for the inception
of the arbitration proceedings or was unable to present his case due to causes
for which he is not responsible; (3) the composition of the arbitral tribunal
or the arbitral procedure was not in conformity with the arbitration rules; or
(4) the matters dealt with by the award fall outside the scope of the arbitration agreement or the power of the tribunal.

Foreign Awards. A party is entitled to apply to the court to cancel a foreign award under the Washington Convention. The combined effect of Articles 53(1), 54(1) and 55 is that, the grounds on which a party may apply to
the court of the country in which enforcement is sought are that the award is
contrary to the public policy, or public interest of that country, or that the
award involves a issue of state immunity.

Interim Award. The Arbitration Law does not state explicitly whether a
party is entitled to challenge an interim award. However, in "Guangzhou
President Hotel Ltd. v. Fast & Care Cargo Services" ①, the hotel asked the
intermediate court of Shenzhen to cancel an interim award. The court held
that an interim award is essentially a procedural ruling, while an arbitration
award capable of challenge under Article 70 of the Arbitration Law or Article 274 of the Civil Procedure Law refers to a final award. Thus the legality
of an interim award is outwith the scope of investigation of the court, and
the application to cancel the interim award had to be rejected.② It can there-

---

① Guangzhou President Hotel Ltd. v. Fast & Care Cargo Services, (1999), heard
by the Intermediate Court of Shnezhen, Second Economic Tribunal, No.164.

② Han Jian, Theory and Practice on Modem International Commercial Law, Beijing: Law Press, 2000, 357-358.

中英仲裁法比较研究
A Comparative Study of the Chinese Arbitration
Law and the Arbitration Laws of the UK

fore be seen that an interim award cannot be challenged under Chinese arbitration law.

2. Procedure for cancellation

Domestic awards. Under Article 58 of the Arbitration Law the competent court in an application to cancel a domestic award is the intermediate court of the place where the arbitration agency is situated. Article 59 provides that an application must be submitted within 6 months of receipt of the award. Article 60 then indicates that the court shall cancel the award or reject the application, within 2 months of receipt of the application.

Foreign-related awards. The competent court is the intermediate court of the place in which the arbitration institution is located.[1] The time limit within which an application for cancellation of foreign-related awards and that within which the court shall render its decision are the same as those apply to domestic awards.

Remitting awards for reconsideration. The Arbitration law allows the court which receives an application for cancellation of a domestic or a foreign-related award to direct that the case be reconsidered by the arbitral tribunal. The court must give the tribunal a certain period of time to take this step, and must suspend the cancellation procedure in the meantime. If the tribunal refuses to re-arbitrate, the court shall resume the cancellation procedure.[2] However, it is unclear how long shall "a certain period of time" is, and there is no clue as to how that question may be decided.

3. Theories of cancellation

Theory of the opposing system of canceling awards. Opponents of system of canceling awards claim that there should be no difference between grounds for canceling awards and those for refusing recognition and enforcement of awards. If a party disagrees with an award, he may challenge the

---

① Article 58 of the PRC Arbitration Law 2017.
② Article 61 of the PRC Arbitration Law 2017.

process of enforcement of the award, and the enforcing court may investigate the award at that stage. Thus, there is no need for a process of canceling awards, which effectively ensures double supervision of arbitral awards. Even if an arbitral tribunal makes computational, clerical or typographical errors, it can itself correct these on the application of the parties or of its own motion. In this case, a process of canceling awards is also unnecessary. Moreover, if there is a process of canceling awards, the dispute is actually not only referred to arbitration but also is dealt with by legal proceedings, which is contrary to the principle that a dispute should be dealt with by arbitration only or litigation only, and the principle that a dispute shall be resolved by a single, final arbitral award.[1]

Theory Supporting System of Canceling Awards. Supporters of the system of canceling awards suggest firstly, that Chinese arbitration law should reflect the reality of China. At present in China the number of arbitration agencies is too large, the qualifications of arbitrators are not very high, and the rules of arbitration need to be improved. Therefore, after an arbitral award is made, court supervision is necessary. Supervision at the stage of enforcement is not enough and a process of canceling awards is necessary. Secondly, canceling awards and refusing enforcement are two different procedures and cannot be regarded as the same legal remedy simply because they proceed on similar grounds. Thirdly, in most of countries in the world, the grounds of canceling awards and refusing their enforcement are actually different, although the grounds of canceling awards and refusing their enforcement are actually the same under the Chinese law, which will be discussed below. Fourthly, maintaining a procedure for canceling awards suits the re-

---

[1] See "Explanation about the Chinese Arbitration Law (Draft)", in "A Complete Set of Material about the Chinese Arbitration Law" compiled by the Section of Civil Law of Legal Working Committee of Standing Committee of the National People's Congress, and the Department of Secretary of Chinese International Economy and Trade Arbitration Agency, Publishing Company of Law,1995,56.

中英仲裁法比较研究
A Comparative Study of the Chinese Arbitration
Law and the Arbitration Laws of the UK

quirement of the system of arbitration, and is in accordance with current trends, being consistent with the arbitration regimes of most of countries in the world.[1] The above seems to be the prevailing opinion. The Director of Legal Working Committee of Standing Committee of the National People's Congress, Gu Angran, observed in "Explanation about the Chinese Arbitration Law (Draft)" that stipulation of a procedure for cancelling awards can help protect the legal interests of the parties and reduce mistakes in conduct of arbitration. The laws of many other countries have stipulated procedures for cancelling awards.[2]

Theoretical Underpinning of the Remitting Awards for Reconsideration. Where the award goes beyond the scope of the arbitration agreement does not resolved some matters submitted to arbitration, canceling the award is a very negative outcome. In the latter case part of the dispute still needs to be resolved, while in the former only part of the award is objectionable. Remitting awards for reconsideration takes less time than bringing the dispute to arbitration anew or referring it to litigation. Thus the process is more efficient. There are two criteria for remitting awards for reconsideration — the court considers the award capable of remission, and that the challengeable award is apt for reconsideration by the arbitral tribunal. The former depends on the court's discretion, which is a subjective criterion; the latter is an objective criterion, which also depends on the judge's estimation and also

---

① See "Explanation about the Chinese Arbitration Law (Draft)", published in "A Complete Set of Material about the Chinese Arbitration Law" compiled by the Section of Civil Law of Legal Working Committee of Standing Committee of the National People's Congress, and the Department of Secretary of Chinese International Economy and Trade Arbitration Agency, Beijing: Publishing Company of Law, 1995, 56-57.

② See "Explanation about the Chinese Arbitration Law (Draft)", published in "A Complete Set of Material about the Chinese Arbitration Law" compiled by the Section of Civil Law of Legal Working Committee of Standing Committee of the National People's Congress, and the Department of Secretary of Chinese International Economy and Trade Arbitration Agency, Beijing: Publishing Company of Law, 1995, 56.

forms the basis of the exercise of the court's discretion.

B. Refusal of Enforcement

1. Grounds for refusing enforcement

[Domestic Awards]

Article 63 of the PRC Arbitration Law provides that the court shall not enforce a foreign-related award if the party against whom an application is made provides evidence proving that the arbitration award involves one of the circumstances prescribed in Article 237 of the Civil Procedure Law which states that the people's court refuse enforcement if it is established that:

a. There was no arbitration agreement;

b. The matter being adjudicated does not fall within the arbitration agreement or the arbitration organ's authority;

c. The formation of the arbitration tribunal or the arbitral procedure violates the law;

d. the evidence on which the award is based is falsified;

e. the other party has concealed evidence which is sufficient to affect the impartiality of the award; and

f. The arbitrator is found to have taken bribes, conducted malpractice, or misused the law in rendering the award.

The court may also refuse enforcement if it would not be in the public interest.

Foreign-related Awards. Article 71 of the PRC Arbitration Law provides that the court shall not enforce a foreign-related award if the party against whom an application is made provides evidence proving that the arbitration award involves one of the circumstances prescribed in Clause 1, Article 274 of the Civil Procedure Law. It can be seen that the grounds for challenging foreign-related awards are looser than those for challenging domestic awards. The party to a domestic award may challenge the award on the grounds that the evidence on which the award is based is false; or that the

中英仲裁法比较研究
A Comparative Study of the Chinese Arbitration
Law and the Arbitration Laws of the UK

other party has concealed evidence which is sufficient to affect the impartiality of the award; or that the arbitrator(s) has (have) demanded or accepted bribes, committed graft or perverted the law in making the arbitral award, whereas a party to a foreign-related award is not entitled to challenge the award on those grounds. In other words, a party to a foreign-related award is not entitled to challenge the award on substantive grounds, but only on procedural grounds, which are: (1) there is no written arbitration agreement; (2) the party against whom the application for enforcement is made was not given notice for the appointment of an arbitrator or for the inception of the arbitration proceedings or was unable to present his case due to causes for which he is not responsible; (3) the composition of the arbitral tribunal or the arbitral procedure was not in conformity with the arbitration rules; or (4) the matters dealt with by the award fall outside the scope of the arbitration agreement or the power of the tribunal.

[Foreign Awards]

New York Convention 1958. Article 269 of the Civil Procedure Law provides that where a verdict rendered by a foreign arbitration organization requires a Chinese court to acknowledge its validity and enforce it, the applicant must apply to the intermediate court where the losing party resides or his property is situated. The court shall then act according to the international treaties to which China is a party, or in accordance with the principle of mutual reciprocity. It can be seen that whether an award is a foreign one depends on whether the award is made by a foreign arbitration agency, which is inconsistent with the common approach of international arbitration laws and practice. For example, the New York Convention of 1958 applies to the recognition and enforcement of arbitral awards made in the territory of a State other than the State where recognition and enforcement is sought. It also applies to arbitral awards not considered as domestic awards in the State where recognition and enforcement is sought.① These different criteria as to what is a foreign award cause no practical problem where an award may is made by a foreign arbitration agency, but within the country in which recognition and enforcement is sought. In this case, in accordance with the New York Convention, the award shall not be deemed as a foreign award, unless the country in which the recognition and enforcement is sought does not consider the award domestic. Chinese law does not consider such an award domestic, thus the New York Convention applies.

However, a problem arises where an award is made by a Chinese arbitration agency outwith China. The award is deemed domestic under Chinese law, but foreign under the New York Convention. In this case, a conflict would then arise, which is whether the rules in Chinese arbitration law regarding domestic awards or the New York Convention which deals with foreign awards shall apply. Thus such an award would be subject to the rather stricter regime which governs domestic award. I recommend that Chinese law should fall in line with the New York Convention.

Recognition and enforcement of the award may be refused, at the request of the party against whom it is invoked, only if that party furnishes to the court where the recognition and enforcement is sought can proof one of the grounds provided by the New York Convention.

Bilateral Judicial aid Agreements. China has made bilateral judicial agreements with many countries so far and most of the agreements contain bilateral agreements for recognition and enforcement.② Most of those agreements have clearly provided that the New York Convention shall apply to

---

① Article 1(1) of the New York Convention 1958.
② Since China has made the first bilateral judicial agreement with France regarding Civil and Commercial matters on May 4th, 1997, China has made more than 30 bilateral judicial agreements with states, including Poland, Belgium, Mongolia, Italy, Roumania, Russia, White Russia, Kazakstan, Ukraine, Cuba, Spain, Bulgaria, Thailand, Egypt, Turkey, Greece, Cyprus, Hungary, Morocco, Kirghizia, Singapore.

中英仲裁法比较研究
A Comparative Study of the Chinese Arbitration
Law and the Arbitration Laws of the UK

mutual recognition and enforcement of awards of the countries who have made the agreement. In fact, most of those countries who have made the a-greements are themselves member states to the New York Convention. For example, Article 26 of the Bilateral Civil and Criminal Judicial Agreement between Greece and China states that each of the two countries shall recog-nize and enforce arbitral awards on commercial disputes made by the other country according to the New York Convention, unless the country has made a declaration or reservation. Equally, Article 28 of the Bilateral Civil Judicial Agreement between Italy and China provides that an arbitral award made in one country shall be recognized and enforced in the other country ac-cording to the New York Convention 1958. Therefore, in these circum-stances, performance of the bilateral judicial agreement turns to be perform-ance of the New York Convention. A few bilateral judicial agreements have not provided that the New York Convention shall apply, but have their own regulations regarding recognition and enforcement of awards. For example, Article 26 of the Bilateral Commercial and Criminal Judicial Agreement be-tween Turkey and China provides that, besides the other provisions in Sec-tion 3 of the chapter, an arbitral award fulfilling the following requirements shall be recognized and enforced:

(1)according to the law of the country of the applicant, the arbitral a-ward deals with a contractual or non-contractual commercial dispute.

(2) There is a written agreement that the parties are willing to refer a specific dispute or a dispute arising from a specific legal relation to an arbi-tration agency. The award is made by the arbitration agency mentioned a-bove within its jurisdiction as provided by the arbitration agreement.

(3) According to the law of the place of the party against whom recog-nition and enforcement is sought, the arbitration agreement is valid.

The Principle of Reciprocity. Article 219 of the Civil Procedure Law, in-dicates that where the state of the applicant has no international treaty or bi-lateral judicial agreement with China, China may recognize or enforce a foreign award according to the principle of reciprocity. The principle of reciprocity is simply a principle, so that no detailed rules are attached thereto.

2. Procedure for refusing enforcement

[Domestic Awards]

Article 237 of the Civil Procedure Law provides that where a party fails to carry out an award, the other party may seek its enforcement in the competent court, without indicating which court is competent. However, Article 256 of "Opinion as to Several Problems on Enforcement of Civil Procedure Law"① indicates that arbitration awards fall within the concept of "other legal documents" recognized by Article 224 of the Civil Procedure Law. This states that "other legal documents" shall be executed by the court in the place where the person concerned resides or where the property concerned is located. Article 224 also provides that a civil judgment shall be executed by the court of first instance. The combined effect of the above provisions is that, as regard enforcement of domestic awards, the competent court is the court of first instance in the place where the person against whom the award is made resides, or the place where the property concerned is located.

Article 239 of the Civil Procedure Law states that the time limit for requesting enforcement is two years. The time limit specified in the preceding paragraph shall be computed from the last day of the period of performance prescribed by the award. Where the award demands that performance to be carried out at different periods, the time limit shall be computed from the last day of each performance period as prescribed. Article 229 of the Civil Procedure Law provides that if the person being executed or the property being executed is in another place, the local people's court may be entrusted to perform it on his behalf. After the entrusted people's court receives the letter of entrustment, it must start execution within 15 days and must not refuse.

---

① "Opinion on Application of the PRC Civil Procedure Law" by the SPC, Law Issue, No.22 (1992),July 14,1992.

中英仲裁法比较研究
A Comparative Study of the Chinese Arbitration
Law and the Arbitration Laws of the UK

After the implementation is completed, the results of the implementation shall be entrusted to the people's court in a timely manner; if it has not been completed within 30 days, the implementation report shall be entrusted to the people's court. If the entrusted people's court does not implement it within 15 days from the date of receipt of the letter of entrustment, the entrusted people's court may request the superior people's court of the entrusted people's court to order the entrusted people's court to execute it. These time limits apply to request for enforcement of domestic awards, foreign-related awards, and foreign awards.

[Foreign-related Awards]

Article 273 of the Civil Procedure Law states that if one party fails to implement a foreign-related award, the other party may apply for enforcement in the intermediate court in the place where the object of the application resides, or where the property is located. It is notable that a "Report System" applies to refusing enforcement of foreign-related awards. The SPC issued "Notice of Problems Relating to Treatment of the People's Court as to Foreign-related Awards and Foreign Awards" on August 28th, 1995.[1] By virtue of this Notice, where a party applies for enforcement of a foreign-related award, if the court finds one of the grounds provided by Article 260 of the Civil Procedure Law to be established, rather than refusing enforcement, the court shall report to the higher court of that area, which shall investigate the award. If the higher court agrees that enforcement should be refused, it shall report its opinion to the SPC. Only after the SPC replies, can the court refuse to enforce the award. The Report System applies to not only foreign-related awards but also foreign awards.

[Foreign Awards]

Bilateral Judicial Agreement. As to refusal of enforcement of a foreign

---

[1] "Notice on the Issues that People's Courts Treat Foreign-Related Awards and Foreign Arbitral Matters" by the SPC, Law Issue, No.18 (1995), August 28, 1995.

awards by virtue of bilateral judicial agreement, the appropriate court is as before. The same is true of time limits for making applications. As regards the time limit for making a ruling, where a bilateral judicial agreement provides that the New York Convention applies, the time limit which applies to a New York Convention Award shall apply. Where a bilateral judicial agreement does not provide that the New York Convention applies, Chinese arbitration law contains no rule as to time limits. The "Report System" again applies in this context.

III. Suggested Improvements to the Chinese Law

1. In deciding whether an arbitral award is foreign-related or not, the rules of the PRC Arbitration Law are different from the rules of "Opinion as to Several Problems on Enforcement of Civil Procedure Law". The conflict between the different rules should be resolved.

2. Whether an arbitral award is foreign should not depend on which arbitration agency makes the award, but on in which country the award is made, so that the conflict between the rules of Chinese arbitration law and the rules of the New York Convention can be avoided.

3. As to domestic awards and foreign-related awards, the Chinese arbitration law does not provide the time limit within which an application for refusal of enforcement shall be made.

4. As to foreign awards to which the New York Convention does not apply, Chinese arbitration law does not stipulate a time limit within which a ruling on enforcement or a ruling of refusal of enforcement shall be made.

5. It is not clear whether an arbitral award can be cancelled in part.

中英仲裁法比较研究
A Comparative Study of the Chinese Arbitration
Law and the Arbitration Laws of the UK

Ⅳ. The Approach of the Laws Operating in the UK

A. Introduction

As ever it is useful to refer to the United Kingdom for a paradigm which offers two models for consideration — the 1996 Arbitration Act and the Model Law. Chinese arbitration law, the Model Law, and the 1996 Act all give the parties the right to challenge an arbitral award. There are similarities among the three laws as to the grounds and procedures for challenging awards, and remedies for challengeable awards. Since there are differences in culture and tradition, there are differences between the three laws as to the detail of challenging an award. One main difference relates to remedies for challengeable awards. There is also difference in the grounds and procedures for challenging awards. Another main difference is that only in the 1996 Act, the court may, on the application of the party claiming enforcement of the award, order the other party to provide security.

B. Cancellation of Awards

1. Grounds for cancellation

[Incapacity and invalidity]

Model Law. By virtue of Article 34, the only recourse against an award is via an action for setting aside①although a party is not precluded from defending himself by resisting recognition and enforcement under Article 36 in proceedings initiated by the other party.② The reason why the Working Group did not consider refusal of recognition and enforcement as a form of

---

① Doc. A/CN. 9/232, para.14.
② Doc. A/CN. 9/246, para.274.

"recourse" is that the term "recourse" has in a number of languages the connotation of a positive initiative or action, such as an "appeal",① Article 34(1) of the Model Law provides that recourse to a court against an arbitral award may be made only by an application for setting aside in accordance with paragraphs (2) and (3) of this article. Article 34(2) provides the grounds on which an award may be set aside. These grounds are divided into two groups. Some grounds are required to be proved by the applicant, whereas the others are required to be found by the court. The importance of the distinction is not only that the applicant is not required as a legal matter to allege these grounds, but also that the court may set aside an award notwithstanding that the applicant is affected by waiver or estoppel under Articles 4 or 16. Article 34(2)(a)(i) provides that an arbitral award may be set aside by the court only if the party making the application furnishes proof that: a party to the arbitration agreement referred to in Article 7 was under some incapacity; or the arbitration agreement is not valid under the law to which the parties have subjected it or, failing any indication thereon, under the law of this State (i. e. the state which has adopted the Model Law).

The final report on the Model Law records that "it was understood that an award might be set aside on any of the grounds listed in paragraph (2) irrespective of whether such ground had materially affected the awards."② Nevertheless, Article 34(2) indicates that the court "may" rather than "must" set the award aside, when any of the grounds are proved,③ so that the court has discretion to decline to set aside an award, where it considers that a procedural defect is unimportant. One must bear in mind the effect of waiver in this context. If a party believes that the arbitration agreement is invalid, he should raise a plea of no jurisdiction before the tribunal under Ar-

---

① Doc. A/CN. 9/246, para.197.
② U. N. A/40/17, para.303.
③ See U. N. A/CN. 9/SR. 318, para.65.

中英仲裁法比较研究
A Comparative Study of the Chinese Arbitration
Law and the Arbitration Laws of the UK

ticle 16(2). If he fails to do so, the travaux preparatoires comment that: [1]
"he should be precluded from raising objections with respect to the existence
or validity or scope of the arbitration agreement also in other contexts... in
particular the post-award stage, i. e. Article 34(2)(a)(i)". Nonetheless, "it
was recognized that the failure to raise a plea could not have the effect of a
waiver in all circumstances, especially where the plea... was that the dispute
was non-arbitrable or that the award was in conflict with public policy". [2] In
the end it was decide not to attempt to deal specifically with this matter,
leaving the question to be interpreted or regulated by states adopting the
Model Law. [3] It submitted that beyond arbitrability and public policy, the
waiver principle should apply. [4]

1996 Act. The 1996 Act does not cite a party's lack of capacity or the invalidity of the arbitration agreement as specific grounds for challenging a-
wards. Yet it may be assumed that incapacity is a form of invalidity. Section
30(1)(a) states that an arbitral tribunal may rule on whether there is a valid
arbitration agreement when it rules on its own substantive jurisdiction.
Thus, if the arbitration agreement is invalid, the tribunal will lack substantive jurisdiction. Section 67(1) provides that a party to arbitral proceedings
may (upon notice to the other parties and to the tribunal) apply to the court
challenging any award of the arbitral tribunal as to its substantive jurisdiction; or seek an order declaring an award made by the tribunal on the merits
to be of no effect, in whole or in part, because the tribunal did not have substantive jurisdiction.

Chinese Law. Chinese arbitration law also stipulates the invalidity of the
arbitration agreement as a ground of challenge without specifically mentio-

---

[1] U. N. A/CN. 9/WG. II/WP. 50, para.16.

[2] U. N. A/40/17, para.288.

[3] U. N. A/40/17, para.289.

[4] Davidson, Fraser P., Arbitration, Edinburgh: W. Green, 2000, 370.

ning incapacity. However, by virtue of Article 17(2) of the Arbitration Law①, "incapacity" is included in "invalidity". Thus Chinese arbitration law need make no amendment in this regard.

[Lack of proper notice or being unable to present case]

Model Law. Article 34(a)(ii) states that it is a ground of challenge that the party making the application was not given proper notice of the appointment of an arbitrator or of the arbitral proceedings or was otherwise unable to present his case. It is clear that in arbitral proceedings with more than one arbitrator, failure to give proper notice of the appointment of any one of them constitutes a ground for setting aside an award.② The first part of the provision contemplates the situation where a party cannot present his case because he has not had sufficient advance warning of an arbitrator's appointment or of the proceedings generally.③ Under Article 3(a) any written communication is deemed to have received, if it is delivered to the addressee personally or if it is delivered at his place of business, habitual residence or mailing address; if none of these can be found after making a reasonable inquiry, a written communication is deemed to have been received if it is sent to the addressee's last-known place of business, habitual residence or mailing address by registered letter or any other means which provides a record of the attempt to deliver it. It is therefore possible that a party may take no part in the proceedings, indeed being ignorant of the appointment of the tribunal, the arbitral proceedings and even the making of the award, without the validity of the award being threatened, provided communications have

---

① Article 17(2) of the PRC Arbitration Law 2017 provides that an arbitration agreement is invalid if the arbitration agreement concluded by persons without or with limited capacity for civil acts.

② Commission Report, para.286.

③ See the English case The Myron [1970] 1 Q. B. 527. See Davidson, Fraser P., Arbitration, Edinburgh: W. Green, 2000, 368.

中英仲裁法比较研究
A Comparative Study of the Chinese Arbitration
Law and the Arbitration Laws of the UK

addressed to him as indicated by Article 3.[1] The second part of the provision deals with the situation where a party is effectively prevented from presenting his case. If a party was unable to present his case due to personal reasons or "could have avoided the situation, he should not be given an opportunity to set the award aside".[2] The provision obviously has a considerable degree of affinity with Article 18, which establishes the fundamental principle that the parties should be treated equally and each given a full opportunity to present his case. Yet a decision that the wording of Article 34(2)(a) (ii) should be aligned with Article 18[3] was later reversed as it was regarded as more important to align Article 34 with Article 36 and thus Article V of the New York Convention than with Article 18.[4] It is perhaps worth recalling that by virtue of Article 18, unequal treatment of the parties or the failure to allow one party to present his case will always be a ground on which the award may be set aside, whatever else happens or may be agreed. Thus the waiver principle cannot preclude an award being set aside on the grounds of a breach of Article 18, even though it might prevent the setting aside of the award in relation to minor procedural defects.[5]

1996 Act. The 1996 Act does not literally state that an award may be set aside on the ground that the application was not given proper notice of the appointment of an arbitrator or of the arbitral proceedings or was otherwise unable to present his case. However, these are serious irregularities and Section 68(1) indicates that a party to the arbitral proceedings may (upon notice to the other parties and to the tribunal) apply to the court challenging an award in the proceedings on the ground of serious irregularity affecting the tribunal, the proceedings or the award. Section 68(2) then specifies what is

---

① Davidson, Fraser P., Arbitration, Edinburgh: W. Green,2000,369.
② U. N. A/CN. 9/SR. 317, paras.39,40.
③ U. N. A/40/17, para.287.
④ U. N. A/40/17, para.302.
⑤ Davidson, Fraser P., Arbitration, Edinburgh: W. Green,2000,372.

meant by serious irregularity. One should always bear in mind that it is a requirement under this section that an irregularity has caused or is likely to cause substantial injustice to the applicant, although the use of the word "irregularity" might suggest that something less than a major failure in procedure or error in the award is sufficient. Section 68(2)(a) refers to failure by the tribunal to comply with Section 33 (general duty of tribunal) to give the parties a reasonable opportunity to put their case, while Section 68(2)(c) refers to failure by the tribunal to conduct the proceedings in accordance with the procedure agreed by the parties. It follows that it is not enough that the arbitrator has conducted the proceedings in a fashion which has caused one of the parties to lose faith in him.[1] Moreover, if the arbitrators have made their award, further evidence is not admissible as the arbitrators are functus, but if the award has not been made and it remains possible for the late evidence to be heard, failure to allow its admission may amount to failure to give a party an opportunity to present his case.[2]

Chinese Law. In Chinese arbitration law, as regards domestic awards, the fact that the composition of the arbitration tribunal or the arbitration procedure is contrary to the legal procedure is a ground for challenge. Article 237 of the Civil Procedure Law specifies exactly the same ground as Article 58. Thus, there is no need for Chinese arbitration law to be amended.

[Beyond the scope of the submission to arbitration]

Model Law. Article 34(2)(iii) states that the award deals with a dispute not contemplated by or not falling within the terms of the submission to arbitration, or contains decisions on matters beyond the scope of the submission to arbitration, provided that, if the decisions on matters submitted to arbitration can be separated from those not so submitted, only that part of

---

[1] Merkin, Robert & Lyde, Barlow & Gilbert, Arbitration Law, London, Hong Kong: LLP Professional Publishing,1991,16-18.

[2] Merkin, Robert & Lyde, Barlow & Gilbert, Arbitration Law, London, Hong Kong: LLP, Professional Publishing,1991,16-18.

中英仲裁法比较研究
A Comparative Study of the Chinese Arbitration
Law and the Arbitration Laws of the UK

the award which contains decisions on matters not submitted to arbitration may be set aside. If only part of the award exceeds the jurisdiction of the arbitral tribunal, only that part need be set aside, provided it is separable from the rest of the award. Once again the waiver principle would apply here.[1]

1996 Act. Section 68(2)(b) provides that the tribunal exceeding its powers (otherwise than by exceeding its substantive jurisdiction) is a ground of challenge. Matters which might fall within Section 68(2)(b) include any exercise of interlocutory powers (e.g. the power to order security for costs) which the parties have agreed the arbitrators are not to possess.[2]

Chinese Law. Article 58(2) of the PRC Arbitration Law 2017 and Article 260(4) of the Civil Procedure Law provide that an award may be challenged on the ground that the matters of the award are beyond the extent of the arbitration. However, there is no provision in Chinese arbitration law dealing with the situation in which the tribunal exceeds its powers. I suggest that the chinese arbitration law should adopt the legislative approach of the 1996 Act and make this a ground for challenging awards in the future amendment.

[Composition of the arbitral tribunal or the arbitral procedure was not in accordance with the agreement of the parties or with law.]

Model Law. Article 34(2)(a)(iv) indicates as a ground of challenge that the composition of the arbitral tribunal or the arbitral procedure was not in accordance with the agreement of the parties, unless such agreement was in conflict with a provision of this Law from which the parties cannot derogate, or, failing such agreement, was not in accordance with this Law. The text of the provision does not clearly reflect the Working Group's decision that an award should be subject to setting aside not only if the composition of the arbitral tribunal or the arbitral procedure is not in accordance with any agree-

---

① See (1983) 8 Yearbook of Commercial Arbitration 386.

② Merkin, Robert & Lyde, Barlow & Gilbert, Arbitration Law, London, Hong Kong: LLP Professional Publishing, 1991, 16-18.

ment of the parties, but also if such composition or procedure, while in accordance with such agreement, violates mandatory provision of the Model
Law. The text says that if the parties' agreement conflicts with mandatory
provisions of the Mode Law, non-observance of the agreement is not a
ground for setting aside, but does not say that observance of such a conflicting agreement is a ground for setting aside.① Yet this is undoubtedly the in-
tent of the provision. The travaux preparatoires explain that:②"where the a-
greement (of the parties) was in conflict with a mandatory provision of this
law or where the parties had not made an agreement on the procedural point
at issue, the provisions of 'this law' whether mandatory or not, provided
the standards against which the composition of the arbitral tribunal and the
arbitral procedure were to be measured." The Model Law is an example of
poor and obscure drafting in this respect, and hardly provides a model to be
emulated.

　　1996 Act. The 1996 Act does not employ the same words as the Model
Law but the combined effect of Section 68(2)(a) which provides that failure
by the tribunal to comply with Section 33 (the general duty of the tribunal)
to adopt procedures suitable to the circumstances of the case avoiding unnecessary delay or expense is a ground of challenge and Section 68(2)(c) which
provides that failure by the tribunal to conduct the proceedings in accordance
with the procedure agreed by the parties is a ground is as the same as that of
Article 34(2)(a)(iv).

　　Chinese Law. Chinese arbitration law simply provides that the party
may challenge an award on the ground that the composition of the arbitration tribunal or the arbitral procedure is contrary to the law. Since Chinese
arbitration law and the CIETAC Arbitration Rules allow the parties to make
their own agreement as to the composition of tribunal and arbitral proceed-

---

　　①　Merkin, Robert & Lyde, Barlow & Gilbert, Arbitration Law, London, Hong
Kong: LLP Professional Publishing,1991,212.

　　②　U. N. A/40/17, para.290.

中英仲裁法比较研究
A Comparative Study of the Chinese Arbitration
Law and the Arbitration Laws of the UK

ings, I suggest that the law should also provide as a ground of challenge that the composition of the tribunal or the arbitral procedure is contrary to the parties' agreement, making it plain that if the agreement conflicts with mandatory law, non-observance of the agreement is not a ground for setting aside while that observance of such an agreement is a ground for setting aside.

[Non-arbitrability]

Model Law. Article 34(2)(b)(i) provides that an award may be set aside if the court finds that the subject-matter of the dispute is not capable of settlement by arbitration under the law of this State. It is important to remember that in terms of Article 34(1) the only recourse against an award is via an application to set it aside, so that the court may not intervene unless such an application has been made.[1]

1996 Act. The 1996 Act does not literally state that non-arbitrability is a ground for challenging, but it is assumed that non-arbitrability would fall within the scope of lack of substantive jurisdiction. The 1996 Act does not divide the grounds of challenging into two types, and any ground must be proved by the applicant.

Chinese Law. Chinese arbitration law does not directly state non-arbitrability as a ground for challenging awards. Yet, Chinese arbitration law provides that if a dispute is not capable of settlement by arbitration, the arbitral agreement is invalid, and the invalidity of an arbitral agreement is a ground of challenge. Chinese arbitration law clearly provides which kinds of disputes cannot be referred to arbitration.[2] So I consider it would not be too hard for the applicant to prove non-arbitrability. Therefore, it is no need to amend the provision of Chinese arbitration law.

---

① U. N. A/CN. 9/SR. 318, paras.7,8.

② The following disputes shall not be submitted to arbitration: 1. disputes over marriage, adoption, guardianship, child maintenance and inheritance, and 2. administrative disputes falling within the jurisdiction of the relevant administrative organs according to law.

[Conflict with public policy]

Model Law. Article 34(2)(b)(ii) indicates that an award may be set a-side if the court finds that the award is in conflict with the public policy of this State. As to the question whether conflict with public policy covered all the stages in the arbitral proceedings during which irregularities might have occurred, the relevant portion of the Commission Report reads as follows:

"It was understood that the term 'public policy', which was used in the 1958 New York Convention and many other treaties, covered fundamental principles of law and justice in substantive as well as procedural respects. Thus, instances such as corruption, bribery and fraud and similar serious cases would constitute a ground for setting aside. It was noted, in that con-nection, that the wording 'the award is in conflict with the public policy of the State' was not to be interpreted as excluding instances or events relating to the manner in which an award was arrived at."[1]

1996 Act. By virtue of Section 68(2)(g), it is a ground for challenge that the award or the way in which it was procured was contrary to public policy. Unlike the Model Law, in the 1996 Act this ground is not to be found by the court, but is required to be proved by the applicant.

Chinese Law. Under Chinese arbitration law, the award or the way in which it was procured being conflict with public policy is a ground for chal-lenging awards, which shall be found by the court. In my opinion, it is bet-ter for this ground to be found by the court, rather than a party, as it might be difficult for the party to consider whether an award or the way in which it was made is conflict with public policy. Thus, Chinese arbitration law needs not to be amended.

[Failure to deal with all the issues]

Model Law. The Model Law does not provide failure to deal with all the issues that were put to it as a ground for challenging an award, although a

---

① Doc. A/CN. 9/SR. 331, para.297.

中英仲裁法比较研究
A Comparative Study of the Chinese Arbitration
Law and the Arbitration Laws of the UK

procedure exists under Article 33(3) whereby a party may apply to the tribunal for an additional award to be made to cover the matters which were omitted.

1996 Act. Section 68(2)(d) states failure by the tribunal to deal with all the issues that were put to it as a ground of challenge.

Chinese Law. Chinese arbitration law does not mention failure to deal with all the issues that were put to it. In my view, where issues are omitted from the award, the better approach is for the party to be entitled to apply to the arbitral tribunal for an additional award to cover the matters which were omitted, since there is no reason why the award need be set aside in such a case.

[Excess of powers by any arbitral institution or other person]

Model Law. The grounds for challenging awards in the Model Law do not include excess of powers by any arbitral or other institution or person vested by the parties with powers in relation to the proceedings or the award exceeding its powers.

1996 Act. Section 68(2)(e) provides that excess of powers by any arbitral or other institution or person vested by the parties with powers in relation to the proceedings or the award exceeding its powers is a ground for challenging awards.

Chinese Law. Chinese arbitration law regards excess of powers by arbitration agency as a ground, without mentioning excess of powers by other arbitral institution or person. Since in Chinese arbitration law, the parties are not free to vest other institution or person with powers in relation to the proceedings or the award, there is no need for Chinese arbitration law to adopt the approach of the 1996 Act.

[Uncertainty or ambiguity as to effect of award]

Model Law. Under the Model Law, uncertainty or ambiguity as to effect of awards is not a ground of challenge, although a procedure exists under Article 33(1)(b) whereby a party may apply to the tribunal for an interpretation of a specific part of the award.

1996 Act. Under the 1996 Act, a party can challenge an award on the ground that uncertainty or ambiguity as to the effect of the award.[1] An award is not to be taken as too uncertain if the obligations of the parties are apparent from it.[2] Under Section 57(3) a party may apply to the arbitral tribunal to correct an award or to make an additional award so as to clarify or remove any ambiguity in the award. By virtue of Section 70(2) which provides that an application or appeal may not be brought if the applicant or appellant has not first exhausted an available recourse under Section 57, the party shall first apply to the tribunal to correct an award or make an additional award before challenging an award before the court.

Chinese Law. In Chinese arbitration law, uncertainty or ambiguity as effect of award is not a ground on which a party may challenge an award. In my view, it is beneficial for Chinese arbitration law to adopt the instance of the 1996 Act and add this ground.

[Award being obtained by fraud]

Model law. Although the Model Law is apparently silent about the consequences of an award being obtained by fraud, such an award would certainly be open to challenge on the basis that it offended against public policy.

1996 Act. Section 68(2)(g) indicates that a party may challenge an award on the ground that the award is obtained by fraud. One obvious situation in which this head of serious irregularity would be applicable is where one of the parties has withheld evidence which is material to the award and which might, if disclosed, have produced a different result. The fact that evidence does subsequently become apparent is not enough for a finding that

---

[1]   Section 68(2)(f) of the 1996 Act.

[2]   Merkin, Robert & Lyde, Barlow & Gilbert, Arbitration Law, London, Hong Kong: LLP Professional Publishing, 1991, 16-18.

中英仲裁法比较研究
A Comparative Study of the Chinese Arbitration
Law and the Arbitration Laws of the UK

the award is obtained by fraud. What is required is fraudulent non-disclosure.[1]

Chinese Law. In Chinese arbitration law, as regards domestic awards, a party may challenge an award on the ground that the evidence on which the award is based is falsified, or the other party has concealed evidence which is sufficient to affect the impartiality of the award, or the arbitrator(s) has (have) demanded or accepted bribes, committed graft or perverted the law in making the arbitral award. Yet, as regards foreign-related awards, Chinese arbitration law does not mention the ground that an award is obtained by fraud. I suggest that award being obtained by fraud should also be made a ground for challenging foreign-related awards.

[Failure to comply with requirement as to form of award]

Model Law. An award which is not in the form stipulated by Article 31 is not an award at all in the eyes of the Model Law, and thus need not be challenged.

1996 Act. Section 68(2)(h) provides that a party may challenge an award on the ground that there is a failure to comply with the requirements as to the form of the award. Such requirements may be agreed by the parties, or in the absence of agreement may flow from the default rules for the form of awards set out in Section 52 of the 1996 Act, which requires the awards to be signed, dated, containing a statement as to the seat of the arbitration and reasoned.

Chinese Law. In Chinese arbitration law, failure to comply with requirements of form is not regarded as a ground for challenging awards. In my view, failure to comply with requirement as to form of the award could be amended in the stage of correction of an award, and no need to regard it as a ground for challenging an award. Thus, it is not needed for Chinese ar-

---

① Merkin, Robert & Lyde, Barlow & Gilbert, Arbitration Law, London, Hong Kong: LLP Professional Publishing,1991,16-18.

bitration law to adopt the stance of the 1996 Act.

[Irregularity admitted by the tribunal or any arbitral or other institution or person]

Model Law. The Model Law does not mention this ground.

1996 Act. Section 68(2)(i) states that a party may challenge an award on the ground that there is any irregularity in the conduct of the proceedings or in the award which is admitted by the tribunal or by any arbitral or other institution or person vested by the parties with powers in relation to the proceedings or the award. It may be that this ground has a very limited role, as procedural errors in the conduct of the proceedings or in the format of the award are caught by the more specific earlier provisions of Section 68(2) of the Act.①

Chinese Law. Chinese arbitration law is silent about this ground. Since, as mentioned above, Section 68(2)(i) has very limited effect, and Chinese arbitration law does not allow the parties to vest other institution or person with powers in relation to arbitral proceedings or the award, Chinese arbitration law does not need to adopt the instance of the 1996 Act in this respect.

[Appeal on point of law]

Model Law. Under the Model Law, a party is not entitled to challenge an award on a question of law.

1996 Act. Section 69(1) provides that unless otherwise agreed by the parties, a party to arbitral proceedings may(upon notice to the other parties and to the tribunal) appeal to the court on a question of law arising out of an award made in the proceedings. An agreement to dispense with reasons for the tribunal's award shall be considered an agreement to exclude the court's jurisdiction under this section. It can be seen that the parties can agree to ex-

---

① Merkin, Robert & Lyde, Barlow & Gilbert, Arbitration Law, London, Hong Kong: LLP Professional Publishing,1991,17-18.

中英仲裁法比较研究
A Comparative Study of the Chinese Arbitration
Law and the Arbitration Laws of the UK

clude the right of appeal. However, in relation to domestic arbitration agreements, exclusion agreements are ineffective unless entered into after the commencement of the arbitral process.① Consideration was given to the question of whether a right of appeal on the substantive issues should be preserved at all. The principle that the parties are free to agree how to resolve their dispute with minimum of court intervention would, prima facie, militate against a substantive appeal. From a commercial point of view, the possibility of long, drawn-out court proceedings involved in a substantive appeal might make the parties choose another arbitral forum. The rationale for a right of appeal on a point of law is that the parties cannot be taken to have agreed that the tribunal would obviously misapply the relevant law. There is also a general interest in enabling a seriously doubtful decision to be reviewed. These are instances of safeguards, necessary in the public interest, that delimiting the freedom of the parties to choose their tribunal and abide by its decision.② Section 69(2) states that an appeal shall not be brought except with the agreement of all the other parties to the proceedings, or with the leave of the court, which leave shall be given under Section 69(3) only if the court is satisfied:

a. that the determination of the question will substantially affect the rights of one or more of the parties;

b. that the question is one which the tribunal was asked to determine;

c. that, on the basis of the findings of fact in the award:

(i) the decision of the tribunal on the question is obviously wrong; or

(ii) the question is one of general public importance and the decision of the tribunal is at least open to serious doubt; and

d. that, despite the agreement of the parties to resolve the matter by arbitration, it is just and proper in all the circumstances for the court to deter-

---

① Section 87 of the 1996 Act.

② Harris, Bruce/Planterose, Rowan & Tecks, Jonathan, The Arbitration Act 1996: A Commentary, 3rd ed. Malden: Blackwell Publishing, Inc., 2003,254.

mine the question.

Chinese Law. In Chinese arbitration law, a party is not allowed to challenge an international or foreign-related award on the substantive issues.① In my view, if substantive issues could be appealed, the scope of intervention of the court would be too great, even with the restrictions which are now built into the 1996 Act. English law is almost unique in allowing appeals on points of law. It has been driven to retain this possibility at least partly because of the pre-eminence of English commercial law, it being thought that dealing with appeals from arbitral awards permits the continued development of English commercial law. China dos not share this need, so that Chinese arbitration law does not need to adopt the approach of the 1996 Act.

2. Procedure for challenging awards

[Bringing forward of an application]

Model Law. There is no specific requirement as to bringing forward of an application under the Model Law.

1996 Act. As to procedures for appeal on point of law, an appeal shall not be brought except with the agreement of all the other parties to the proceedings, or with the leave of the court.②

Chinese Law. Chinese arbitration law does not allow a party to challenge an award on point of law, so there is no need to consider what requirement shall be fulfilled to make such an appeal.

[Time limits]

Model Law. By virtue of Article 34(3), an application for setting aside may not be made after three months have elapsed from the date on which the party making that application had received that award or, if a request had

---

① With respect of a domestic arbitration award, however, a party is allowed to present a challenge on the grounds of the errors of law or fact. See Article 58 of the PRC Arbitration Law 2017 and Section 20 of the "Interpretation of the SPC on Application of the PRC Arbitration Law", Law Interpretation, No.7(2006), Sept. 8, 2006.

② Section 69(2) of the 1996 Act.

中英仲裁法比较研究
A Comparative Study of the Chinese Arbitration
Law and the Arbitration Laws of the UK

been made under Article 33 (which refers to the correction and interpretation of awards and the making of addition awards) from the date on which that request had been disposed of by the arbitral tribunal. The Model Law does not provide a time limit within which a court should make decision whether to set side an award. Remitting awards for reconsideration by the tribunal is not allowed under the Model Law, thus there is no time limit in this respect.

1996 Act. Under Section 70(3), any application or appeal must be brought within 28 days of the date of the award or, if there has been any arbitral process of appeal or review, of the date when the applicant or appellant was notified of the result of that process. Where only a part of the award is tainted by ambiguity, that part must be referred back in light of Section 57, and the remainder appealed immediately, and indeed the appeal is governed by the 28-day time limit in Section 70(3).[1] By virtue of Section 80 (5), the court has power to extend any time limit, but an application to the court for an extension must state the basis on which the applicant seeks an extension, and the respondent has seven days from service on him to file written evidence contesting the extension of time.[2] This power would be useful to overcome the difficulties arising form the tribunal exercising its power to withhold the award until payment, pursuant to Section 56. If the award is not released until the time limit for challenge or appeal has expired, then an application to the court for an extension of time under Section 80(5) would be appropriate. However, where the difficulties have arisen because of the applicant's failure to pay for and collect the award promptly, the applicant will have a heavy burden placed upon him to justify his conduct and thus obtain an extension.[3] Section 71(3) states that where the award is remitted to the tribunal, in whole or in part, for reconsideration, the tribunal

---

[1]　Gbangbola v. Smith & Sheriff Ltd [1998] 3 All ER 730.

[2]　CPR r 62.11.

[3]　Harris, Bruce/Planterose, Rowan & Tecks, Jonathan, The Arbitration Act 1996: A Commentary, 3rd ed. Malden: Blackwell Publishing, Inc., 2003,259.

shall make a fresh award in respect of the matters remitted within three months of the date of the order for remission or such longer or shorter period as the court may direct. One must also bear in mind that Section 79 gives the court power, unless the parties otherwise agree, to extend any time limit agreed by them in relation to any matter relating to the arbitral proceedings or specified in any provision having effect in default of such agreement.① The 1996 Act does not provide any time limit for the court to make a decision whether to set aside an award.

Chinese Law. Chinese arbitration law does not give the court power to extend the time limit for application. If the Chinese arbitration law does not adopt the approach of the 1996 Act to give the tribunal power to withhold awards, there is no need for Chinese arbitration law to give such power to the court. If Chinese arbitration law attempts to adopt that approach, it is suggested that the approach of giving the court power to extend the time limit should also be adopted.

[Exhausting available arbitral procedure]

Model Law. The Model Law does not require a party to exhaust available arbitral processes before challenging an award.

1996 Act. Section 70(2) provides that an application or appeal may not be brought if the applicant or appellant has not first exhausted any available arbitral process of appeal or review, and any available recourse under Section 57 (correction of award or additional award).

Chinese Law. In Chinese arbitration law, there is no requirement that arbitral process of appeal or review should be first exhausted. The reason of this lack is probably that no arbitral process of appeal or review is provided by the Chinese arbitral rules, including the CIETAC Rules. From my point of view, the Chinese arbitral rules should recognize arbitral processes of ap-

---

① Section 79(1) also provides that this section does not apply to a time limit to which Section 12 applies (power of court to extend time for beginning arbitral proceedings).

中英仲裁法比较研究
A Comparative Study of the Chinese Arbitration
Law and the Arbitration Laws of the UK

peal or review, so that the will of the parties to refer the dispute to arbitration could be respected and the intervention of the court restricted. Moreover, where the seat of arbitration is within China, the parties may choose to apply a set of arbitral rules which is not Chinese. In such circumstances, if the rules chosen provide for a process of appeal or review, Chinese law's failure to require that such process be exhausted before an award may be challenged is unsatisfactory. Therefore, I suggest that the Arbitration Law adopts the stance of the 1996 Act in this matter.

[Ordering the tribunal to state reasons]

Model Law. The Model Law does not empower the court as described below.

1996 Act. Section 70(4) states that if on an application or appeal it appears to the court that the award does not contain the tribunal's reasons, or does not set out the tribunal's reasons in sufficient detail to enable the court properly to consider the application or appeal, the court may order the tribunal to state the reasons for its award in sufficient detail for that purpose.

Chinese Law. Under Chinese arbitration law, the court has no power to order the tribunal to state reasons for that purpose. Since this power is mainly concerned with appeals on a point of law and the Chinese arbitration law does not allow an appeal on this ground, I suggest that there is no need for Chinese arbitration law to adopt this approach of the 1996 Act in this regard.

[Costs of application or appeal]

Model Law. Under the Model Law, the court has no power as described below.

1996 Act. Section 70(6) states that the court may order the applicant or appellant to provide security for the costs of the application or appeal, and may direct that the application or appeal be dismissed if the order is not complied with.

Chinese Law. Chinese arbitration law does not give the court the power to order an applicant or appellant to provide security for the cost of application or appeal. In my view, ordering the applicant or appellant to provide such security could, to some extent, prevent or reduce abusive applications or appeals. Therefore, Chinese arbitration law might beneficially adopt such power.

[Court's decision]

Model Law. By virtue of Article 34, the court may set aside an award on the grounds provided by the Law. Also, the court may, where appropriate and so requested by a party, suspend the setting aside proceedings for a period of time determined by it in order to give the arbitral tribunal an opportunity to resume the arbitral proceedings or to take such other action as in the arbitral tribunal's opinion will eliminate the grounds for setting aside.① This power can only be exercised if a party so requests.

1996 Act. As to challenge of lack of substantive jurisdiction, the court may under Section 67(3) confirm the award, vary the award, or set aside the award in whole or in part. As to challenge of serious irregularity affecting the tribunal, the proceedings or the award, the court may under Section 68(3) remit the award to the tribunal, in whole or in part, for reconsideration, or set the award aside in whole or in part, or declare the award to be of no effect, in whole or in part. The court shall not exercise its power to set aside or to declare an award to be of no effect, in whole or in part, unless it is satisfied that it would be inappropriate to remit the matters in question to the tribunal for reconsideration. Assuming that some action is to be taken, the main objection to setting aside, as opposed to remission, is that the parties are put to the expense of a full rehearing of their dispute. In a number of situations set out in Section 68(2), remission of the award to the arbitrators is the obvious remedy, e. g., where the award is incomplete or uncertain or ambiguous, or does not comply with statutory or agreed requirements of form, or where there is an admitted error in the award. Setting aside the a-

---

① Article 34(4) of the Model Law.

中英仲裁法比较研究
A Comparative Study of the Chinese Arbitration
Law and the Arbitration Laws of the UK

ward may, however, be the only sensible option in exceptional circumstances where the serious irregularity relates to the conduct of the proceedings and further aggravating circumstances render remission inappropriate.① Setting aside the award does not affect the validity of the original arbitration agreement between the parties, nor does it automatically operate to affect the status of the existing arbitrators.② Where an award has been remitted, the hearing will generally take place before all of the original arbitrators.③ Even if there is reason to doubt the ability of the existing arbitrators to reach a fair decision, the court has no jurisdiction under the 1996 Act to remit the award to a fresh panel. The effect of a remission is not to impose upon the arbitrators the obligation to make a fresh award even in respect of the matters not remitted to him. As to appeal on point of law, the court may under Section 69(7) confirm the award, vary the award, remit the award to the tribunal in whole or in part for reconsideration in the light of the court's determination, or set aside the award in whole or in part. Again, the court shall not exercise its power to set aside an award, in whole or in part, unless it is satisfied that it would be inappropriate to remit the matters in question to the tribunal for reconsideration. The decision of the court on an appeal on point of law shall be treated as a judgment of the court for the purposes of a further appeal.④ The leave of the court is required for any appeal from a decision of the court regarding all kinds of challenge of awards.⑤ In light of Section 71(2), where the award is varied, the variation has effect as part of the tribunal's award. In light of Section 71(4), where the award is set aside

---

① Merkin, Robert & Lyde, Barlow & Gilbert, Arbitration Law, London, Hong Kong: LLP Professional Publishing, 1991, 18-19.

② Merkin, Robert & Lyde, Barlow & Gilbert, Arbitration Law, London, Hong Kong: LLP Professional Publishing, 1991, 18-20.

③ This applies even where the original award was reached by a majority decision: Richard Clear & Co. Ltd. v. Bloch (1922) 13 L1 LR 462.

④ Section 69(8) of the 1996 Act.

⑤ Section 67(4), Section 68(4), Section 69(6) of the 1996 Act.

or declared to be of no effect, in whole or in part, the court may also order that any provision that an award is a condition precedent to the bringing of legal proceedings in respect of a matter to which the arbitration agreement applies, is of no effect as regards the subject matter of the award or, as the case may be, the relevant part of the award.

Chinese Law. In Chinese arbitration law, the court has power to confirm, set aside, or remit an award for reconsideration by the arbitral tribunal. The court is not allowed by the Chinese law to vary a challengeable award. From my point of view, giving the court power to vary an award would allow too much scope for court intervention. Moreover, since the court can remit an award to be reconsidered by the arbitral tribunal, I consider there is no need to allow the court to vary an award. The Chinese Arbitration Law does not mention whether the party can appeal a decision of the court regarding challenge of awards, but certain legal explanations of the Supreme Court deal with the issue. "The Supreme Court's reply about whether a party could appeal against the decision of the court as to set aside an award or dismissal of an application for setting an award aside"① states that the party is not allowed to appeal against the court's decision on this issue. "the Supreme Court's Reply about whether the Court shall Accept an Application for Appeal Against the Court's Decision as to Setting an Award Aside" provides that where the court orders an award to be set aside, if the party appeals to the court, the court shall dismiss the application.② Giving parties the right to appeal against the court's decision may protect their legal interests. However, in China arbitration is not extremely developed, so such right is very likely to be abused, while the finality and efficiency of arbitra-

---

① See Law Reply [1997] No.5, April 23rd, 1997.

② See the "Official and Written Reply to the Matter on whether the People's Court Accepts the Petition for Re-hearing Presented by the Party who is not subject to the Ruling of the People's Court on Setting Aside an Arbitration Award" by the SPC, Law Interpretation, No.6(1999), Jan. 29,1999.

中英仲裁法比较研究
A Comparative Study of the Chinese Arbitration
Law and the Arbitration Laws of the UK

tion will be adversely affected. Therefore, considering the stage of the development of Chinese arbitration, I suggest Chinese arbitration law does not give parties the right to appeal against the court's decision as to setting aside an award.

C. Resisting enforcement

[Grounds for resisting enforcement]

The grounds for resisting enforcement under the Model Law are identical to the grounds for setting it aside, both being based on the grounds for resisting enforcement under the New York Convention. Since the United Kingdom and China are both parties to the New York Convention, the laws in the two systems, being based on the New York Convention, are identical. Thus, the grounds for resisting enforcement of awards in the three laws are identical, and no amendment should be made to this part of Chinese arbitration law.

V. Conclusion

It has been suggested that Chinese arbitration law should adopt some of the grounds for challenging an award contained in the 1996 Act, such as the tribunal's failure to deal with all the issues put to it, uncertainty or ambiguity as to the effect of an award, and an award being obtained by fraud. Secondly, if Chinese arbitration law adopts the approach of the 1996 Act in giving tribunals power to withhold awards, it is suggested that the approach of giving the court power to extend time limits should also be adopted, so as to avoid the problem of awards being released after the time limits for challenges or appeals have expired. Thirdly, Chinese arbitration law should adopt the stance of the 1996 Act and give the court power to order the tribunal to state the reasons for its award in sufficient detail, to allow the court to consider properly applications or appeals. Finally, the 1996 Act gives the court power to order the applicant or appellant to provide security for the costs of applications or appeals. Chinese arbitration law should confer such power to help prevent or reduce abusive applications or appeals.

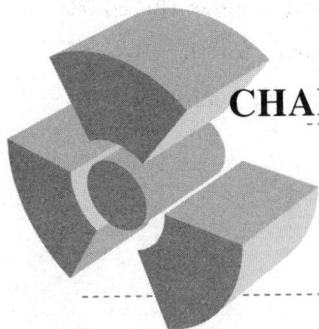

中英仲裁法比较研究
A Comparative Study of the Chinese Arbitration
Law and the Arbitration Laws of the UK

CHAPTER 13

CONCLUSION

It can be seen from the thesis that some provisions of Chinese Arbitration Law and the CIETAC Rules (2015) are far from perfect. In some areas, the level of judicial control is too high, while in some other areas the level of courts support is insufficient. Moreover, agencies of the state play a very intrusive role in the arbitral process. As a result, the independence of the arbitral tribunal and the efficiency of the arbitral process may be adversely affected, while the autonomy of the parties might not be properly respected. Additionally, some provisions are obscure or contradictory. Such defects would tend to make parties lose confidence in the Chinese system and choose an alternative arbitral forum to the detriment of China's developing trade relations. Therefore, to give the parties, particularly foreign users, confidence in the Chinese system, reform is vital. Through comparing the Model Law and the 1996 Act with Chinese arbitration law, I suggested that Chinese law be reformed as follows.

Firstly, regarding the nature and form of the arbitration agreement, the requirement of Chinese arbitration law that parties choose an arbitration agency to regulate the arbitration has two main disadvantages. It prevents ad-hoc arbitration, while imposing on both the arbitral tribunal and the court a heavy burden to examine the validity of the arbitration agreement. I suggest that Chinese arbitration law should abandon this requirement. At the same time Chinese arbitration law requires that arbitration agreements be in writing, but is not clear as to what constitutes "writing". This problem could be removed if China simply abandons requirement of writing.

Secondly, regarding the staying of legal proceedings, if China adopts the principle of competence-competence, Chinese law should require the court to stay its proceedings, rather than dismiss the action, where a challenge to the tribunal's competence is made. The courts in this context should have discretion whether to examine the validity of the arbitration agreement.

Thirdly, regarding the creation of the arbitral tribunal, Chinese law might make an arbitrator's lack of agreed qualifications a ground for both removing arbitrators and challenging awards, and in this context the arbitration commission should be given the power to revoke the appointments already made.

Fourthly, regarding the revocation of arbitral authority and its consequences, in Chinese arbitration law, the court does not play a role in the challenge procedure and in most cases the Chairman of the arbitral agency shall make rule on the challenge, his decision being final. Where the challenge is unsuccessful, the challenging party therefore has no recourse. Chinese law should permit the court to review the Chairman's decision and provide necessary supervision of the arbitral process. Also the law should specify grounds on which the court may remove the arbitrator. The parties should have the power to agree whether a substitute arbitrator shall be appointed, and, where a new tribunal is constituted, whether the previous proceeding shall stand. Obvious gaps in the Chinese law should be filled, as to such matters as the liabilities and entitlement to fees of an arbitrator who resigns, the effect of the death of an arbitrator or the person who appointed him, and the effect of an arbitrator's ceasing to hold his position on any appointment

中英仲裁法比较研究
A Comparative Study of the Chinese Arbitration
Law and the Arbitration Laws of the UK

made by him.

Fifthly, regarding arbitral immunity, arbitrators should be liable for damages in negligence like other providers of professional services. However, it should be possible for arbitrators to be granted immunity from suit by agreement with the parties. In the situations where there is no such agreement, a party should be obliged to provide security before bringing an action against an arbitrator.

Sixthly, as regards questions of jurisdiction, the principles of competence-competence and separability should be adopted, and should be regarded as mandatory and interdependent. Chinese law should offer clarification as to how jurisdictional objections should be raised and the stage at which this should be done.

Seventhly, as regards the conduct of the proceeding, Chinese arbitration law should permit the parties to preclude the arbitral tribunal from collecting evidence on its own initiative. It might be useful to give the court the power to collect evidence, subject to the agreement of the parties. However, the tribunal should be given power to order interim measures of protection, and the court should be able to enforce with the peremptory orders of the tribunal.

Eightly, as to the arbitral award, the tribunal should be able to interpret ambiguities in an award unless otherwise agreed by the parties. The court might be allowed to extend the periods within which an arbitral award, or an application for correction or an actual correction, may be made. As far as enforcement is concerned, the court should be allowed not only to enforce an award in the same manner as a judgment, but also issue a judgment in terms of the award. The arbitral tribunal might be given power to withhold an arbitral award in case of non-payment of fees, while the court should be able to order the tribunal to deliver the award on the payment into court by the applicant.

Finally, as regards challenging awards, the Chinese arbitration law should add new grounds for challenging an award, i. e. the tribunal's failure to deal with all the issues put to it, uncertainty or ambiguity as to the effect of an award, and an award being obtained by fraud. If the law gives tribunals power to withhold awards, it might also give the court power to extend time limits within which challenges should be made. The court should have power to order the tribunal to state the reasons for its award in sufficient detail, and to order the applicant or appellant to provide security for the costs of applications or appeals.

It is suggested that if Chinese arbitration law is reformed as described above, it will achieve an appropriate balance between the autonomy of the arbitral process and the legitimate interests of the Chinese legal system. Thus China would become a more modern, more attractive arbitral forum, to the benefit of its developing trade relations.